ISOCARP Review 06

Sustainable City / Developing World

2010

 **ISOCARP**

Copyright © 2010
International Society of City
and Regional Planners

Published by ISOCARP

Organisers
Architectural Association of Kenya
AAK Town Planners Chapter
International Society of City
and Regional Planners ISOCARP

Partners
Government of Kenya
City Council of Nairobi
UN Habitat
World Urban Campaign
ISDR - United Nations International
Strategy for Disaster Reduction
IIUD - Institute for International
Urban Development
OECD - Organisation for Economic
Co-operation and Development

Green Sponsor
Siemens

Sponsors
Arnaiz Consultores
Holcim Foundation

Media Partner
Urban World

Strategic Partners
University of Nairobi
KPDA - Kenya Property
Developers Association

ISOCARP Strategic Partners
City of Antwerp, Belgium
Fundación Metrópoli, Spain
INVI, Poland

Editor
Chris Gossop

Secretary General ISOCARP
Pablo Vaggione

Coordination
Gaby Kurth, ISOCARP

Design and Layout
Ricardo Moura, Portugal
www.ricardomoura.org

ISBN: 978-0-415-61715-4
[Routledge, Main Distributor]

ISBN: 978-94-90354-07-7
[ISOCARP]

Copy-Editor
Andrew Hitchen, United Kingdom

Cover Photo
Nigel Pavitt, John Warburton-Lee
Photography JWLP-00023427-001
Title: Nairobi in late afternoon sunlight
with Uhuru Park in the foreground

Printed in the Netherlands
Drukkerij Aktief b.v.

Library
University of Texas
at San Antonio

Contents

6	Foreword by the ISOCARP President
Ismael Fernández Mejía
7	Foreword by the Chair of the Local Organising Committee
Mairura Omwenga
8	Sustainable City/Developing World
An Introduction to Review 06
Chris Gossop
19	**Part 1 – Focus on Africa**
20	Kenya: Urban Settlements and Development Profile
Mairura Omwenga
34	Project Preparation and its Crucial Role in Enabling More Effective and Sustainable Development – The South African Experience
Mark Misselhorn
52	Urban Africa – Challenges and Opportunities at a Time of Climate Change
Laura Petrella
79	**Part 2 – A Global Challenge**
80	Climate Change, Cities and the IPCC
Jean-Pascal van Ypersele
90	Sustainable Urbanism in Abu Dhabi
John P Madden
118	Energy Saving and Emission Reduction: Chinese Low Carbon Strategy in 11th Five Year Plan Period
SHI Nan and YU Taofang
142	Low Carbon Kunshan: Towards a Sustainable Future
Zhang Quan

167	**Part 3 – New Methods and Strategies**
168	The Carbon Footprint of UK Cities: 4 M: Measurement, Modelling, Mapping and Management *Kevin J Lomas et al*
192	Rebuilding after a Natural Disaster: Using the Opportunity to be 'better than ever' *Dhiru A Thadani*
212	The Loss of Green Spaces in and around City Areas: Learning from Syria *Peter Ross*
228	Cultivating the Capital: How the Planning System is Vital to London's Ability to Grow its Own Food *Jenny Jones and Rosie Boycott*
245	**Part 4 – The ISOCARP Awards for Excellence** *Dirk Engelke*
260	**About the editor**
261	**About the authors**

Foreword One

Ismael Fernández Mejía
ISOCARP President (2009 - 2012)

Knowledge for Cities and dissemination of knowledge in urban science are the main objectives of our Society. In this line it has been developing several instruments in order to achieve this goal; amongst them is ISOCARP's publications program.

The publication of documents is related to most of our activities, which goes from the UPAT (Urban Planning Advisory Teams) and YPP (Young Planning Professionals) Programmes up to other documents related to the scientific life of the Society. From all these publications the ISOCARP Review is the Flagship. This publication started in 2005 as a compendium of papers prepared by our members in relation to the subject matter of our annual congress.

This year is no exception. Review 06 has included within its pages the view of several members, experts in their field, who have contributed their views on the subject of this year's Congress theme Sustainable Cities, Developing World.

This subject matter is part of a sequence that the Society has been interested in looking at for a number of years now. The central point on the last three congresses has been sustainability and its effect in different facets of the city life and structure. So, we have reviewed city sprawl, low carbon cities and, on this new opportunity, how the developing world can take advantage of the lessons in sustainability, without the need of going through all the stages that cities in the developed world have followed, that maybe some times were not the best answer to the needs of their inhabitants. Of course, there are also lessons that cities in the more developed regions have to learn. The participation of authors presenting cases from all over the world enhances this Review in such a way that the reader can learn how things are being done in various latitudes and in which way the sustainability concept is understood and applied in a global context. Cases from Kenya, China, Abu Dhabi, Syria, South Africa, very interesting collaborations from UN-Habitat and the IPCC, views on the carbon footprint, and urban food growing from the UK and the sheer opportunity of rebuilding after disasters, surely enrich the content of this Review.

Finally, I want to thank, personally and in the name of the Society, all the authors and the people involved in the preparation, editing and publication of this Review. I want to congratulate them all for the fine work and the achievement of producing this interesting document. It will be added to our series of Reviews, disseminating knowledge on urban planning and giving the generations to come the chance to learn and understand how we in 2010 approached and generated Knowledge for Cities.

Foreword Two

Mairura Omwenga
Chairman of the Local Organising Committee

ISOCARP Review is the premier annual publication of the International Society of City and Regional Planners. In the last few years, the Review has grown in terms of world distribution and readership. This year the ISOCARP Review 06 has indeed captured global issues that require the attention of planners.

The 46th ISOCARP International Congress 2010 in Nairobi is focused on the theme – Sustainable City/Developing World. This Congress is indeed special to ISOCARP – (i) This is the first ISOCARP Congress in Sub-Saharan Africa; and (ii) The world's attention is focused on rapid urbanisation in the South and developing countries in general.

ISOCARP Review 06 has been organised in three main parts – (i) Focus on Africa, (ii) The Global Challenge, and (iii) New Methods and Strategies. We want to recognize and thank the contributors of the various papers for their hard work. In alphabetical order, we acknowledge the following:

Jenny Jones and Rosie Boycott – Cultivating the Capital: How the Planning System is Vital to London's Ability to Grow its Own Food

K J Lomas et al – The Carbon Footprint of UK Cities: 4 M: Measurement, Modeling, Mapping and Management

John P Madden – Sustainable Urbanism in Abu Dhabi

Mark Misselhorn – Project Preparation and its Crucial Role in Enabling More Effective and Sustainable Development – The South African Experience

Mairura Omwenga – Kenya: Urban Settlements and Development Profile

Laura Petrella, UN HABITAT – Urban Africa – Challenges and Opportunities for Planning at a Time of Climate Change

Peter Ross – The Loss of Green SpaceS in and around City Areas: Learning from Syria

SHI Nan and YU Taofang – Energy Saving and Emission Reduction: Chinese Low Carbon Strategy in 11th Five Year Plan Period

Dhiru A Thadani - Rebuilding after a Natural Disaster: Using the Opportunity to be 'better than ever'

Jean-Pascal van Ypersele – Climate Change, Cities and the IPCC

Zhang Quan – Low Carbon Kunshan: Towards a Sustainable Future.

This time, the review also includes a summary of the outcome of the 2009 ISOCARP Awards for Excellence Programme, summarizing the jury report and the three winning entries from China and the UAE.

We also wish to appreciate the great efforts of many people in the preparation of this publication. These include in particular Chris Gossop, Vice President Publications, and in the ISOCARP Secretariat, Gaby Kurth, to whom we are thankful for their hard work. Our heartfelt thanks also go to UN-Habitat, the Government of Kenya, and the City Council of Nairobi for accepting to co-host the 46th ISOCARP Congress. Secretary General Pablo Vaggione deserves special appreciation for his tremendous energy and efforts in organising this unique Congress. To the Local Organising Committee, the Architectural Association of Kenya, and AAK Town Planners Chapter in particular, we say: "you have made it". Thank you!

Sustainable City/Developing World
An Introduction to Review 06

Chris Gossop

This book complements its predecessor *Low Carbon Cities* (Review 05) which was published alongside ISOCARP's congress on that subject held in Porto, Portugal in October 2009. Most of the case studies presented in Review 05 concerned the countries and the cities of the developed world which have, in the past, been the main contributors to greenhouse gas (GHG) emissions, the growing levels of which pose such a threat to the future of mankind and to the millions of other species with which we share this planet.

Review 06 switches emphasis to the developing world, to the world's poorer states – for instance, many of those on the African continent, and to the rapidly industrialising countries, the foremost example of which is China. It addresses sustainable development in all its aspects - the economic, the environmental and the social, although considerations, specifically, of climate change and the low carbon agenda are never far away. Indeed they permeate almost all of the essays and, in some cases, they are the central theme.

There is an acceptance on the part of most world leaders that, to prevent truly catastrophic climate change, our planet's average temperature should not be allowed to rise by more than 2^0C above its pre-industrial level. Unfortunately, however, those leaders have, as yet, shown themselves unable to agree the necessary comprehensive deal to secure this; while some progress was made there, for the most part, last December's Copenhagen summit was a sadly missed opportunity to forge a new, greener path for the Earth.

But we must keep trying, because the problem will not go away, and time is short. Individual countries and cities must persist with, and scale up, their current low carbon initiatives and adaptive measures despite the seeming vacuum, for the time being, at international level. And we must learn from each other about the things that succeed (and about those approaches that may work less well); spreading such messages is one of the key purposes of ISOCARP, of our Review series, and of our international congresses which bring together planners and related professionals from all over the world.

In the meantime, the signs that the world's climate is changing, that we are entering an era of greater extremes, are becoming increasingly apparent. This editorial is being written as the full implications of the events along the Indus Valley in Pakistan are being revealed - as the effects of flood surge devastate one region after another, overwhelming the hastily erected defences. Millions of families have been displaced, losing their homes and their livelihoods, often all they possess. This is a massive humanitarian and environmental crisis for Pakistan and the world, another warning sign – the biggest yet in recent times

- of our vulnerability in the face of forces that we cannot control. And there have been plenty of other disasters, for example the mudslides that led to the huge losses of life in Zhouqu county, China.

Such weather induced events can overwhelm the capacity of any one nation to tackle them, indeed international, pooled resources are becoming increasingly stretched as the new priorities brought about by the Pakistan tragedy are superimposed upon the continuing commitments left by the Haiti earthquake. They pose immediate, massive challenges upon governments, national international agencies and other bodies but, equally, there is the medium and the longer term to think about, the question of rebuilding the settlements that have been destroyed, or relocating the affected communities to places that are deemed to be safer and carrying out the rebuilding there.

Either way, this will be a huge task for planners, designers and other professionals who will need to build much greater resilience into these replacement neighbourhoods and settlements and, as a precaution, into existing vulnerable places. This will be an essential part of the adaptation strategies that, alongside mitigation, must be part of our response to climate change. In its third section, Review 06 includes a case study on the plans developed for devastated coastal towns in Mississippi, in the wake of Hurricane Katrina. This is a good example of a 'bottom up' approach to community rebuilding, an approach that is likely to be translatable to other post disaster situations.

We are all in this together. In terms of mitigation - intervention to reduce the output or to enhance the sinks of greenhouse gases – initially, the developed countries must bear most of the burden. For it has been their historic development since the industrial era began, and the increasingly affluent lifestyles of most of their citizens, that have been the principal cause of a rise in atmospheric carbon dioxide levels of some 40% over the last 250 years. They must achieve big cuts in GHG emissions very quickly, at least of the order of those committed by the European Union of 20% by 2020 (compared to 1990 levels). And by 2050 those cuts by the developed countries will need to be of the order of 80%.

But the developing world will have to take responsibility too, especially the rapidly industrialising countries whose per capita emissions are rising at a fast rate. They are becoming major contributors to the greenhouse effect and that contribution will become more significant unless their economic growth can be achieved with a far lower impact in carbon terms. The part that the world's planners and urban designers can play will be to foster patterns of development, and individual buildings that are inherently low carbon; thus their contribution to mitigation will be one of their priorities. A second will be in respect of adaptation, to ensure that plans for existing and future communities incorporate that resilience to climate change effects referred to earlier.

Further details on ISOCARP's stance on climate change, and the planning response to it, are set out in its Porto Statement *Seven Ingredients for Low Carbon Cities* (www.isocarp.org). It is likely that these conclusions will be further developed in the light of the debate at the Society's 2010 congress in Nairobi, Kenya *Sustainable City/ Developing World.*

The eleven rich case studies presented in ISOCARP Review 06 are divided into three parts. Thus, Part I focuses on Africa, as is appropriate given the location of ISOCARP's 2010 World Congress. Part II broadens the perspective to a global one, commencing with a paper from the Vice Chair of the Intergovernmental Panel on Climate Change (IPCC). Part III is about new methods and strategies and it concludes with a study about the importance of using urban land for food growing, in this case, London.

Review 06 contains one further section. This is about ISOCARP's 2009 Awards for Excellence and the winning entries.

The Case Studies – A Guide

Part I – Focus on Africa
We start with a case study on Kenya, a country that has much to teach planners about the challenges that face Africa's cities generally in this era of rapid change. In his essay **Kenya: Urban Settlements and Development Profile**, Mairura Omwenga focuses upon the rapid expansion of Nairobi, Mombasa and other Kenyan cities, arising both from natural growth, and migration, as rural dwellers move in to seek the undoubted, though often elusive, economic opportunities. Among the outcomes are the increasing sprawl of poorly serviced informal housing, and worsening environmental conditions. Faced with a fast growing population with its associated poverty, and a deteriorating infrastructure, the public authorities struggle to cope.

A principal message is that planning must receive greater emphasis as the key to leading and guiding urban growth and development. Here, the recent decision by the Kenyan Government to establish a Ministry for Nairobi Metropolitan Development is an important initiative, for among its tasks is the development and implementation of an integrated metropolitan area growth and development strategy. The Ministry's publication, *Nairobi Metro 2030*[1], sets out a vision for a region that will grow from an estimated 6.1 million population in 2007 to reach towards 12.1 million by 2030. The vision is of a world class African metropolis, a regional and global services hub that offers an improved quality of life without burdening future generations.

Clearly, the effective planning and upgrading of the Nairobi region, and of Kenya's other cities, will be a huge task for the planners and other decision makers involved. As Omwenga concludes, it should involve the allocation of significant resources for housing, coupled with a new priority to the upgrading of slum areas. As so often in planning, this is about 'squaring the circle' so that the vision of strategies such as *Nairobi Metro 2030* can become a reality. But that requires a commitment to effective implementation, an area where, world-wide, the results so often fall short of what is needed, and are a long way from what we intended to happen.

This is why the messages of Mark Misselhorn's perspective from South Africa, **Project Preparation and its Crucial Role in Enabling More Effective and Sustainable Development**, are so important. This essay is about getting implementation right, and bridging the gap between the wider strategic vision for a settlement and what appears on the ground. It includes a key diagram – 'The Project Preparation Cycle' which is about the process that leads up to implementation and, while drawn up in a South African context, it is clearly of much wider applicability. The six steps that it identifies are pragmatic ones, charting a rightly cautious approach to project preparation that, at several stages, may lead to a finding that a project should not proceed.

The Cycle commences with 'Project Identification and Prioritisation', which is especially important whenever resources are clearly limited. Among the other stages is 'Pre-Feasibility' whereby an investigating team would prepare a risk profile covering, for example, site suitability, and any legal constraints. A broad concept would next be drawn up, together with capital and operational costs. If then the project were seen to be viable, it would then proceed to a more detailed Feasibility Stage in which design details and detailed costings would be worked out, leading to funding applications.

The article concludes with two important case studies from eThekwini in the Durban area. They concern, in one case, the provision of basic services to a slum development of 76,000 households and, in the other, a precinct development including new basic housing. They are good examples of well directed, cost effective schemes that can significantly improve the local quality of life, and they demonstrate the merits of systematic project preparation.

We conclude the first part of Review 06 with a broader look at the African continent and its planning needs. The article by UN HABITAT's Laura Petrella, **Urban Africa – Challenges and Opportunities for Planning at a Time of Climate Change**, complements an earlier article by the Agency that appeared in Review 05[2]. That looked at the world's cities as a whole and drew attention to their inextricable link to climate change.

In her focus, this time on Africa, Petrella highlights the fact that while this remains the least urbanised continent, it is the place where urbanisation is proceeding fastest. With three cities of over five million people, and an urban population projected to increase from some 370 million to some 750 by 2030, Africa is no longer the overwhelmingly rural continent that it once was. Also, much of the urban growth is poverty led, rather than being consequent upon industrial development as in other world regions. National approaches to land use planning need to reflect these trends and patterns.

But there is still a considerable emphasis on planning systems that are the legacy of colonial days, and these may be of limited relevance to the circumstances of today. The essay describes new pragmatic approaches that seek to link planning and development in a context of limited resources. City Development Strategies represent one such approach, while South Africa's Integrated Development Plans, which focus on policy co-ordination at local government level, are another.

The fundamental need to address the causes and effects of climate change is viewed by UN HABITAT as a potential integrating factor in planning strategies. While Africa generates only 3% of world GHG emissions, and therefore contributes only minimally to global warming, that statistic hides huge inequalities; on the one hand, there are the poor, having minimal access to modern forms of energy and requiring it in the future and, on the other, the elite who enjoy western lifestyles and whose activities create similar levels of emissions per capita to those of the rich countries. Moreover, Africa and its cities are very vulnerable to the effects of climate change, with slum areas often most in the firing line. Effective planning has to work towards reducing that vulnerability, improving infrastructure such as public transport and countering the extensive sprawl that is so prevalent.

Africa's cities of tomorrow will need to reflect all aspects of the sustainable development agenda, the environmental, the social, and the economic, as well as cultural factors. What will they be like?

Part II – A Global Perspective
Climate change poses a serious threat to Africa and, indeed, to every world region. That is the continuing message of the IPCC, and of the next article of this Review by its Vice Chair, Jean-Pascal van Ypersele. In **Climate Change, Cities and the IPCC**, he gives five succinct messages that draw upon the work of the world's best climate scientists. Contrary to the impression that

has been given by certain parts of the media and other detractors, the IPCC's conclusions have emerged through an extremely painstaking review process, they reflect scientific consensus and uncertainties, where they remain, and they tend towards conservatism.

Even so, the first three of the messages are stark enough. They are that climate change is happening now, that its impacts are likely to be increasingly felt as GHG concentrations build up, and that, while adaptation can help societies adjust, we must reduce emissions if we are to tackle the worst potential impacts of climate change. That leads to the fourth message, which is that we humans have the ability to rein in our emissions through a combination of lifestyle and behavioural change, technological advancement and the application of appropriate policies. The caveat is that this will need to be driven by appropriate carbon price signals. The final message concerns the programme of work for IPCC in the years ahead. This will now turn to addressing the regional aspects of climate change impacts and vulnerability, adaptation and mitigation at that level.

The work of the IPCC has profound implications for our future, and its results ought to be studied by every planner[3]. This brings us back to the low carbon agenda and, in particular, the future shape and organisation of our cities – their density and their land use mix, and how we manage our energy and other resources. At a finer grain level, it also involves the design of our built environment and of the green spaces that should be integral to our cities, towns and neighbourhoods.

The three case studies that follow explore attempts at different levels to move in such a direction. Thus John Madden's text **Sustainable Urbanism in Abu Dhabi** gives an overview of the efforts being made to define a sustainable framework and an integrated design approach for this rapidly expanding city, the capital of the United Arab Emirates. It describes the urban structure framework plan 2030, and it then focuses on two strategic projects –the Capital District, the home of national government and commercial uses, and the ground-breaking Masdar development, with its embedded carbon neutral and zero waste structure.

Abu Dhabi's planning is impressive for its long term vision. Formerly linked to the exploitation of its abundant oil reserves, the Emirate now seeks a diversified economy and an approach to development based on sustainable urbanism. That spatial vision includes an ambitious integrated transport system, a more human scale for its streets guided by a new design manual and a comprehensive approach to the design and delivery of infrastructure, including significant provision of renewable energy.

Through the Estimada programme[4], the Emirate aims to embed sustainability principles into daily life and into decisions on the use of resources. Its 'Pearl Rating' guides all new physical development. This is a multi-faceted system specially tailored to the extreme heat and humidity of a coastal desert area, and one element of it is building orientation, both as a way of channelling coastal winds through a development and as a means of creating shade. Increasingly, Abu Dhabi is showing itself to be an important laboratory, where new approaches to spatial planning and design can be tested. This article contributes to the spreading of knowledge about it.

The next two essays are about China. Visiting that huge country, one can only marvel at the scale of its urbanisation which is being driven by high speed economic growth. That massive development, and meeting the needs of a population that stood at some 1.3 billion in 2003 (with a natural growth rate of 6%) poses huge challenges for the country, and for planning in its broadest sense. In particular, there are major resource issues that will need to be tackled. These include land supply where the demands of urbanisation contradict the need to retain good arable land, shortages of water in many areas (and the quality of that water) and energy, where growing consumption means a continuing dependence upon indigenous coal which is a major source of China's rising greenhouse gas emissions[5].

An approach towards ultimately reducing dependence upon such fossil fuels is outlined in the paper by Shi Nan and Yu Taofang, **Energy Saving and Emission Reduction: Chinese Low Carbon Strategy in 11th Five Year Plan Period**. The strategy of Energy Saving and Emission Reduction (ESER) is part of a continuing focus by China to improve its efficiency and to work towards less polluting energy. The ambition of China's current 5 Year Plan is to reduce its energy intensity[6] by 20% by 2010. But it is important to realise that China's gross emissions are increasing and that this seems destined to continue for the time being as the country develops. The fundamental challenge for China, together with other fast developing countries, is how to break the link between high emissions and economic growth.

However, there are grounds for optimism in some areas, at least. As the paper outlines, China is developing a substantial renewable energy sector, and other important steps towards ESER have been taken, for example the setting up of a National Energy Committee and a start on carbon trading. The authors view China's road to urbanisation as providing a potential opportunity for ESER, and as a starting point for solving the problems. They foresee increasing demands to reduce both local environmental pollution and carbon emissions. To that end, city planners and decision makers should resist American style suburbanisation and pursue compact and greener forms of urbanisation, and lower carbon cities.

Kunshan is a good example of a place that is seeking such a route. In his paper **Low Carbon Kunshan: Towards a Sustainable Future**, Zhang Quan describes a city on the edge of the Shanghai conurbation that has expanded massively over the 30 years, from a population of 80,000 in the 1980s, to the present 1.2 million. The city is regarded as a major success in terms in terms of its economic and social development; thus, as one of the first Chinese cities to open itself up, it has attracted numerous international businesses and there has been a major improvement in living conditions.

But there is also a recognition that, while energy intensity has been reducing, overall energy consumption (and hence GHG emissions) have risen considerably during this period of growth. Thus, Kunshan will need to change its development mode if it is to become more sustainable in the context of world climate change. So that will be an added challenge for the years ahead. The paper outlines a package of measures embracing cleaner energy (including the development of renewables), spatial planning on compact city lines, and transport measures that place considerable emphasis on parking restraint and the use of public transport. The big question is the extent to which these and other measures being pursued by Kunshan will be enough to counter the trends towards rising emissions. Can Kunshan become a genuinely low carbon city?

Part III – New Methods and Strategies

Cities around the world, Kunshan included, are putting in substantial efforts to improve their local environmental conditions, and hence the health and overall well being of their citizens. This is likely to have economic spin offs too in terms of business investment. These areas – the environmental, the social and the economic represent, of course, the main pillars of sustainable development but, given the imperative of tackling the sources of climate change, we will need to achieve far more on the environmental front if we are to secure cities that can genuinely be said to be sustainable.

The path towards that state will be a long and difficult one that, crucially must involve big reductions in carbon emissions. But how should we measure our progress along that path, what specific steps should we take and how should we prioritise our investments? And in practical terms what is our starting point, what is the carbon footprint of an individual city?

ISOCARP is pleased to be able to publish the interim results of a major research programme conducted by five UK universities. In their paper, **The Carbon Footprint of UK Cities: 4M: Measurement, Modelling, Mapping and Management,** Kevin Lomas and 17 other researchers seek to advance knowledge and practice by addressing the complex realities of a functioning, dynamic city. They base their '4M' studies on Leicester, the UK's 15th largest city. This has a population of some 280,000 living in some 110,000 homes, some 70,000 non domestic buildings and a clearly defined boundary. Some 57% of its land is green space, a figure that includes domestic gardens.

Now half way through its four year programme, the multidisciplinary 4M team has been measuring the carbon emissions from buildings and transport, as well as biological carbon storage and sequestration in soil and vegetation. They aim to create a bottom up, practical methodology for urban carbon footprinting, to develop models and mapping showing the relationship between human activities and emissions, and to predict the likely impact of carbon management practices.

The essay includes a useful summary of national priorities for carbon reduction and of what is expected of the various sectors. In respect of housing, UK building regulations are being progressively tightened so that, by 2016, new homes will have to be carbon neutral. But the existing housing stock, which is often very poorly insulated, presents a far bigger challenge and the paper provides some sobering evidence of the scale and difficulty of the task. It is not an impossible one, but the retrofitting effort will have to be much more ambitious than anything that has been achieved before.

That contrast between the planning of the new, and how we deal with our existing built environment - its restructuring and its remodelling - to secure lower carbon emissions and a better energy performance is one key message from this paper. It reminds us that planners and decision maker will have to think and act very broadly indeed if we are to lower those carbon footprints. This is an important study that should provide new insights into the likely gains and cost effectiveness of pursuing different measures. For example, is the refurbishment of homes more effective than traffic management and what priority should be attached to district heating or carbon sequestration initiatives?

Earlier, this Introduction referred to the natural disasters that appear to be increasing in their frequency and their intensity, and to the role of planners and designers in deciding upon suitable approaches to the replacement and rebuilding of devastated areas. In **Rebuilding after a Natural Disaster: using the opportunity to be better than ever**, Dhiru Thadani sets out his experience of an intensive planning and design exercise that took place in the wake of Hurricane Katrina. But rather than New Orleans, its focus was on eleven gulf coast cities in Mississippi where over 200,000 residents were left homeless.

Under the Mississippi Rebuilding Forum, designers, planners and other professionals from the Congress of the New Urbanism worked intensively with local officials, stakeholders and citizens from the area. The purpose of this six day brainstorming exercise was to plan for the rebuilding in a better, more community oriented way, based upon the principles of the New Urbanism. So, instead of the sprawl of the pre-Katrina era, the aspiration was to create compact, walkable communities, having a clear spirit of place. The author led the team that worked on the City of Long Beach. His beautiful sketches outline a clear vision for the revival of this seaside settlement.

Sadly, the early momentum achieved through this innovative way of working was not sustained and the pace of rebuilding has been disappointingly slow. Undoubtedly, the recent BP oil disaster will have compounded the delays. Nevertheless, many of the necessary precursor plans are in place to enable that rebuilding, as are funding mechanisms to assist the development.

Looking ahead to the inevitable disasters of the future, the approaches that have been pioneered in Mississippi are, doubtless, of wider applicability, as experience from which we can borrow in comparable situations.

In his article, **The Loss of Green Spaces in and around Cities: Learning from Syria,** Peter Ross describes how satellite images have been used to gain an insight into the extent to which urban greenspace has been lost through the expansion of Syria's cities. Those cities have seen major growth over recent decades, including many refugees from neighbouring countries, and this has swamped the ability of the country's formerly effective planning systems to cope. The result has been significant informal development falling outside the planning system. That system was unable to move quickly enough to create the plans able to guide such development and ensure its quality.

Under the EU/Syrian Government funded Municipal Administration Modernisation Programme (MAM), attempts have been made to improve the quality and effectiveness of local government, in particular in its ability to manage growth. Thus over more than four years, MAM has delivered a series of action plans covering legislative, financial and administrative reform and its work strands have included urban planning and related topics. Specifically, the MAM programme has assisted the Syrian Government with the introduction of its first regional planning legislation, one of the main aims of which is to protect green areas through the better regulation of urban growth, especially in respect of the informal areas.

Ross describes how Syria's Ministry of Local Administration has been able to use Landsat images from 1988 and 2007 to quantify the changes across six Syrian cities in terms of the spread of development and the loss of green space. These images are of medium resolution which are more readily available to developing countries than high resolution ones, and they are often free of charge. But, as the illustrations in the article reveal, they provide sufficiently good information for policy conclusions to be drawn. They certainly show that there have been very considerable losses of green space between the two dates.

The promising news is that Syria's urban planners now have two important tools to guide the city growth of the future, regional planning legislation and the cost effective technique of using medium resolution satellite imagery.

The final essay in this Review is about the vitally important topic of food availability and food security. Increasingly, the world struggles to feed its growing population, as more people convert to grain intensive western diets, as grain is diverted to provide fuel for cars and as crops fail through the extremes of drought and flooding. The failure of the Ukrainian wheat crop this summer is a recent example.

At the same time, there are growing concerns about the environmental costs of consuming food transported from distant locations – i.e. the food miles. For this and other reasons, such as the desire for healthier eating, consumers in western countries are now beginning to favour locally grown produce, food that they grow themselves or food produced by nearby farmers and often sold through farmers' markets. Over time, this could lead to considerable savings in energy use and related carbon emissions.

So, is this an area that planners have neglected, and could individual cities do more to boost local growing as part of their planning strategies? In **Cultivating the Capital: How the Planning System is Vital to London's Ability to Grow its Own Food,** Jenny Jones of the London Assembly writes about a key investigation into London's potential to grow more of its own food. That investigation pointed to the acute dependence of London on distant food sources, to lengthy supply chains that are vulnerable to disruption, and to the major implications of those supply patterns in terms of transport and food miles.

Thus, London should become more self sufficient in food supply terms, making much greater use of the open land of the Green Belt and of other available land within its built up area. Paradoxically, it has been the planning system that has thwarted some potential farming initiatives and, for the future, greater flexibility is required. Thus, changes to the London Plan are proposed, a step that is being supported by the Mayor of London.

The essay also contains some interesting case studies about local food growing and marketing initiatives in London and a contribution by Rosie Boycott, of the London Food Board about Capital Growth a scheme to create 2012 Growing Spaces by 2012. These are community based schemes, providing considerable social benefits as well as the benefit of fresh, local produce.

Part IV – The ISOCARP Awards for Excellence

In this final part of the Review, we describe the three winning entries from our 2009 Awards scheme.

We hope that you will enjoy reading this latest issue of our popular publication on international planning.

—

Endnotes

1. Ministry of Nairobi Metropolitan Development 2008 *Nairobi Metro 2020 – A World Class African Metropolis.*

2. UN HABITAT 2009 *Cities and Climate Change; The perspective of UN HABITAT.* ISOCARP Review 05 05;*Low Carbon Cities* October 2009

3. www.ipcc.ch

4. Estimada being the Arabic word for sustainability

5. Shao Yisheng, Shi Nan et al (2008) *Some Observations Concerning China's Urban Development* China Architecture and Building Press

6. Energy intensity is energy consumed per unit of GDP

01
Focus on Africa

Kenya: Urban Settlements and Development Profile

Mairura Omwenga

Nairobi, Central Business District
Souce: Julius Mwelu/UN Habitat

1. Introduction

1.1. Overview

This paper presents a development profile of a sample of urban settlements in Kenya. Kenya is experiencing very rapid population growth, particularly in urban areas. The number and size of urban settlements has grown rapidly in the last 30-40 years. This rapid urbanization generates tremendous development potential and opportunities in the country. It has also generated serious social, economic and spatial challenges.

The paper highlights the development potential and challenges facing urban settlements in Kenya. The development profile of the towns covers economic activities, housing, infrastructure and utilities, transport and governance issues. The paper then concludes by highlighting proposals on the way forward.

1.2. Location

Kenya is situated on the eastern coast of Africa. Tanzania borders the country to the South, Uganda to the West, Ethiopia and Sudan to the North, Somalia to the Northeast, and the Indian Ocean to the East. Kenya covers an area of 582,646 km2. 20% of the country area is good arable land but 80% is arid and semi-arid land.

1.3. Kenya - Physical and Climatic Features

From the Indian Ocean, the low coastal plains rise to the central highlands. The highlands are bisected by the Great Rift Valley and also the home to Mount Kenya (5199m) - the second highest mountain in Africa – Plate 1-1. To the West of the country lies Lake Victoria.

Kenya has a primarily tropical climate. The country receives about 250mm of rainfall annually in the north eastern semi-arid region and above 1,800mm in the wet western and central Kenya highlands.

1.4. National Population

For the last 30-40 years, Kenya has experienced rapid population growth. At a growth rate of 3.2 – 3.4% per annum, the country's population rose from 11 million people in 1969 to about 40 million in 2010. In the last 20 – 30 years, Kenya has also experienced very rapid urban population growth (UN-Habitat, 2008, p.102). Whereas the worldwide urban population is expected to double in 42 years, East Africa's urban population is likely to double in 17 years. Kenya's urbanization level is currently at 25% of total national population.

1.5. The Country's Economic Base

Agriculture is the backbone of Kenya's economy. The main exports include tea, coffee, and horticultural produce. Indeed Kenya is known for its world quality coffee and tea (Plate 1-2). In the last few years, horticulture production has also increased tremendously and today horticulture exports are among the top foreign exchange earners (Plate 1-3).

Heavy manufacturing industry and commercial establishments are concentrated in the main urban centres of Nairobi, Mombasa, Kisumu, Nakuru, and Eldoret. Kenya is also a leading tourist destination in Africa, with a wide range of tourist attractions. These attractions include coastal beaches, wildlife parks and game reserves, beautiful landmarks and year-round good weather. Kenya boasts the 8th Wonder of the World – the great migration in Masai Mara – Plate 1-4.

Plate 1-1: Mt. Kenya - A Key National Landmark

Plate 1-2: Large Scale Tea Plantation in Kericho

Plate 1-3: Flower Farming in Naivasha

Plate 1-4: Wildebeest Migration in Masai Mara

2. Kenya - Urbanization Trends

2.1. Urban Population

In 2010 Kenya's population is estimated at 40 million people. In 1999, Nairobi, the capital city, had a population of 2,143,000. In the same year, Kenya's second largest city and port of Mombasa had 665,000 people. The national and urban population distribution of the main urban centres in Kenya, including Nairobi Metropolitan Region (NMR) is shown below (Table 2-1).

Year	1999	2007	2012	2017	2022	2027	2030
Total National Population, Million	28.7	36.3	41.5	47.2	52.9	58.7	62.1
Total Urban Population, Million	5.4	9.0	12.3	16.9	23.1	31.7	38.2
Urban % of National Population	18.8	24.8	29.6	35.8	43.7	54.0	61.5
NMR Population, Million	4.8	6.3	7.6	9.0	10.8	12.8	14.3
NMR % of National Population	16.7	17.4	18.3	19.1	20.2	21.7	22.8
NMR % of Urban Population	88.5	70.3	61.7	53.3	46.3	40.2	37.0

Table 2-1: National, Urban and Nairobi Metropolitan Population Up to 2030

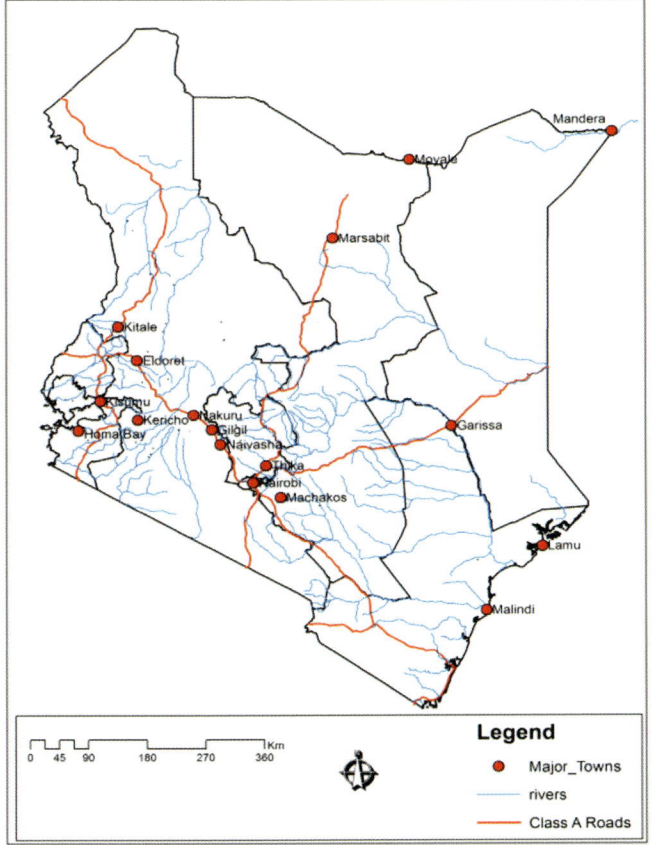

Figure 2-1: Distribution of Main Urban Centres in Kenya

2.2. Number and Distribution of Urban Centres

It is, estimated that there are about 2,500 – 3,000 urban centres in Kenya. Beyond Nairobi and Mombasa, Kenya's major towns include Kisumu, Nakuru, Eldoret, Nyeri, Kakamega, Embu, and Garissa. The distribution of the main urban centres is shown below (Figure 2-1). The majority of these are concentrated in the areas of good arable land and adjacent to the main road and railway line along the Mombasa/Nairobi/Kisumu transport corridor..

2.3. Category and Hierarchy of Urban Centres

The hierarchy of urban centres in Kenya is split into several categories, namely (Kenya, 1986) – (i) city council; (ii) municipal council; (iii) town council; (iv) urban council; (v) rural centre; (vi) market centre; and (vii) local centre.

Nairobi is the only city council in the country. The 44 municipal councils include Kisumu, Kakamega, Eldoret, Nakuru, Nyeri, Murang'a, Thika, Machakos, Embu and Meru.

There are sixty three (63) town councils; these include Keroka, Kendu Bay, Yala, Mumias, Lodwar, Narok, Kajiado, Isiolo, Chuka, and Kangundo. At the moment there are no operational urban councils as all former urban councils were upgraded to town councils.

Elsewhere, county councils are responsible for the administration of the three other tiers of settlement, namely rural centres, market centres, and local centres (Plate 2-1).

3. Nairobi Metropolitan Region
3.1. Background

Nairobi is the capital city of Kenya and the main commercial and service centre in Eastern Africa. Nairobi is a Masai name that translates as "the place of cool waters" and is popularly known as the "green city in the sun". It was founded in 1895 as a campsite for white settlers and, in 1899, became a depot during the construction of the Kenya-Uganda railway. The city is at an altitude of 1,795m and has a comfortable weather temperature of 12/25 degrees centigrade and annual rainfall of 1,200mm.

As a city, Nairobi has some unique and strategic features. These include (i) Nairobi National Park - the only city in the world with a natural wildlife park (Plate 3-1); and (ii) its United Nations (UN). Thus, Nairobi is the world headquarters of the United Nations Environmental Programme (UNEP) and UN-HABITAT. Nairobi is the only city in the South and developing world that has global headquarters for UN lead agencies (Plate 3-2).

Plate 3-1: Nairobi National Park is within the City

Plate 2-1: Kenol Market Centre in Thika District

Plate 3-2: UN Headquarters in Nairobi

3.2. Nairobi Metropolitan Region

The city of Nairobi covers 686 km2. It has experienced very rapid growth and expansion into the neighbouring regions. In 2008, the Government created the Nairobi Metropolitan Region in order to effectively manage the city and the city region activities. This metropolitan region brings together 15 local authorities – (i) The City Council of Nairobi; (ii) The Municipal Councils of Thika, Ruiru, Kiambu, Limuru, Mavoko and Machakos; (iii) The Town Councils of Karuri, Kikuyu, Kajiado, and Kangundo; and (iv) County Councils of Thika, Kiambu, Ol Kejuado and Masaku.

3.3. Urban Development Opportunities

Nairobi and its metropolitan region is experiencing the highest and most rapid rate of urbanization and spatial growth in East Africa. Nairobi Metropolitan Region has enormous development potential and opportunities:

- It is strategically located within the local, regional and international transport linkages.
- Nairobi is served by, and is at the midpoint of, the Great North Road that links Cape Town and Cairo.
- Nairobi's Jomo Kenyatta International Airport (JKIA) is within 5/6 hours of all major cities in Africa.
- The city acts as a convenient gateway to many parts of Eastern, Central and Southern parts of Africa.
- Nairobi is the global and regional headquarters of UN HABITAT, and UNEP.
- The city is also headquarters to many international and regional corporate organizations; these have a heavy industrial and commercial investment presence in the city.
- The metropolitan region has a large population base of 6.3 million people (2007) and a projected population of 14.3 million people in 2030. This population base provides the labour force to run the economy in the metropolitan region.
- The metropolitan region has a large pool of universities and research institutions to provide the knowledge, skills and technology required for sustainable city development (Plate 3-3).

3.4. Urban Development Challenges

Despite its great development achievement, Nairobi and its metropolitan region is faced with a wide range of problems and challenges:

- The metropolitan region cannot meet the needs of the large population and rapid population growth rate. There are rising unemployment and poverty levels in the metropolitan region. The performance of the economy lags behind the population growth. (MoNMD, 2008, p.24).
- There is an inadequate housing supply with a projected deficit of 45-70% below the demand, particularly for the low income population. In Nairobi City, for example, 60% of the population lives in deplorable and deprived housing conditions (MoNMD, 2008, p.24) (Plate 3-4).
- The infrastructure is inadequate. Many households in Nairobi and its metropolitan region do not have adequate access to water, sanitation and electricity.
- There is poor provision of, and access to, community and social services including schools, health facilities and sport/recreational facilities.
- The transport system is inadequate. The city experiences long motor vehicle traffic jams, poor and expensive matatu public transport services, and a poor safety record.
- The system of governance is poor, ineffective and uncoordinated. Development plans, activities and projects among government ministries and local authorities are not well planned, coordinated, financed and executed.

- There is a deterioration in the general quality of the environ

3.5. The Way Forward

The Government, local authorities, private sector and non-governmental organizations in the metropolitan region are undertaking several projects aimed at improving the economy and services in the Nairobi metropolitan region. These projects include (MoNMD, 2008; 2009):

- The establishment of the Ministry of Nairobi Metropolitan Development (MoNMD) in 2008 to integrate and co-ordinate development plans and the execution of projects within the metropolitan region.
- The release by the Ministry in 2008 of Nairobi Metro 2030, a strategic and policy document to coordinate activities within the 15 local authorities.
- The current preparation by the Ministry of the strategic spatial plan for the metropolitan region (MoNMD, 2009).
- The expansion and moderization of Jomo Kenyatta International Airport to handle increased traffic.
- The expansion and modernization of main trunk roads and by-pass roads – Mombasa Road, Uhuru Highway, Thika Road, Northern by-pass and Southern by-pass.
- The initiation and development by the government of an ICT hub in Machakos/Mavoko to serve Nairobi.
- The instigation by the government of a number of housing improvement projects (Plate 3-6).

Plate 3-3: University of Nairobi

Plate 3-4: Mathare Informal Settlement

Plate 3-5: Deterioration of Environment

Plate 3-6: Slum Upgrading Program in Kibera

4. Mombasa – Coastal Province

4.1. Background

Mombasa is the second largest urban centre in Kenya after the city of Nairobi. The town, which is about 500 km south east of Nairobi, is situated on Mombasa Island and in 1999 it had a population of 727,842 people (GoK, 2001). Its historical development dates back to the 15th century during the Arabian rule of the coastal strip. Mombasa is also home to the historic Fort Jesus, built as a military base by the Portuguese in the 16th Century. The average rainfall in Mombasa is 1,200mm per annum and the average temperature range is 20/31 degrees centigrade.

Plate 4-1: Kilindini Harbor

4.2. Main Development Opportunities and Activities

Mombasa has the largest harbour in Eastern Africa with good sheltered harbour facilities at Kilindini port, and is the gateway to the East and Central African region (Plate 4-1). Within that region, Mombasa has the second largest port in terms of tonnage and containers handled after Durban in South Africa. The total cargo traffic through the port is about 14 million tons a year. It is served by 17 shipping lines and has direct connections to over 80 world ports. It is also served by Moi International Airport. The major industrial activity is associated with the petroleum refinery in Changamwe (Plate 4-2).

Plate 4-2: Changamwe Oil Refinery

Mombasa is a major tourist destination in Kenya and Africa due to its clean coastal beaches. The main points of interest in Mombasa town are the ocean beach, Old Town and Fort Jesus (Plates 4-3, 4-4, and 4-5). There are several luxury hotels on these beaches.

Plate 4-3: Mombasa Beaches

Plate 4-4: Symbolic Elephant Tusks - Mombasa.

Plate 4-5: Fort Jesus – Mombasa

4.3. Development Challenges

The main development challenges facing Mombasa include:
- The fact that Mombasa does not have a current and strategic town development spatial plan. The last master plan for Mombasa was prepared in 1962 (MMC, 1963).
- The congestion at Kilindini Port. The port facilities, road and railway system have not been expanded enough to cope with the rising demand.
- The congestion of vehicular traffic on the island and also along the 3 links to the mainland at Likoni Ferry, Makupa Causeway and Nyali Bridge.
- The increasing pollution of the coastal beaches due to poor collection and disposal of waste.
- The inadequate supply of housing and supporting infrastructure – water, sewerage etc.

4.4. The Way Forward

In order to improve the development of Mombasa, a number of projects are being undertaken and/or are on the drawing board. These include:
- The construction of a permanent bridge across Kilindini harbour at Likoni to replace the ferry services.
- The construction of a by-pass road to the western side of Mombasa, linking the South Coast and the Mombasa-Nairobi highway.
- The preparation by Kenya Ports Authority (KPA) of a master plan for the port in order to expand port facilities, rail, and access roads and ease traffic congestion.
- The initiation by the Ministry of Local Government, Ministry of Lands, and the Municipal Council of Mombasa of the process of preparing the strategic long term plan for Mombasa.

5. Kisumu - Nyanza Province
5.1. Background

Kisumu, the third largest urban centre in Kenya, is the headquarters of Nyanza Province (Plate 5-1). It has developed progressively from a railway terminus and internal port in 1901, to become the leading commercial/trading, industrial, communication and administrative centre in the Lake Victoria basin. The town covers an area of approximately 417 km^2 The average rainfall in Kisumu is 1,500 mm per annum and the average temperature is 15/30 degrees centigrade.

Plate 5-1: Kisumu Town with Lake Victoria Visible in the Background

5.2. Population
Kisumu had a population of approximately 360,000 people according to the 1999 national population census (GoK, 2001). Its estimated population growth rate is 2.8% p.a.

5.3. Main Economic Development Activities
Kisumu is the main commercial and industrial centre in the Western and Lake Victoria region. The main industrial establishments include Kicomi Textile Mills, Equator/Coca Cola Bottlers, and several bakeries. In the immediate sugar belt hinterland, the town benefits from the presence of many sugar factories like Miwani and Muhoroni. Kisumu also has great potential in the fishing industry.

Kisumu is the centre for the Western Kenya and Lake Victoria tourism circuit and boasts several tourist class hotels. It also serves as a transportation hub for road, water and air transport. It operates the main regional airport in Western Kenya as well as the main terminal for the lake steamer service that serves Kenya, Tanzania and Uganda.

Kisumu is the home of a number of colleges, universities and research institutions. These include Maseno University, Great Lakes University, Tom Mboya Labour College, Kisumu Polytechnic, Kenya Medical Research Institute and the Centre for Disease Control.

5.4. Development Challenges
The main development challenges facing Kisumu include:
- The high population growth rate and increasing incidence of poverty..
- An inadequate housing provision. About 60% of the population live in poor and informal settlements that lack basic services.
- The inadequate provision of infrastructure and utilities, including water and sanitation services.
- The lack of a current town development plan and the uncontrolled growth of urban sprawl.
- The existence of poor transport services. The railway and lake steamer services are poor. The internal transport system is also inadequate and unsafe, particularly for non-motorised traffic (Plate 5-2).

Plate 5-2: Motorists and Boda Boda Cyclists Competing for Space

5.5. The Way Forward
The following projects are taking place to improve the development of Kisumu:
- The preparation of a strategic spatial plan for the town. This is a joint effort by the Municipal Council, Ministry of Local Government, and the Ministry of Lands.
- The establishment by the Municipal Council of a town planning department and the recruitment of technical and professional town planners.
- The initiation of a housing improvement program which is focusing on those with low incomes and on informal settlements.
- The implementation of a water and sanitation improvement project by the Municipal Council, and Kisumu Water and Sewerage Company.
- The expansion of Kisumu Airport to international standards.
- The rehabilitation of the port facilities and lake steamer services

6. Nakuru – Rift Valley Province

6.1. Background
Located about 150km west of Nairobi in the Great Rift Valley, Nakuru is the fourth largest city in Kenya after Nairobi, Mombasa and Kisumu. It gained municipality status in 1952 and covers an area of 290km2, of which the Lake Nakuru National Park takes up 188km2 MCN et al., 1999). Nakuru is the provincial headquarters for the vast Rift Valley Province. The average rainfall is 900 mm per annum and the average temperature range is 10/26 degrees centigrade.

6.2. Population
Nakuru town is estimated to have a population of approximately 550,000 in 2010 (GOK, 2001). The high population growth rate (7% per annum) continues to exert pressure on the fragile ecosystem and the limited urban infrastructure and services.

6.3. Economic Development Opportunities
Nakuru is the location of key industries, commercial establishments, and provincial government offices in Rift Valley. Tourism, agriculture and agro-based industries are the primary contributing sectors to the economy. Known as the 'farmers' capital' of Kenya, Nakuru is a renown hub for dairy and agro-based industrial and manufacturing activities.

Nakuru and its environs are endowed with numerous natural and ecological features that attract tourists to the town. These tourist attractions include Lake Nakuru National Park (Ramsar site), and one of the world's largest bird sanctuaries hosting flamingos and pelicans (Plate 6-1).

6-4. Development Challenges
The main development challenges in the municipality include:
- The uncontrolled development and urban sprawl.
- The high population growth rate and rising incidence of poverty.
- The inadequate housing and poor provision of infrastructure and utilities.
- The Increasing pollution of Lake Nakuru, the drying up of feeding rivers and reduced water level in the lake.
- The related loss of animal and flamingo populations.

6.5. The Way Forward
The municipal council and government are undertaking several projects to support sustainable development in the town. These include:
- The redevelopment of housing and slum upgrading in low and middle income areas.
- The expansion of the water and sewerage system in the town.
- Environmental improvement and waste management schemes in low and middle income areas.
- The expansion and improvement of the main Nairobi/Eldoret highway.
- The proposed development of the local airport.
- The initiation by the Municipal Council and Ministry of Local Government of a strategic spatial plan for the municipality.

Plate 6-1: Flamingos in Lake Nakuru

7. Eldoret – Home to Sports Champions
7.1. Background
Eldoret is the administrative centre of Uasin Gishu District in Rift Valley Province. The population was 193,830 in the 1999 census (GoK, 2001). Eldoret has an average rainfall of 1,100mm per annum and the average temperature range is 9/22 degrees centigrade.

7.2. Home to Sports Champions
Eldoret is the hometown of legendary Kenyan runners and world champions (Plate 7-1). The high altitude is an ideal training ground for many middle and long distance athletes. The runners from Eldoret have contributed significantly to the economy of Eldoret town (Plate 7-2).

7.3. Economic Activities and Opportunities
The economy of Eldoret is based on large-scale agriculture and livestock farms. Major industries include textile, wheat, pyrethrum and maize. The town has a large market created by major institutions like Moi University, Eldoret Polytechnic, Moi Teaching and Referral Hospital (MTRH), and Eldoret International Airport.

7.4. The Main Development Challenges
The development challenges facing Eldoret include –
- Inadequate housing to meet demand.
- Inadequate infrastructure services and utilities.
- Poor transportation, particularly for non-motorized traffic.
- The economic slowdown due to the 2007/8 community clashes and collapsing industrial establishment.
- Uncontrolled and unplanned development and expansion
- Inadequate utilization of Eldoret Airport

7.5. The Way Forward
The following projects are currently being undertaken in Eldoret –
- The preparation of the strategic spatial plan for the town, which is near completion..
- The improvement of low-income housing areas in Langas, Huruma etc.
- The improvement and expansion of the sewerage and drainage system..
- The expansion and improvement of access roads, parking facilities and street lighting.

Plate 7-1: Kenyan Runners are World Champions

Plate 7-2: Eldoret Tow

8. Conclusion and Recommendations

8.1. Urban Settlement Potential and Opportunities

A survey of urban settlements in Kenya confirms that there exists great development potential and investment opportunities. These are greater in the larger municipalities and in particular, the Nairobi metropolitan region. This is because the larger urban centres enjoy greater economies of scale and have a stable economic base. But it is important that the planning and development of the urban centres is well integrated with the rural hinterland of this agricultural country.

Kenya enjoys a strategic position within the African continent. The country acts as the gateway to many parts of east, central and southern Africa. Kenya also enjoys unique and attractive features that appeal to tourists. These attractions also act to boost and support the development of sustainable urban centres in Kenya. The urban housing sector provides a great investment opportunity as the supply barely meets 20% of the demand.

8.2. Development Challenges

It is also true that the growth and development of urban centres in Kenya are faced with many problems and challenges. These challenges include (i) widespread urban sprawl, uncontrolled growth and haphazard development in urban areas; (ii) an inadequate supply of housing and mushrooming of informal slum settlements; (iii) an inadequate supply of water; (iv) poor sanitation, poor wastewater drainage and solid waste disposal; (v) an inadequate supply of infrastructure services such as electricity and ICT services; (vi) a poor transport and road network system; (vii) poor administration and management systems in local authorities; and (viii) limited community and social services such as schools, health facilities, open and recreational space.

8.3. Recommendations

The following recommendations are proposed in order to achieve sustainable urban development and planning in Kenya:

- That urban growth and development should be coordinated and integrated with town and country planning. Indeed this planning must lead and guide urban growth and development in Kenya. Special attention should be given to the metropolitan regions of Nairobi, Mombasa, Kisumu, Nakuru, and Eldoret.
- That as a priority, the country must proceed to prepare spatial development plans at all levels - national, regional, and local.
- That as a matter of urgency there should be coordination and integration of the key institutions responsible for urban development and spatial planning – the Ministry of Local Government, the Ministry of Lands and various local authorities.
- That adequate resources should be allocated for low-income and middle-income housing. Priority should also be given to slum upgrading projects.
- That adequate resources should be allocated to the improvement of community facilities, infrastructure services and utilities e.g. schools, health centres, water, sanitation, electricity etc.
- That Government, local authorities, and the community should work together to improve the general environment in urban areas. This includes proper solid waste management, improved air quality, and protection of water sources.

Reference and Bibliography

Central Bureau of Statistics (CBS) (2004), Kenya Demographic and Health Survey 2003, Ministry of Health, Nairobi

Government of Kenya (GoK) (2001), 1999 Population and Housing Census, Government Printer, Nairobi

Kenya National Bureau of Statistics (2009), Kenya Demographic and Health Survey 2008/2009, Preliminary Report, Nairobi

Kenya National Bureau of Statistics (KNBS) (2009), Statistical Abstract, the Government Printer, Nairobi

Kenya National Bureau of Statistics (KNBS) (2010), Economic Survey, Nairobi, Government Printer

Kenya, Republic of (1986), Local Government Act (Cap 265), Nairobi, Government Printer

Kenya, Republic of (1996), the Physical Planning Act (Cap 265), Nairobi, Government Printer

Municipal Council of Nakuru (MCN), Republic of Kenya, UNCHS (1999), Strategic Structure Plan: Action Plan for Sustainable Development. Vol. II., Nairobi

Ministry of Lands and Settlement (MLS) (1971), Town Planning Handbook, Nairobi, Unpublished

Ministry of Lands and Settlement (MLS) (1978), Human Settlement in Kenya, Strategy for Urban and Rural Development, Government Printer, Nairobi

Ministry of Lands (2009), National Land Policy, Sessional Paper No.3 of 2000, Government Printer, Nairobi

Ministry of Lands (2010), National Spatial Plan, Draft Concept Paper, Department of Physical Planning, Nairobi

Ministry of Nairobi Metropolitan Development (MoNMD) (2008), Nairobi Metro 2030, A World Class African Metropolis, Government Printer, Nairobi

Mombasa Municipal Council (1963), Mombasa Master Plan, Printing and Packing Corporation, Nairobi

UN Habitat (2003), Kenya Urban Sector Profile, UN-Habitat, Nairobi

UN Habitat (2008), The State of African Cities 2008, UN-Habitat, Nairobi

Project Preparation and its Crucial Role in Enabling More Effective and Sustainable Development – The South African Experience

Mark Misselhorn

Typical greenfields, mixed income housing development to the north of Durban (Parkgate Project)

Community rental housing project at Umlazi providing City-owned rental housing stock for those with very low income levels.

A typical informal settlement in eThekwini – this one at Cato Crest in Cato Manor.

A typical informal settlement upgrading process utilizing a double storey attached low cost typology and a 'rollover' upgrading approach (i.e. site developed in small 'rollover' phases to minimize temporary relocations requirements) (Cato Crest).

Introduction

Since the advent of democracy in South African in 1994, significant strides have been made in bringing about political, socio-economic and built environment transformation. Amongst other achievements, rigorous frameworks for governance and development planning have been legislated and significant programmes of state expenditure put in place in order to address historical developmental backlogs arising from the apartheid era. In some respects, South Africa may be regarded as a case study for good practices in this regard. However, notwithstanding the world-class planning and governance frameworks in place, there have also been significant challenges in respect of the planning and implementation of developmental projects which provide rich lessons, not only for South Africa, but also for other developing countries.

| Concept & Feasibility (Project Preparation) |  | Detailed Design (Specification & Costs) |  | Impl... |

Project Preparation Cycle

NOTE: This cycle is generic & is based mainly on the preparation process for state or donor funded housing & infrastructure projects. The primary stages are 2, 3 & 4. Some adaptation of this generic process may be required depending on specific circumstances & project types, especially for projects which are non-infrastructural in nature. All figures are in South African rands.

1. Project Identification and Prioritisation

Answers the question: Which projects or initiatives should be prioritized?

Purpose & scope: Appropriate where project demand exceeds available resources & rational choices need to be made. Projects assessed against defined selection criteria & prioritized via an initiation timetable. Typically undertaken at the programme level (a group of potential projects or geographic area) to ensure that local level spatial planning is in synch with prioritized projects.

Cost: Variable, but typically R10K to R50K.
Timescale: 1 to 6 wks.

6. Monitoring and Review

Answers the question: Was project preparation effective & how can it be improved in future projects?

Purpose & scope: Project preparation effectiveness reviewed. Feedback given to stakeholders.

Cost: Typically R2K to R6K per project.
Timescale: Variable.

5. Follow Through with Investors

Answers the question: Has implementation funding been secured?

Purpose & scope: Outstanding funder requirements & queries are met. Funding approvals or agreements with implementation partners are concluded.

Cost: Variable.
Timescale: Highly variable - from a few weeks to over a year.

Feasibility

Answers the question: Is the project fe... and supported, what is the concept & much will it cost to implement?

Purpose & scope: More detailed ... undertaken by a team of suitably ... professionals to resolve any outstanding ... define planning, design, institutional & ... parameters (capital & operational) ... preliminary level. Project concept finalize... support from all key stakeholders. E... project is feasible, appropriate & sustain... Comprehensive applications to implemen... / capital funders made. Scope & costs m... considerably depending on stakeholder & ... requirements.

Cost: Variable, but typically R100K to R60C...
Timescale: 2 to 6 months

 © Project Preparation Trust of KZN

Cycle

Commission and Handover (& Review) → **Operating and Maintenance (& Review)**

Preliminary Assessment

Answers the question: Should preparation funding be released & what are the main risks that require mitigation?

Purpose & scope: Lightweight, upfront assessment (pre-screening) of a specific project by a suitable professional. Identifies key risks & opportunities prior to commencing with full scale preparation. Includes collection of available information, desktop assessment, initial stakeholder consultation & site visit. Defines scope & budget for detailed preparation phases to follow.

Cost: Typically R4K to R8K.
Timescale: 1 to 3 wks.

Project Viable?
- NO → Terminate OR Take Special Action
- YES →

Pre-feasibility

Answers the question: What is the project's risk profile, can the risks be mitigated & what is the preliminary project concept?

Purpose & scope: Risks assessed by a team of suitably skilled professionals. Assessments usually include site suitability (land legal, bulk services, geotechnical, topography, environmental etc), stakeholder support & funding availability. Broad project concept & rough capital & operational costs are defined.

Cost: Variable, but typically R40K to R100K.
Timescale: 2 to 6 months.

Project Viable?
- YES
- NO → Terminate OR Take Special Action

Graph showing declining influence and increasing cost of change over time

(Axes: Level of Influence, Cost to Change; Phases: Concept, Design, Implement, Commission; curves: Level of Influence, Potential to add value, Cost to Change)

(Ref "Project Management & Control Techniques": Rory Burke. Promatec, 1999)

Figure 1: Project Preparation Cycle showing different phases, their purposes and broad scope

Aerial photograph of a typical informal settlement.

Typical double storey low income housing units in eThekwini (Uganda settlement)

One of the most prominent of these lessons is the need for more effective project preparation in order to provide the necessary link between local level spatial plans (which are typically 'broad brush' in nature), budgetary allocations for capital expenditures, and the delivery of viable and appropriate projects.

Despite the obvious need for development projects and interventions to be properly conceptualized, prepared and planned, the reality remains that they all too often occur in a reactive and sometimes haphazard fashion. This is especially apparent with projects which focus on addressing poverty, basic infrastructure provision and the inclusion of the urban poor into cities. It is also not a uniquely South African phenomenon.

Why does this occur and how can this situation be remedied? This short paper explores the issues and provides some answers, based on Project Preparation Trust's (PPT's)[1] extensive experience in preparing various developmental projects in South Africa, ranging from informal settlement upgrading, housing and infrastructure to special needs, livelihoods and local economic development.

What is Project Preparation?

Project preparation can be broadly defined as the entire social, technical and financial work required to ensure that a proposed project is feasible and appropriate and that it can be successfully implemented. The preparation process ensures the identification and elimination of key risks at the earliest possible time and maximises development opportunities by ensuring that projects are well conceptualised. Typical preparation activities include: the identification of funding sources, needs assessments, community and stakeholder consultations, the development of project concepts, assessments of site suitability (e.g. topography, geotechnical and environmental conditions, bulk service availability and land legal issues), land availability negotiations and agreements, participative planning, preliminary design, estimates for capital and operational costs and applications / proposals to funders or implementation partners. Most of this work takes place during the pre-feasibility and feasibility phases. The project preparation process and its various phases are outlined in more detail in Figure 1.

The Planning and Governance Framework in South Africa

The planning and governance framework in South Africa is characterized by principles of strong local government, integrated local development planning and the budgeting of state resources on the basis of such plans. Legislation in South Africa[2] requires municipalities to develop and maintain Integrated Development Plans (IDP's) which are required not only to determine the broad spatial planning themes for a specific municipality (typically over a five year period), but to also go further in terms of identifying specific projects and initiatives which are to be prioritised over the period. In theory the linkages between the overarching IDP and the delivery of projects are achieved by means of sector plans which identify and prioritize specific projects in various different sectors (e.g. housing, water, sanitation, key social facilities). It is envisaged that sector forums constituting key sector stakeholders (including municipal and provincial line department representation) create such sector plans. Examples of such sector plans are Consolidated Infrastructure Plans (CIP's) and Housing Sector Plans (HSP's). In theory, such plans guide and inform the Medium Term Expenditure Frameworks (MTEF's) of government and enable the rational and effective allocation of state resources. The different responsibilities, powers and functions of different spheres of government (national, provincial and local government[3]) are legislated and the re-demarcation of municipalities in 1998[4] ensures egalitarian 'wall to wall' local municipalities covering both urban and rural areas with no separate 'town councils' except for Metros (which themselves typically encompass some peri-urban and rural hinterland).

What are the Challenges to the Effective Implementation of the Framework?

There are of course a range of other challenges to the successful implementation of the above-mentioned planning and governance framework, the most important of which are outlined in Figure 2 and obviously some are more easily overcome than others. There is, however, one challenge which is inherent in the framework itself but which is also relatively easily addressed, in which case it can play a catalytic role in overcoming or mitigating most of the other challenges. This is the challenge of entrenching and mainstreaming more effective project preparation.

One of the paradoxes of the current framework is that it necessitates project selection and medium term budget allocations in the absence of adequate up front project assessment and feasibility work in order to determine the viability and appropriateness of such projects and to inform budgetary allocations. In addition, there is typically a lack of project preparation funding to enable such up front work to be undertaken. Most project assessment and feasibility work is therefore undertaken 'at risk' by private sector service providers which compromises its effectiveness and creates the potential for an inherent conflict of interests. Service providers working at risk understandably often undertake the minimum level

Challenges	Project Preparation Mitigation Role
A) Insufficient skills and human capacity within various spheres of government, especially at the level of local municipalities[5]	Procuring external, private sector and NGO expertise into the critical early stages of the project cycle augments limited state capacity at a time when critical conceptual and strategic decisions are made, including decisions on the allocation of significant capital funding.
B) A tendency towards patronage and the politicization of development and planning processes	Systematic project preparation provides a more rigorous and technically informed basis for the selection, prioritisation and conceptualization of projects and in so doing offsets and counter-balances politically driven processes.
C) Difficulties in ensuring effective and unbiased procurement of services, contracts and tenders	Project preparation confirms not only the feasibility of a project but also provides a specification and cost for its implementation. This enables the preparation of more effective tender documentation which clearly specifies the standards, requirements and criteria that must be met by a prospective contractor. Such a 'pre-planned' procurement approach can enable more effective and accountable results.
D) An over-emphasis on implementation and capital expenditure relative to project preparation and planning	If enshrined in planning and governance frameworks, systematic project preparation ensures that the early stages of the project cycle, where conceptual and strategic decisions are made, receive the necessary 'pride of place'.
E) Poor co-operation between different spheres of government and between different government departments[6]	The technical and social / participative work undertaken during project preparation provides both the technical information as well as the process to make co-operation between different spheres of government and / or departments significantly easier and less risky.
F) A tendency towards top down policy and strategy formulation, including the design of development grants which tend to be prescriptive and rigid	Project preparation quickly indicates where policies, strategies or the configuration of grants are out of sync with real project needs on the ground and enables useful feedback to the higher spheres of government to make the necessary adjustments (including where grants need to be more flexible).

Figure 2: Challenges facing the effective implementation of planning and governance frameworks in South Africa and the role which more systematic and institutionalized project preparation can play in mitigating these challenges.

of technical work in order to minimize costs and risk. They also have a perverse incentive in proving projects to be viable as this is the only basis upon which they have a chance of recovering their risk and making some profit on the detailed design and implementation phases (even though government procurement regulations make the prospects of down-stream procurement uncertain). Furthermore, because project preparation is not sufficiently institutionalized and funded by government, in most instances there are no established specifications and cost norms for the preparation of different types of projects, nor established mechanisms for ensuring the quality thereof.

There are of course a range of other challenges to the successful implementation of the above-mentioned planning and governance framework, the most important of which are outlined in Figure 2 left. This table also indicates the manner in which more effective and systematic project preparation can address or offset these challenges. For this to be achieved, systematic project preparation would ultimately need to be made an inherent part of the state's planning framework and up front funding for it would need to be provided.

Why is Preparation Typically Neglected?

Given the obvious need for systematic project preparation and the significant value it adds, the question must be asked as to why it remains neglected, not only in South Africa, but also elsewhere in the developing world. Experience in South Africa suggests that the following are some of the main factors:

- Project preparation is generally poorly understood in terms of its need, function and form (e.g. its specification and cost). Further reference should be made to Figure 1 in this regard.
- Feasibilities and business plans are often regarded as administrative 'tick boxes' or formalities which need to be complied with before projects can be implemented or funding allocated and consequently project preparation is not appreciated as being a critical and value adding phase of the project cycle.
- Politically prioritised projects tend to be subjected to insufficient rational scrutiny.
- There is a tendency to 'hurry' into implementation. This is especially so in the case of programmes where there is high capital spend and where there is pressure to address significant developmental backlogs (as in the case of South Africa and other developing countries).
- Relatively short budgetary cycles (e.g. of a year) place extreme pressure to rapidly spend allocated budgets or face the risk of losing them.
- There is typically no up front 'seed' funding for project preparation and project planning (both from state and donor sources).
- There is often limited appreciation of the significant (multi year) timeframes for the delivery of many projects, especially those which are complex and capital intensive. Unrealistic project timetables (schedules) are typically produced, often influenced by political aspirations, which are unrealistic from the start. Efforts are therefore often made to 'fastrack' projects (even though such 'fast-tracking usually compromises project outcomes and can often result in projects becoming stalled at a later time).

Why is Effective Project Preparation Critical and What are the Benefits?

Effective project preparation fulfils several critical functions. Firstly, it ensures that only viable and appropriate projects are taken forward into the resource intensive process of detailed design and implementation. Secondly, it ensures that project risks are identified, investigated and mitigated at the earliest possible time in the project cycle. Thirdly, it ensures that a project concept is developed which is robust, appropriate and acceptable to key stakeholders (based on a mix of technical, social and financial inputs).

It is noteworthy that the 'leverage' achieved by project preparation is massive, both financially and in terms of improved project outcomes. The typical financial leverage on project preparation funding for housing and infrastructure projects is in the region of 1:60. This means that, on average, every rand invested in project preparation results in the leverage of R60 in capital / implementation funding on viable and appropriate projects. More importantly, there is also significant qualitative leverage in the sense that well prepared projects afford better and more predictable project outcomes.

In addition, preparation also helps to optimize the allocation of scarce resources through:
- Ensuring the allocation of funding to those projects which are most appropriate, strategic and necessary.
- Significantly reducing the incidence of project failures and the related wastage of finances and other resources.
- Ensuring that projects are carefully conceptualized including, where necessary, the comparative assessment of different projects approaches or solutions to ensure innovation and the implementation of the best project solution available.
- Introducing suitably skilled professionals into the project process early on. Their specialist inputs can then be used to better inform and enrich the strategic and planning decisions of politicians and government officials at a stage when project concepts are still being formulated.
- Enabling more predicable and reliable project timetables (schedules) with associated budgeting and cash-flow benefits.

The Relationship Between Project Preparation and More Sustainable Urban Planning

Project preparation plays a critical role in ensuring that spatial planning (at city or precinct level) remains congruent with project level planning (which incorporates layout planning and urban design elements) and that fruitful developmental outcomes are the result. On the one hand it ensures that projects or initiatives identified through higher level spatial planning processes are subjected to sufficient assessment before they are taken forward at the project level. On the other hand it ensures that project level planning work does not take place in isolation from other necessary preparation activities and that planning elements do not get out of sync with others which are equally important (e.g. securing bulk services or land availability). There are many examples of planners going quite far with project level plans, such as layouts, without sufficient prior work such as bulk services investigations, land acquisitions and geotechnical investigations having been undertaken. Planners are in fact well positioned to play a leading role in the preparation phase of projects as they typically possess the necessary overall spatial, conceptual and interdisciplinary skills required. They are also well positioned to provide practical project level feedback to inform those involved in broader spatial planning processes.

Preparation and Participative Planning

The trend towards more participative planning in recent years, and a growing awareness of what this entails, is welcome. Meaningful engagement with and feedback from project beneficiaries, investors and other affected stakeholders is obviously critical during the preparatory and planning stages. However, on a cautionary note, care also needs to be taken in respect of the timing and intensity of such participation. In the case of pro-poor developmental projects, particular care should be taken not to enter into any process of intensive engagement until some level of technical evaluation of project risks and constraints has first been undertaken (typically at the pre-feasibility level). Such technical work is necessary to inform participative planning processes and to prevent the development of concepts and developmental aspirations which are not possible from a technical perspective[7] and within the available resource constraints. The development of unrealistic concepts, heightened expectations and political pressure may otherwise become a new and problematic project risk requiring additional management and mitigation. There is a trend within some NGO and participative planning circles to enter into a relatively intensive process of 'people driven' planning process right from the outset of projects but without undertaking all of the necessary preparatory technical work. Effective project preparation requires that processes of engagement and participation are always balanced with the relevant technical and financial work by suitably qualified professionals and that appropriate engagement occurs between such development professionals and project beneficiaries (along with other stakeholders) by means of a structured, transparent, and properly facilitated process.

Project Preparation in the Context of Informal Settlement Upgrading

A systematic and rigorous project preparation methodology has been developed in South Africa for the preparation of informal settlement upgrading projects focusing both on conventional, full upgrading[8] as well as the provision of interim services[9] (even if this methodology is not always adhered to). This methodology is informed by extensive experience by a range of stakeholders in preparing and implementing a range of diverse informal settlement upgrading projects over a period of more than 20 years, utilising both state and donor funding sources. There are potentially valuable lessons from South Africa for other developing countries in this regard. Two short case studies from the City of Durban (eThekwini Municipality) are presented in this paper in order to provide some insights to the reader.

The Context in eThekwini Municipality (City of Durban)

It is noted that the informal settlement pattern within eThekwini is characterized by large numbers of settlements scattered throughout both urban and peri-urban parts of the city as opposed to being concentrated in only a small number of massive settlements, as is the pattern in many other African cities.

Approximately a quarter of eThekwini's total population of approximately 3.5million reside in urban and peri-urban informal settlements[10]. Against this backdrop, the use of systematic project preparation methodology has for many years played a key role in the success of eThekwini's programme of providing mass, state subsidized low income housing (along with services and tenure). It has also more recently assisted the municipality in investigating and conceptualising additional pro-active programmes aimed at addressing the basic services needs of those informal settlements for whom mass housing cannot be provided in the near future.

Case Study 1: Interim Basic Services for 76,000 households in 166 prioritised informal (shack) settlements in eThekwini (Durban) Metro

eThekwini's Interim Services programme is a good illustration of how systematic preparation processes applied at the programme level can result in innovation, more effective resource allocation and more effective long term urban restructuring. Preparatory work undertaken on this programme has resulted in the investigation and modeling of different delivery models in order to determine the one which is likely to deliver the greatest benefit. Criteria taken into account included the need for long term spatial restructuring, promoting greater inclusion of the urban poor and addressing basic health, safety and basic services needs of informal residents.

The resultant interim services programme provides a mix of: a) sanitation via communal ablution blocks; b) water supply via communal standpipes; c) a prioritized road infrastructure network consisting of both main transportation routes as well as small access ways and pedestrian footpath; d) the connection of shacks to the main electrical grid and e) plans for the provision of key social facilities (including fire and police stations, clinics, schools, sports-fields and community halls).

The application of preparation methodology to the road infrastructure component has been of particular interest and has resulted in a shift from an initial paradigm driven primarily by the provision of minimum (and fairly high) level of service to individual settlements, to one focused more on spatial restructuring and urban inclusion at the level of entire informal settlement precincts ('clusters' of informal settlements). Importantly the new road networks in informal settlement precincts will now be informed by preliminary spatial plans. Instead of providing a high level of investment in only a few selected settlements at a time, road investment will now take place at a precinct level according to a prioritised road hierarchy and in a more spatially coherent and sustainable fashion.

Informal settlement showing interim road infrastructure

Installation of communal sanitation blocks at an informal settlement in eThekwini Municipality.

Typical communal sanitation blocks located at an informal settlement in eThekwini Municipality. The units are converted containers and are plumbed into water mains and trunk sewers. There are separate blocks for male and female residents. Each block contains toilets, hand-basins and showers.

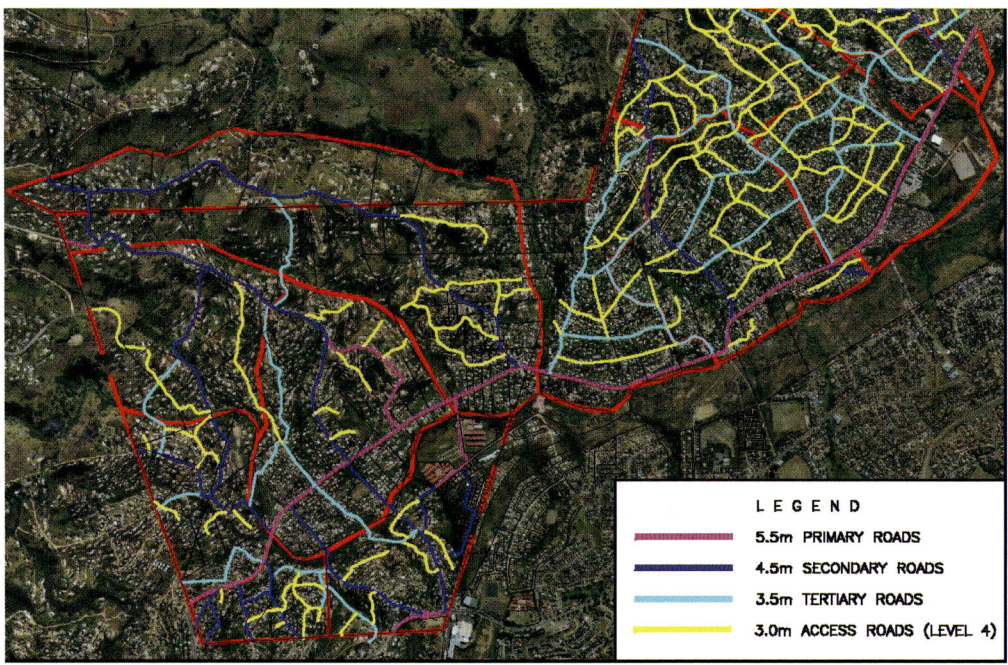

Prioritised road hierarchy at Amaoti, home to more than 14,000 households residing exclusively within informal settlements. This hierarchy has been informed by Spatial Development Framework for the precinct. The hierarchy is significant because it enables phased road investment in a spatially coherent fashion over time.

Spatial Development Framework for Amaoti which has been utilised to assist in the development of a prioritised and phased road investment hierarchy.

Case Study 2: Kenville Informal Settlement Precinct Restructuring Project

The preparation of the Kenville Project is a good illustration of how systematic project preparation can enable better and more innovative developmental solutions such as better integrated planning, alternative (more pedestrianised) planning layouts and alternative housing typologies (in the form of low cost double story units arranged in spatially efficient yet people-friendly 'superblocks'). The Kenville precinct has a prime location within eThekwini (Durban), being located approximately 7km north of the CBD. It is home to a population of approximately 7,500 households of which over 2,500 reside in six 'infill' informal (shack) settlements. The area is predominantly a low-middle income residential suburb and abuts the prime Springfield Park light commercial and light industrial precinct. It is however characterized by steep slopes, challenging geotechnical conditions and limited developable land relative to the existing informal settlement population.

Preparation of the Kenville Project was undertaken at precinct level in order to enable more integrated development and to optimize the resultant urban form. This was especially important given the prime location of the site within the City and its close proximity to job opportunities and other amenities. This integrated precinct level approach is in contrast to the usual trend in South Africa in terms of which informal settlements tend to be dealt with from a narrow housing perspective and in isolation from the greater urban environment in which they are located.

Work undertaken in the preparation of the Kenville project included the following elements:
- an up front status quo assessment with the participation of local residents in order to better understand the area and its people (including focus group interactions with informal residents to probe specific socio-economic issues);
- an assessment of a range of technical site constraints including preliminary investigations into geotechnical, environmental, slope, bulk services and land legal / land availability aspects;
- the development of a preliminary town plan, urban design and architectural concept for the precinct which focuses on creating a functional and people centered urban form whilst maximizing housing yield via a partially pedestrianised layout and the use of a double storey low income housing arranged in 'superblocks';
- the preliminary design of the necessary road, storm-water, sewer and water reticulation;
- the development of preliminary cost estimates for the above and related financial modeling to determine the overall affordability of the project to the city and other funders.
- the commencement of a land acquisition process;
- careful consideration by the city's decision making structures leading to a decision to commence with the implementation of the project.

Aerial view of a typical informal settlement in the Kenville precinct located on steep, marginal land.

Urban design elevation and architectural concept for the Kenville precinct project showing innovation in respect of achieving higher densities and more efficient utilization of scarce land via double storey low cost housing and a more pedestrianised layout on a site characterized by steep and moderately unstable slopes.

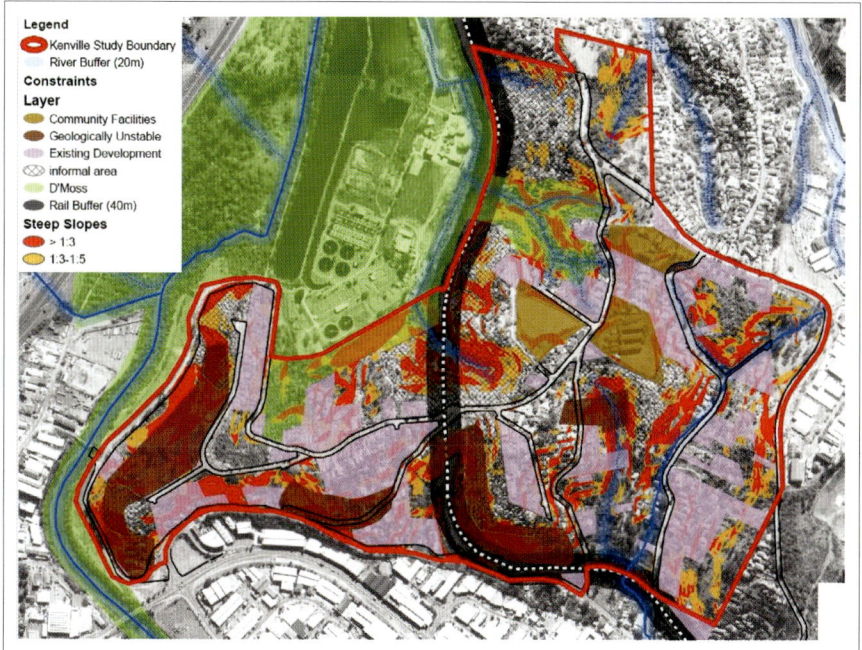

Constraints map for the Kenville precinct arising from pre-feasibility investigations showing land not suitable for development due to slope, geotechnical conditions, environmental factors and servitudes.

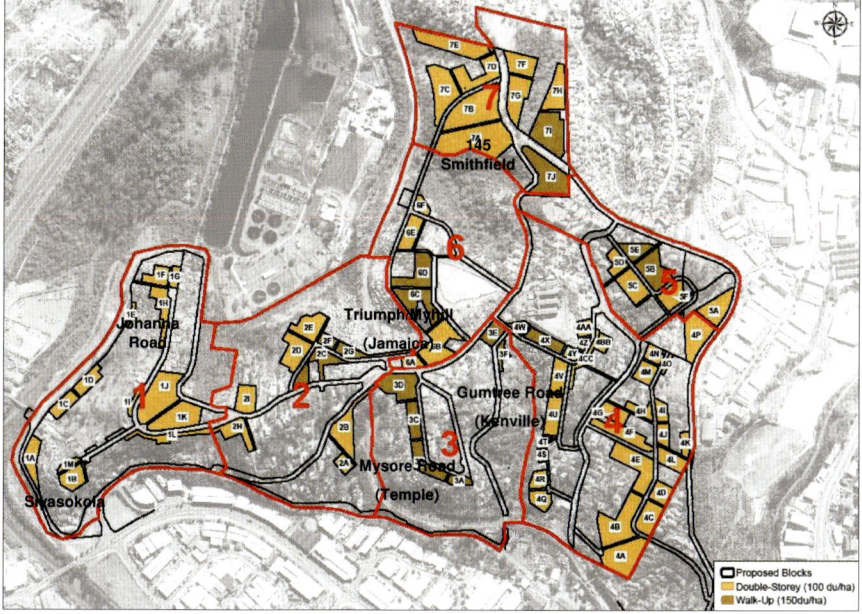

Block layout for the provision of low income housing for residents of informal settlements Kenville precinct as informed by the above constraints map.

Concluding Remarks

It is hoped that this short paper will assist in engendering a greater appreciation of project preparation and the critical role it can play in enabling more effective and sustainable change in developing countries such as South Africa. Development professionals such as town planners can undoubtedly play an important role in helping to create greater awareness in this regard and in helping to mainstream project preparation within government and donor funded programmes alike. Not only is it important that upfront funding for project preparation be made available through such development programmes, but the thinking and approach of project funders and other major stakeholders needs to change. Whilst there are typically established national and international norms and processes in place for project implementation, it is notable that this does not always pertain to the all important preparatory and conceptual stages of projects. It is hoped that a clearer definition of the concepts and processes involved will go some way towards bringing about change in this regard.

—

Endnotes

1. Project Preparation Trust specializes in the preparation of a wide range of developmental projects. PPT is not for profit and was established in 1993 in order to assist in promoting transformation and socio-economic restructuring in South Africa, with a particular focus on poor and disadvantaged communities and augmenting state capacity in the area of project preparation. (www.pptrust.co.za)

2. In particular the Municipal Structures Act (1998), the Municipal Systems Act (2000) and the Municipal Finance Management Act (2003).

3. Consisting of Metro's, district municipalities and local municipalities.

4. Via the 1998 Municipal Demarcation Act.

5. National (central) government in SA recognizes that many local municipalities are under-capacitated or dysfunctional and as a result they developed a Local Government Turnaround Strategy which was finalized in November 2009. The Strategy identifies 58 of SA's 283 municipalities as being in financial distress with 95 having more than 70% of their population not yet having received basic services. A more recent report indicates that approximately 80 municipalities are regarded as being 'low capacity'. In FY2008/9, only 107 (38%) of all municipalities received unqualified audits. Many municipalities are thus either unable to meet development targets or undertake basic functions such as financial management and the operation and maintenance of existing infrastructure, let alone champion complex spatial planning and project functions.

6. E.g. in respect of co-ordinating land acquisition, infrastructure and housing funding from different departments with differing requirements for a single project.

7. E.g. Relating to land legal issues, bulk services availability, geotech and slope stability etc

8. I.e. the provision of a subsidized house with complete infrastructural services and a title deed.

9. I.e. the provision of a lesser, basic level of services such as standpipes, communal ablutions, a limited road network and solid waste removal.

10. Most of these settlements are located on 'marginal' land (e.g. steep and / or geotechnically unstable).

Urban Africa — Challenges and Opportunities for Planning at a Time of Climate Change

Laura Petrella

This century has seen the shift of the majority of the world population to an urban setting/environment. Africa is still the continent with the lowest level of urbanization. At the same time, it is also the continent where urban growth is happening at the fastest rate. Despite these facts, policy makers and the donor community continue to portray Africa as a rural continent and to focus the largest part of their development efforts on rural areas. In general, too little attention is paid to the urban reality of the continent, to understanding its drivers and profile, and to confront properly the challenges, but also embrace the opportunities these trends present for the overall development agenda in the continent.

This paper will summarise the present urbanization and urban policy trends in Africa, its key challenges, and how some innovative urban development planning approaches have been deployed to address them. On this basis, the paper will look at more recent concerns related to climate change and analyse their relevance for the continent's cities in terms of direct and indirect impacts. Finally, it will try to present how urban planning actors and in particular cities are responding to these challenges. It will conclude with reflections on a possible agenda for action.

An overview of Nairobi City, Kenya 2007

Urban Africa – Urbanization Trends in Africa amidst Local and Global Constraints

An urbanizing continent

Data from UN-HABITAT[1] shows that in 2007, with 38.7% of its population living in cities, Africa was still the least urbanised continent of the world. However, it is also the one where urbanization is fastest. With a growth rate of 3.31 % per year, the urban population of Africa is expected to double from 370 million to over 750 million between 2007 and 2030. In East Africa, the world's fastest urbanising region, the urban population will double in only 9 years. In Southern Africa, where the population was 45.6% urbanised in 2007, growth rates are lower, but still far outstrip those of the rural population. In general, migrations from rural areas into cities comprise a reducing share of the new urban population while natural growth from within the cities now plays an increasing role.

Africa's three largest cities of Cairo, Lagos, and Kinshasa had more than 5 million inhabitants each in 2007, while over two thirds of the urban population reside in small and intermediate centres, below 1 million inhabitants, and 60% in cities of less than 500,000 inhabitants. The latter are the centres that are growing at the fastest rate. The African urban structure has two main characteristics. The first is the

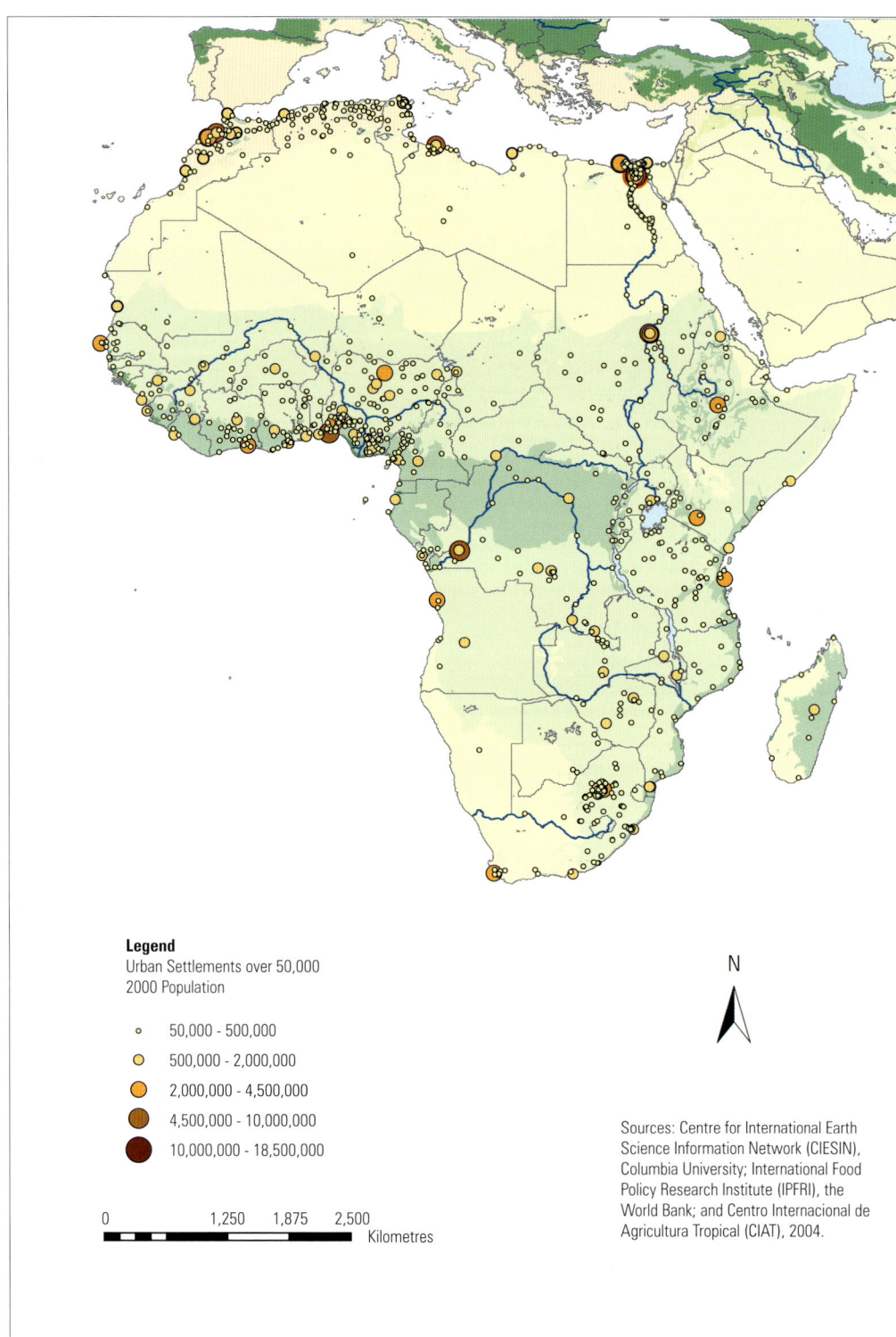

African cities

disproportionate concentration of population, activities, resources and investments in the largest city in the country to the detriment of other cities and towns. The second is the emergence of urban corridors, with large metropolises in relative proximity merging in huge regional systems (such as along the Gulf of Guinea or in the Gauteng Region in South Africa).

Despite these trends, national development policies have focused for a long time on rural development, aiming at reducing migrations. More recently the promotion of territorial rebalancing has aimed at retaining migrants in middle sized cities. But in general, urbanization has taken shape largely in a void of policy interventions. It has also happened in a context of low economic growth, and scarce financial and human resources, in general afflicted by weak governance, social strife and, in a number of countries, armed conflicts.

Poverty in the continent remains quite prevalent, with 40% of Africans living on less than 1 US$ a day and urbanization is to a large extent a poverty driven process, not the industrialization induced socio-economic transformation experienced by other regions of the world. Related to this, inequality is a characteristic feature of many African cities with centres such as Johannesburg and Nairobi displaying some of the greatest extremes between the rich and the poor.

As a direct consequence of this poverty fuelled urban growth, self-help urbanization and uncontrolled spatial development are key features of urban centres. All over Africa, the resultant slums[2] have grown at the same pace as cities as a whole. These informal settlements are home to over 61% of Africa's urban residents.

Graph slums

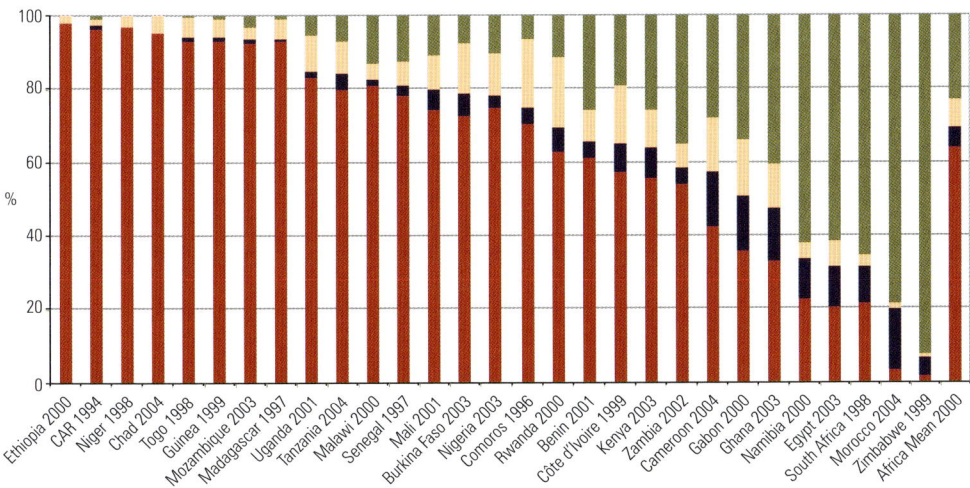

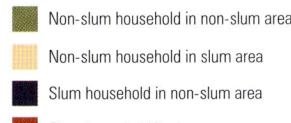

This ratio varies considerably from less than 20 % in countries in North Africa, to more than 90% in Sudan, the Central African Republic and Chad.

Nairobi Slum

Many countries in the continent lack urban policies that define the role of urban centres within the national development agenda and set a long term vision for their management and growth. Also, amidst a relatively slow process of administrative and political decentralization, only major cities, and possibly the capital city, have access to capacities and resources of a significant, if not adequate, scale. Moreover, in several countries corruption is deeply embedded in local government, affecting service provision, and other functions.

In general, planning and managing have also proven quite inappropriate – in particular, urban master plans proved incapable of controlling growth or providing for the associated infrastructure development. Plans were also not updated and not enforced, except for central areas in some instances, and continued to reflect colonial ideas, with zoning and other provisions being modified on an ad-hoc basis. In many instances urban plans have also been consultant (and donor) driven, while capacity to control, enforce and update them remained limited locally. Land management remained also largely unaffected by the plans, as corruption and customary practices remained widespread.

The result of this ineffective planning has been spatial fragmentation, land speculation and urban sprawl. Where economic development creates sufficient markets and interest for prime land occupied by slums, evictions for redevelopment are another feature of urban land management.

Despite this, the cities have continued to expand their economies and to provide real opportunities for their residents due to the presence and creativity of the urban informal sector, the concentration of population and functions, and the opportunities for access to education, information and civic participation[2].

Urban planning innovations in the region

Acknowledging these opportunities and the important mismatch between available tools and needs, cities and countries across the continent have developed innovative approaches, which constitute a rich laboratory of experiences, and have produced lessons which should be documented and discussed more widely. These innovations have included urban governance mechanisms, as well as management approaches and urban planning. They also acknowledge that the overall traditional objective of urban planning – development control – may be unrealistic and even counter-productive in this context. In any case urban planning has not been able to deliver better cities and more equitable development, having instead created perverse effects and put large shares of the urban residents 'outside the law'.

The focus has, therefore, moved a great deal to how to link urban planning and development in a context of limited public resources and within the above-mentioned constraints. The linkages have taken various forms – strategic urban planning focused on priority issues and in many instances oriented to investment planning; integrated planning focused on coordination and rationalization of public action within a specific set of development priorities. Strategic urban plans with a specific entry point, and a city-wide scope have also been developed, through various initiatives, in particular looking at environmental management and at the prevention of violence and crime.

These forms of planning have emerged in the last few years. They initially focused on improving governance mechanisms around urban decision making through consultative processes aimed at identifying a shared development agenda. However, the approach has developed into a tool for focused planning of feasible urban development actions, concentrated on critical hot spots and responding to a shared vision. The City Development Strategy (CDS) approach[3] in particular focuses on investment planning and mobilization of resources, including locally available ones. Adopted by many cities across the continent, this approach has enabled – in the best cases – the development of ‚bankable' projects and served as an entry point for private and public investments, as well as donor support. CDS has also assisted in prioritising appropriate infrastructure and primary services, and the upgrading of informal settlements.

The Rapid Urban Sector Profiling and subsequent strategic action planning, promoted with European Union funding by UN-HABITAT in 54 cities in 18 countries in Africa, also utilises a similar strategic approach. It is focused on slum upgrading and prevention and on integrated actions at national and local level, on a number of sectors, including basic urban services delivery and housing, as well as land. Over time, it has also been adapted to respond to specific issues and priorities at local level, such as violence prevention, or disaster preparedness depending on local needs.

Strategic urban plans that have incorporated strong citizen participation and participatory budgeting approaches have managed to ensure more focus on the reduction of poverty and inequalities, as opposed to plans that have focused more on the economic positioning of the city within the national context and on the leverage of competitive advantages in this sense.

The success of these participatory planning approaches largely depends on the involvement and drive created by stakeholders' participation and on the institutionalization of the plans. As a more flexible and pragmatic tool than traditional master plans, strategic urban plans have remained in many instances separate from the formal planning systems which still refer to master plans and related regulations, and maintain authority in terms of formal urban management. The reform of those planning systems has proved to be much more difficult in terms of governance, legislation and procedures. This, coupled with poor land registration and corruption, has created in some instances blockages related to land availability or long procedures. Strategic plans have also been implemented only to a limited extent, investments not always being easy to mobilise.

In the few example of reforms of planning systems in the region, when strategic urban planning has been merged with formal land use planning and master planning, as has happened in Egypt, this has created a powerful combination of strategic and land related instruments. However, the limited progress in decentralization and the limited availability of implementation tools at local level, including those related to financial planning and investment mobilization, still represent a major obstacle to implementation.

In South Africa, integrated development plans (IDP) have been introduced by law with a focus on interdepartmental coordination at the local government level. The IDP is a medium-term development plan linked to a five-year political cycle, although certain aspects of the plan, including the vision and the spatial development framework (SDF) have a longer-term horizon. The SDF is a city-wide descriptive plan, similar to a strategic spatial plan, and can indicate specific projects at local level. Its role is to coordinate spatially the sectoral plans, where line-function departments align their plans and projects. Its ambition is to change the way sectoral plans are developed and managed. However, these practices are still not fully developed and land use planning and zoning is not integrated in the system as yet, continuing often to operate through older and mostly outdated systems and ordnances.

While no final judgement can be made, this experience is very telling of the difficulties of modifying engrained mechanisms and introducing innovative institutional approaches, and this despite the relatively well endowed situation of South African local governments.

Despite such advances in both formal and non-formal planning, many cities lack up-to-date planning mechanisms and continue to rely on traditional master planning documents which fail to deliver what is needed.

African Cities and Climate Change

In Africa, the unprecedented challenges of the emerging climate crisis and energy crisis impose additional constraints on options for urban development, as they clearly indicate that the usual paths of development are becoming impracticable. They also reorientate the resource flow from outside the continent, as increasing priority is given to the offsetting of carbon emission, or to innovative projects in the field of environmental conservation, energy efficiency and technological innovation. The global economic crisis also results in shrinking financial flows towards developing countries. In general, this new conditionality finds many African countries and cities ill prepared and equipped, and coping with the huge backlog of services, housing and capacities and with the ongoing increase of the urban population becomes even more challenging. The next sections of this paper will try to look at how the global challenge of climate change translates in the African cities and how they are preparing to cope with it.

A marginal contribution to emissions, characterized by inequality and inefficiency

At present, Africa's contribution to global warming is insignificant, amounting to less than three percent of the world's total emissions of greenhouse gases. The majority of African countries emit only minimal quantities of 0.1-0.3 tons of CO_2 per inhabitant per year. Despite the unavailability of disaggregated data, we may estimate that cities in Africa produce the largest share of GHG emissions of the continent, as is the case in other continents. By contrast, Germany's per capita emissions are estimated at 10 tons per annum. However, this admirable emission profile of African cities does not mean that they are models of environmental sustainability and efficient energy use. In fact, there are several facts that the bare figures do not directly tell about the situation and its possible evolution.

African emission level is directly linked to poverty levels and in particular it can be traced back to the low access to energy for the population (up to 80% of urban population does not have access to modern forms of energy) and low levels of industrial and productive activities. The overall limited scale of the formal building market for instance results in the large majority of the houses being built with poor materials, often recycled. Similarly few individuals own private cars and therefore the contribution of private vehicles to emission levels is limited.

However, the African urban elites (often less than 10% of the urban population) do have lifestyles and access to technologies and energy similar to those of any city dweller in developed world. At the same time, public services are inefficient (for instance as far as collective transport is concerned), and proper policies are lacking (which result in a large share of electricity produced using fossil fuels in many countries) and there is limited awareness of environmental issues. In this situation, the urban elites and the growing middle class in African cities are as energy consuming as their counterparts in other parts of the world.

For instance, because of the limited availability or poor quality of public transport, coupled with urban sprawl, individual transport, when accessible, is the preferred transport mode to cope with the limited availability of collective services.

Air pollution in Lagos

In the case of buildings, the lack of regulatory framework, the limited access to technology and the adoption of design and planning models that are not appropriate to the climatic conditions create a huge demand for energy, particularly for cooling. This is the case even if less than 30% of the population lives in modern buildings, and the climate conditions would allow low-carbon energy options (in particular the use of solar energy). Finally, cities that have grown without proper land use and service planning, do not have open green spaces, lack waste management and sewage treatment plants, and the unchecked urban sprawl has depleted the natural carbon sinks and other ecological systems which have a climate mitigating role (such as wetlands).

Already many cities in Africa suffer from environmental degradation and inefficiencies related to the prevalence of badly maintained second-hand cars (as in Kampala, Uganda) and the bad state of roads, the use of fuelwood, charcoal or kerosene for cooking in most urban households, the lack of water conservation and recycling, the depletion of tree cover and the disappearance of open areas. Without specific policy choices, it will be the individual choices of the growing African elites, as well as the inefficient choices that the urban poor are forced to make for lack of options, that will have the biggest impact on emissions from the continent.

In a scenario of economic growth, and in a context of policy delay, emissions are bound to further increase as more people will be able to pursue unsustainable consumption patterns. Although these are marginal issues compared to the global patterns of emission, alternative models of consumption, mobility and production still need to be identified and tested. These will only be acceptable so long as they provide for continuing human development and improvements to the lot of Africa's urban poor.

In this context, development patterns have to change and issues of mitigation and resource conservation should be addressed as part of the management of the growth of urban areas in Africa i.e. avenues have to be found that break the link between GDP growth and emission growth (or reduce the direct relation very few in urban areas.

UN-HABITAT has been pioneering practices at city level in the continent, initially through its Sustainable Cities and Local Agenda 21 programmes, currently through the Cities and Climate Change Initiative. Through environmental planning and management projects, UN-HABITAT has supported city-wide environmental strategies, in which citizens prioritized support to non motorised forms of transport in Kisumu, Kenya,

Kisumu

which is prevalent in today's development patterns). In this way it would be possible to have a significant impact on the future scenarios.

Cities in Africa are not well equipped to take up this challenge. There is only limited experience of approaches that have been able to address inefficiencies and inequities at the same time, and to access global funding mechanisms. For instance, the city of Dar es Salaam has accessed the Clean Development Mechanism (CDM) funds as part of its waste management initiatives under the local environmental management programme. This is one of the few CDM projects in the continent, and one of the the reorganization of public transport in Dar es Salaam, Tanzania, and the improvements to the cycle of waste management (for instance through the introduction of recycling of materials in St Louis, Senegal), among many others. The experiences initiated by UN-HABITAT aim to the reduction of future emission, and of the emission of particular sectors (building, transport), linking service delivery and savings in GHG (waste, water, energy, etc.) and the promotion of green building practices in different countries in Africa. (see BOX).

Green Building Councils in Africa

Green buildings reduce carbon emission and also produce other environmental gains. Recently UN-HABITAT held, in collaboration with the World Green Building Council, an African workshop to discuss the dissemination of green building rating in Africa. The workshop highlighted the existence of several GBC in the continent, and discussed how to further develop the network of professionals of the built environment on green building, the specification of green building adapted to Africa, and support mechanisms.
As a result several countries have initiated the development of national GBC and a regional African Network of Green Building Councils is being developed. The challenge remains of the limited size of the formal market in most countries to which such rating system could be applied, as well as the need for strong client awareness for the rating to be effective and grow as practice in the region.

First GreenBuilding in S.Africa Nedbank

Stablished Earth Blocks

In relation to energy efficiency in the housing and services sectors, interventions have focused on the development of regulatory frameworks and incentives for the adoption of energy efficiency and renewable energy in the housing sector (such as in Morocco, Kenya, Uganda, Tanzania, Burundi and Rwanda).

The challenge remains to bring interventions to scale (from pilot, to local and to national) and to enforce national policies. Experience of environmental planning has demonstrated that a systemic approach to city environmental management can maximise durable economic gains and minimise environmental impacts. Building on such experiences, which for instance have been promoted in several cities across Africa by the Sustainable Cities Programme and Local Agenda 21, local governments could integrate mitigation within urban development initiatives, monitor emission and assess in terms of emission the future plans and urban projects.

Unfortunately to date the understanding among urban actors and local governments in particular remains relatively low compared to the scale of the problem and of the opportunities for sound environmental management. Very few national reports on climate change refer to urban issues and, overall, there is inadequate awareness of the urban dimension of climate change in Africa.

High vulnerability to climate change impacts, and low response capacity
African cities are already feeling the impact of climate change and, although their contribution to it has been minimal, many have high degrees of vulnerability to climate change effects coupled with low response capacity.

Among the climate change impacts, cities in Africa are being affected by storms, tidal surges and flash flooding (also in countries with traditionally very little rain, such as Burkina Faso, Mauritania and Niger). Movement of populations due to drought has affected in particular southern Africa and the Sahel. Shortages in water supply are significant in the Arab states and in southern Africa. Food shortages or the increase in food prices, health problems related to shortage or pollution of water, as well as malaria are affecting cities across the region.

Banks of Nairobi River

Korogocho slum in Nairobi

Coastal cities are particularly at risk due to sea level rise. Numerous African capitals and major cities along the coast host some of the most advanced economic hubs, and a large share of urban population will be seriously affected by sea level rise. About a total of 10 million people would be displaced were sea levels to rise by 30cm, in Abidjan, Alexandria, Conakry, Cotonou, Dakar, Lagos, Luanda, Maputo, Mogadishu, Monrovia and Port-Harcourt[4].

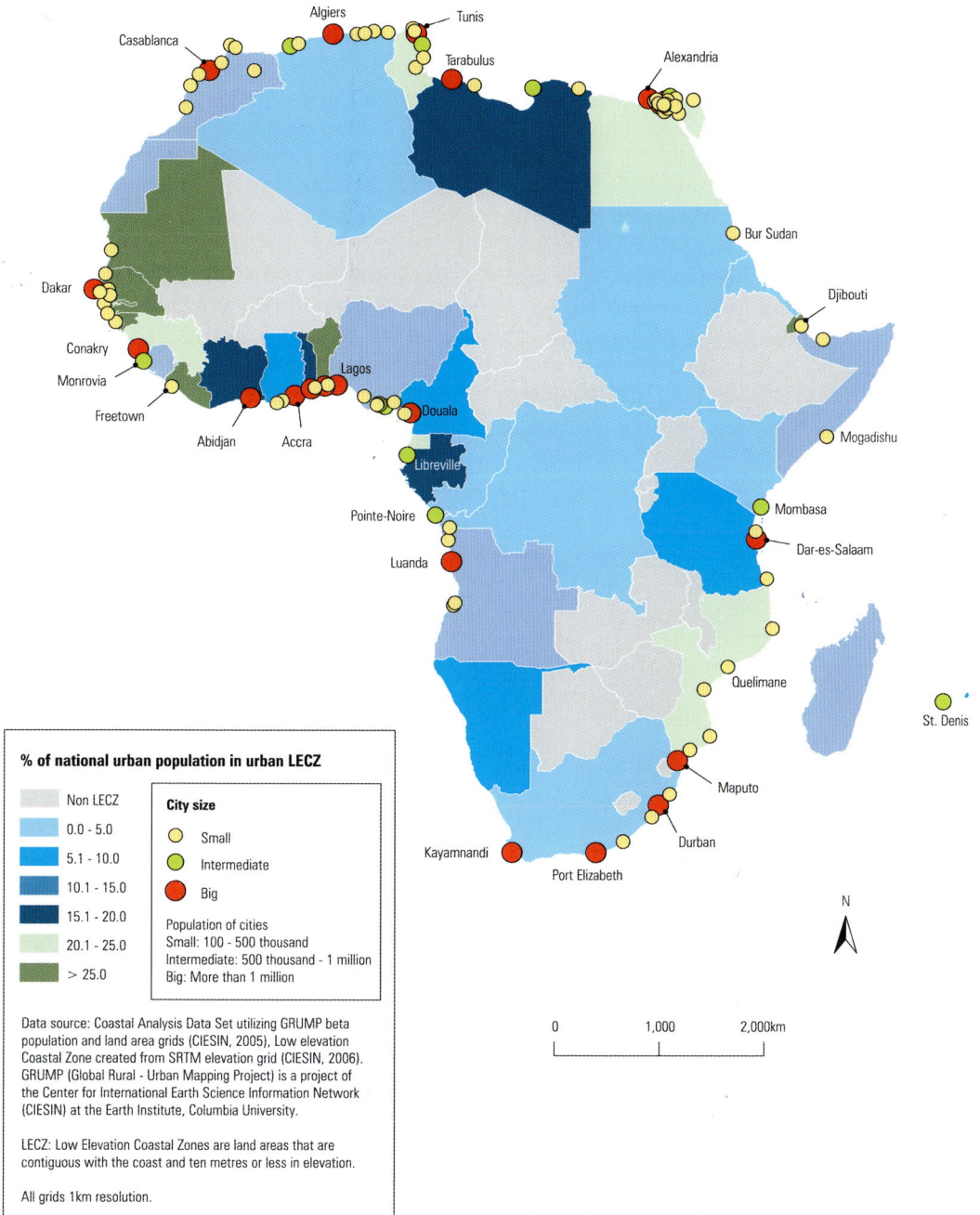

Africa-Cities at risk

The vulnerability of African cities is due to many factors, among which poverty, the existent backlog in investment and infrastructure, the poor housing conditions and failed land markets, as well as the fragility of livelihoods and the great inequalities which are reflected in access to resources and opportunities, play key roles. Ecological systems are quite fragile. In addition, the uncertainty and coarse-grainedness of current climate change projections makes long range urban planning for climate change difficult[5].

Planning has in many cases failed to play a positive role in such contexts and its failure has exacerbated poverty and vulnerability. Corruption, land grabbing, vested interests influencing land use decisions, a lack of decentralization and consolidation of the urban management function at the local level, and often inappropriate planning approaches and lack of enforcement capacity have resulted in many cities expanding without decision-makers paying due consideration to risk (coastal areas, river beds, hills, slopes, etc.) or adopting unsustainable measures of environmental management (canalization of rivers, elimination of tree cover, etc.). The fact that urban expansion is made up to a large extent of sub-standard buildings compounds the existing risks.

In Africa's cities, infrastructure (roads, railways, energy and water distribution networks, or wells) and urban systems such as transport and mobility, or waste management are also particularly vulnerable because of their physical state and in some cases inadequate design.

In addition, African cities and their communities have limited preparedness to cope with the unexpected. Climate change impacts will affect the basic infrastructure. Social and economic impacts, in particular loss of livelihoods, will also be important. There are usually limited opportunities for those affected to move to alternative locations or to

Floods in Congotown in Liberia

reconfigure their livelihoods.

Vulnerability, therefore, in African cities is not just being closer to the disaster, but also being farther from appropriate response and recovery. In this sense even 'flash events' will have long term impacts. Indeed the amount of resources climate related crises and disasters will absorb will reduce the ability of African local governments and other actors to provide services, and will further weaken management systems.

Environmental risks & vulnerabilities in Kampala, Uganda

Located in Central Uganda, on the northern shores of Lake Victoria, Kampala is the Capital City of the Republic of Uganda. Covering an area of 195 sq.km and at an average altitude of 1120 meters above sea level, it is situated on about 24 low flat topped hills that are surrounded by wetland valleys, characterized by an imprint of scattered unplanned settlements.

Kampala City is faced with urban sprawl and increased growth of informal settlements and slums due to the ever increasing population pressure and inadequate land use planning. This has resulted in settlements being located in high risk areas especially those prone to flooding and poor sanitation. Due to the high water table, most of the wells/springs are contaminated mainly by fecal materials and this puts safe water coverage at about 55%. The situation is further exacerbated by the low collection rate of solid waste, which currently stands at 55% and causes blockages of the drainage systems in the city. Scarcity of urban land means that construction is taking place on the hill tops. The lack of water harvesting mechanisms and hard paving have caused degradation of the fragile hill slopes.
As a result, flash floods have become more frequent and violent and the city dwellers are exposed to water borne diseases such as malaria, bilharzia and other related ailments such as respiratory tract infections.

Source: UN-HABITAT Cities and Climate Change Initiative

**Environmental risks & vulnerabilities
in Maputo, Mozambique**

The capital of Mozambique, is located in the south of the country, with an area of 300 km2, and a population of about 1 million (2007). With a density of 3700 hab/km2, the city held 45% of the total Mozambican urban population of which about 50% was considered to live below the poverty line. In Maputo, recent data indicate an increasing rural-urban migration contributing to higher poverty and vulnerability levels.

Coastal zones are the most affected by global warming factors including sea level rise. Maputo is no exception and suffers frequent flooding. The Avenida Marginal within Maputo City along the coast is gradually disappearing. There is also a reduction of sand strips throughout the beaches due to continuous movement of the sea, thus creating serious coastal erosion problems and impacting negatively on economic activities. Although Mozambique's contribution to the world's emissions is insignificant, global warming effects are starting to become visible in the Maputo municipality. The city's three islands located a few kilometers from the coast show clear evidence of climate change effects which include the
1) disappearance of mangroves (in the case of Inhaca Island, a reduction from 10 hectares to only 1 hectare);
2) slow degradation of water quality in wells thus contributing to potable water scarcity;
3) desertification due to drought, exposing sand dunes and worsening wind erosion, causing loss of coastline; and
4) lack of arable land for domestic agriculture.

There are clear signs that the sea level is rising, which creates expensive coastal management problems for Maputo City Municipality. The phenomenon is resulting in salt water intrusion, negatively impacting on agricultural activities, thus contributing to the current urban poverty.

Source: UN-HABITAT Cities and Climate Change Initiative

Adaptation to climate change in African Cities

Given the human settlement conditions and the level of vulnerability to climate change, adaptation is the most important response for the continent's cities. Adaptation needs to focus on the most vulnerable population and settlements. In many cases these are slums or marginal settlements, developed on unsuitable land, outside urban planning provisions, where climate change exacerbates pre-existent risks.

Risk assessment at city level is the first step to identifying those communities and parts of the city that are especially vulnerable. Experience has shown that these exercises can beneficially draw upon local knowledge of the environment; such participation can also result in higher awareness in the community.

A plan for adaptation and risk reduction, coupled with disaster preparedness and response, should include interventions directed to specific groups and parts of the city and its systems, as well as awareness, monitoring and alert mechanisms. Adaptation strategies will need to recognise the many uncertainties about how a particular area might be affected. They should have the capacity to respond both to immediate needs and to longer term concerns. In many cities, one of the priorities will be the improvement of water management beyond drought periods. This should include management of water demand, reclaiming and protection of buffer zones and green areas for water retention and run-off control, and management of waste and pollutants, sanitation improvements, improvement of drainage systems and water harvesting.

Land management to remove specific risks, such as through relocating vulnerable settlements, allocating uses that have a positive impact (parklands, urban agriculture, recreation areas), restoring specific ecosystems (mangroves in coastal areas) and protecting the coastline, are also an important part of adapatation efforts. More appropriate regulatory approaches and mechanisms to ensure unsuitable areas are not built up and occupied shall include the enforcement of 'no-invasion' policies of lands within the lowest parts of floodplains. The reclaiming of threatened areas also requires significant investment and well coordinated efforts involving various public and private actors, as in the case of Eko Atalantic City in Lagos, Nigeria. (BOX - Lagos Eko Atlantic City).

In addition, community resilience needs to be supported by improving health conditions and livelihoods. Participation and awareness and fair enforcement mechanisms are also crucial to avoiding failures such as the situation when residents who were moved to higher ground in Mozambique to protect them from floods returned to their original locations, making them vulnerable once again.

Cities and communities need to function well in order to respond to the challenges of climate change – to be able to absorb climate refugees, to withstand changing climate patterns, to recover from climate induced shocks and to be able to adapt. The fight against urban poverty and for better planned cities is therefore important in making cities in Africa resilient to climate change.

Despite the indifferent results of past planning approaches to limit disasters and direct development towards more sustainable patterns, the scope for a renewed role for planning is huge given the type of problems described above. It will be possible to reap an adaptation dividend from many poverty reduction interventions.

A broad adaptation agenda needs to consider several key dimensions of the cities of Africa to be relevant and sustainable.

First of all it should **work with informality**. This requires flexible and

Eko Atlantic City, Lagos, Nigeria

Over the years Bar Beach in Lagos has been steadily eroded until it was almost completely lost to the Atlantic Ocean. As efforts to stop the erosion had failed, flooding from surges of the ocean waters had started to eat up the major road running along the beach. To avoid the complete loss of Victoria Island, the Lagos State Government has embarked on a massive reclamation effort, to salvage and stabilise the beach and to turn it into a viable economic development. Eko Atlantic City, a new mixed use development project on Bar Beach involves the reclamation of 820 hectares of beachfront 6.5 kilometers long. The design of the new city will be a sustainable city, clean and energy efficient with minimal carbon emissions.

The urban design was produced by Dutch consultants, while an international advisory team is working with the developers and investors to oversee standards. Funding for the project is coming from private equity and loans from financial institutions, as well as the Lagos State Government.

The intervention is modelled on the sea reclamation seen in Dubai, and debate is still open on whether this model is sustainable in the present development constraints. In any case expectations are high that it will provide a permanent protection from water rise for Nigeria's major city and space for high quality urban services and infrastructure which are much needed in Lagos.

Source: www.lagosstate.gov.ng, and UN-HABITAT (2008)

supportive mechanisms which tap into the creativity and productivity of the informal sector and provide avenues for their better organization and contribution to urban development. This will not only strengthen livelihoods but engage the informal sector in innovation as actors of adaptation.

Secondly, adaptation needs to be supported by mechanisms that **guide urban growth in a proactive** way towards less vulnerable areas. Provision of suitable urban land on a large scale avoids the occupation of high risk areas and can reduce damage to valuable ecosystems. Once such mechanisms are in place, the enforcement of controls on land use in sensitive areas would be easier and less controversial.

Thirdly, the upgrading (and when needed, relocation) of slums, together with improved housing and infrastructure standards and access to services, are key adaptation strategies. Slum dwellers should be enabled to play a key role in these processes. Stronger communities and established practices of community involvement will also open more reliable and efficient channels for disaster response and awareness.

Finally, regulatory mechanisms should be seen as complementing the dynamic management and adaptation approaches. This requires a new focus on managing growth and change as opposed to regulating it – through strategy planning approaches that respond to and accommodate development.

Hergeisa Market, Somaliland

Urban Sprawl - Housing density Dar-es-Salaam

Linking Adaptation and Mitigation – A planning agenda for climate change Mitigation and Adaptation in Africa

In the scenarios of mitigation and adaptation presented above, it is clear that the international agenda, which is to a large extent focused on mitigation, differs from the immediate agenda and concerns of African cities.

Very aggressive reductions of emissions, through commitments made by the developed and emerging countries, would ultimately reduce the scale of the climate change threat for the region. However, some effects of climate change are now inevitable due to the temperature increases already recorded and African cities urgently need to be in a position to cope with these. They also need to identify development strategies that are compatible with lower relative emissions, in the long term.

Such convergence towards more 'green' development would allow African cities to truly leapfrog into the future, skipping the carbon intensive development model that has underpinned the growth and development of northern countries. In this respect, urban planning can play an important role. In particular it can act as a facilitator of the debate on development options and visions, taking into account the following points:

1. Climate change responses need to be pro-poor and integrated in the development agenda (i.e. provide explicit development gains). Climate change as an entry point can be linked systematically with other dimensions of development where the contribution assessed is not exclusively to climate change but more in general to environmental sustainability, social equity and economic growth and development. Concepts such as the green economy provide powerful integrative tools in this respect.
2. The Adaptation and Mitigation agenda needs to converge as long and short term objectives (adaptation in the short and long terms for current and future risks, and mitigation in the long term for future emissions) both lead to innovative urban forms, and development planning in a context of scarce resources. Given the unrealistic (because unsustainable) option of filling the development gap in conventional ways, green or low-carbon development opportunities are an attractive option in Africa.
3. Responses driven by the participation of stakeholders, which can make explicit the interests and conflicts related to resources and development options are more likely to achieve equitable development. Community participation approaches, as well as the strengthening of local actors, such as local governments, should play an important role.

Cities in Africa, with the support of the international community are moving in this direction, and some steps have already been undertaken.

It will be important to integrate climate change concerns in urban planning approaches, particularly in the new forms of planning mentioned in the first section of this paper, such as City Development Strategy and Urban Profiling. Both City Alliance and its main partners (World Bank and UN-HABITAT, together with UNEP) have plans to adapt the methodology of CDS in this sense. Revision of the Urban Profile approach, and of its formal adoption at country level (such as in Egypt), are also planned. In addition, UN-HABITAT is working to develop urban planning oriented guidance on climate change, for urban planners, and to promote methodologies for vulnerability assessment and for a greenhouse gases inventory (in collaboration with UNEP and the World Bank), for use by cities[6].

It is also crucial to influence simultaneously national policies and capacities, and international and national

Community Meeting, Tanzania

Current Climate Change Response and Resilience in Maputo

The Maputo Municipality, in collaboration with a local educational and research institution, has very recently launched the Rapid Urban Assessment project which aims at evaluating the levels of emissions within the municipal territory as well as its surrounding areas. This assessment will facilitate rapid decision making on measures to be adopted to help fulfill the recommendations of the United Nations Framework Convention on Climate Change, without hampering economic activities.

Two new departments, for environmental inspection and management, respectively, have been created within the framework of the current restructuring of the Municipality to strengthen the role of the Municipal authorities in the enforcement of mitigation and adaptation measures. The current reconstruction of the National Disaster Management Institute will seek to address the gap between emergency humanitarian response and long-term reconstruction within the current disaster risk reduction government policies, strategies and institutional setting.

Source: UN-HABITAT Cities and Climate Change Initiative

CCCI Process Model

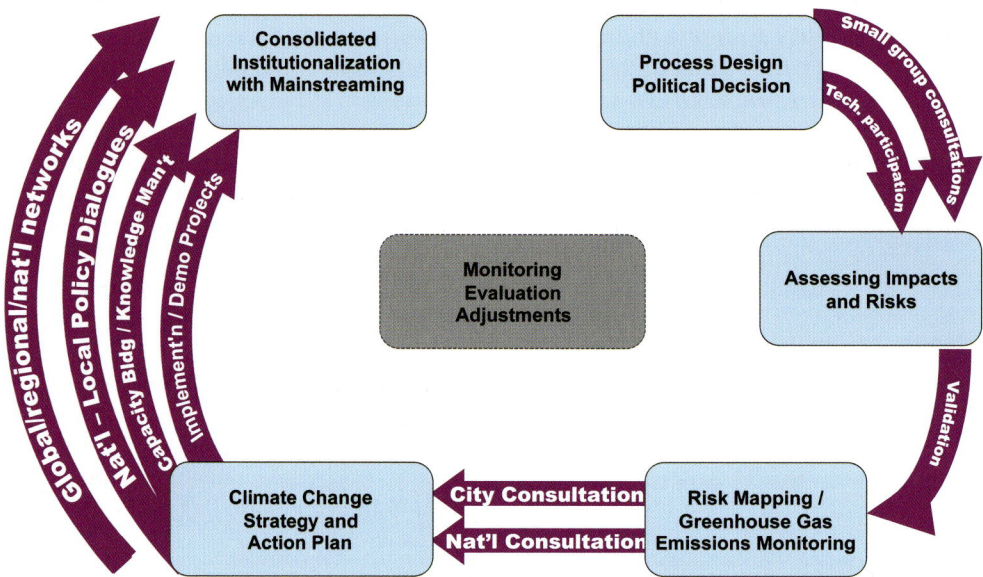

UN-HABITAT work on Climate Change — Cities and Climate change Initiative (CCCI)

UN-HABITAT is focusing its work on climate change in the following areas:
- Advocacy, policy dialogue and policy change
- Tool development and application
- Piloting climate change mitigation and adaptation measures
- Knowledge management and dissemination, through, amongst others, the UN-HABITAT partner universities and the partnership with UN-HABITAT's Local Government Training Institutes Network.

Initially 7 cities in Africa (Kampala in Uganda, Maputo in Mozambique, St Louis in Senegal, Bobo Dioulasso in Bukina Faso, Welvis Bay in Namibia, Mombasa in Kenya and Kigali in Rwanda) plus Esmeraldas in Ecuador, and Sorsogon in the Philippines participate in the Cities in Climate Change Initiative as key partner cities. At the same time best practice from other cities around the world are being collected and will be promoted.

financing mechanisms. In particular, national dialogue linking national climate change mechanisms (in many countries facilitated by the Ministry of Environment) and cities, has been identified as a key precursor of more urban relevant national policies and plans. It is hoped that this will also result in countries preparing national reports that are more aware of the specific challenges of climate change in urban areas.

Finally, a great deal of attention needs to be paid to capacity development around these themes. Environmental management and planning experiences have proved to be a very good basis for climate change responses in countries of the North[7]. In Africa, Dar es Salaam with its long history of urban environmental management, is one of the few cities that has been able to access CDM funding. Capitalising on existing capacities, supporting human resources development within institutions, research bodies and the private sector, clarifying institutional mandates (and levels of decentralization) and ensuring that plans are embedded within supportive institutional and resource allocation mechanisms, are all important components of capacity building in this context.In line with the considerations discussed above, the UN-HABITAT Cities and Climate Change Initiative is working with several African cities focusing on awareness and policy change, localizing national climate change plans, the development of local relevant tools, and the testing of approaches and their evaluation and dissemination, together with relevant training (see box). Urban planners have the great challenge of being at the forefront of the longer term shaping of our cities, and of integrating the different concerns mentioned above within such a future. They also have the skills and experience for forecasting the impact of adaptation and mitigation approaches on the viability of cities in the future. All this knowledge is dearly needed to put in motion a transition to sustainable and climate conscious urban development.

Conclusions
The climate change agenda brings to the debate about, and to the practice of, urban development. a very strong environmental conditionality. In this sense, it provides a strong argument for urban sustainability to be pursued and planned for, and has indeed provid ed impetus for reflection and experimen tations on low-carbon and adaptation initiatives. It also makes available resources for the implementation of ap propriate climate change interventions.

Climate change as an entry point into the contemporary urban development agenda, is a potential vehicle for truly sustainable development. This will be possible if the long term priorities of urban development, short term adaptation and future mitigation are all factored in a robust and integrated response which is cognizant of the key demands and needs of the target cities.

If the climate change agenda is not reduced to mere accounting for GHG and mere reinforcement of infrastructure size (both in themselves important components of any climate change response strategy), but is used as an opportunity to rethink development mechanisms and to reinvent urban sustainable development in its more holistic sense, there will be gains on more than the climate front and better cities for all.

Climate change is objectively a serious challenge for African cities, and a key threat to sustainable urban development at all scales. At the same time, the 'climate change conditionality' is becoming central to development aid, as well as to private investment, and will soon become an important criterion of the offer of options to the growing number of individuals seeking access to better services and goods. In the capacity to adopt more climate sensitive patterns of urban development, housing, mobility and consumption in general, lies the opportunity for developing world cities, and for Africa in particular, the possibility of addressing future challenges and of accessing new development opportunities.

The fact that such an opportunity is only being slowly taken up by Africa is just a further indication of the need for more attention to long term trends and prospects in a continent beset by recurrent crisis and an emergency culture, even when talking of urban planning[9].

—

Endnotes

1. Data are derived from UN-HABITAT (2008), State of African Cities 2008, Nairobi and UN-HABITAT (2009) Global Report on Human Settlements 2009, London, Earthscan

2. UN-HABITAT definition of slums is that of a contiguous settlement where the inhabitants are characterised as having inadequate housing and basic services; a slum is often not recognised and addressed by public authorities as an integral part of the city. The definition of slum households is a household that lacks one or more of five elements: access to improved water, access to improved sanitation, security of tenure, durability of housing, and sufficient living area.

3. Kassides, Christine (2006), The Urban Transition in Sub-Saharan Africa: Implications for Economic Growth and Poverty Reduction, Washington, The City Alliance.

4. The City Development Strategy approach has been developed and supported by the City Alliance, a joint World Bank and UN-HABITAT initiative addressing urban development and slum upgrading with support from several donors.

5. Data from Center for International Earth Science Information Network (www.ciesin.org) elaborated by UN-HABITAT Global Urban Observatory. Quoted in UN-HABITAT (2008), State of African Cities 2008, Nairobi

6. UN-HABITAT, UNEP and The World Bank jointly developed 'Draft International Standard for Determining Greenhouse Gas Emissions for Cities' was presented and discussed at the World Urban Forum in Rio de Janeiro in March 2010. It is available at: www.unep.org/urban_environment/PDFs/InternationalStd-GHG.pdf

7. This is discussed in: Robert Kehew (2009), "Projecting Globally, Planning Locally: A Progress Report From Four Cities in Developing Countries", in Climate Sense, World Meteorological Organization.

8. Cases such as those in Portland or Malmo presented in the Review 05 Low Carbon Cities testify to this.

9. Copyright for pictures: Picture on p. 62 (c) GLH Architects, p. 73 (c) TAWLAT, all other pictures (c) UN-Habitat.

02

A Global Challenge

Climate Change, Cities, and the IPCC

Jean-Pascal van Ypersele

Porto, Portugal, the venue for ISOCARP's 45th International Congress on Low Carbon Cities in October 2009, picture taken by Chris Gossop

Article written at the invitation of ISOCARP, following their 2009 Congress in Porto.

Key messages:

1. Climate change is happening now, mostly as a result of human activities.
2. The impacts will be felt everywhere, including cities, with most damage in developing countries.
3. Adaptation measures can reduce some of the negative impacts, but they have limitations and costs.
4. Together with lifestyle and behaviour changes, known technologies and policies can reduce greenhouse gas emissions at reasonable costs, but effective policies, including an effective carbon-price signal would be required.
5. The IPCC will devote increasing attention in its next report into the regional aspects of climate change impacts, vulnerability and adaptation, as well as mitigation, and cities will form an important aspect of this.

Introduction

Before discussing the substance using the last IPCC report as a reference, I would like to quickly remind you what the IPCC is. The Intergovernmental Panel on Climate Change (IPCC) was established in 1988 by the World Meteorological Organization and the United Nations Environment Programme to provide the world with a clear, balanced view of the present state of understanding of climate change. It is the leading body for the assessment of climate change. The IPCC doesn't do research itself: it reviews and assesses the scientific, technical and socio-economic information published in the scientific literature. It takes about 4 years to complete a new IPCC assessment report. The first was published in 1990, and the most recent one, completed in 2007 and called AR4, is the fourth.

If the IPCC has acquired the weight it has, I believe it is essentially because of three factors: 1) a large number of the best scientists are involved in the writing of its reports, 2) three cycles of reviews take place (by experts and governments) with thousands of comments that are taken into account (90000 for the AR4), and 3), the final approval Plenary for the Summary for Policy Makers involves both the main authors of the report and official delegations of over 120 countries, which means that the consensus at the end reflects not only the scientists' viewpoints, but also the policy makers'. Please note that, because of the elaborate review procedure, and because of the efforts by some delegations to dilute the SPM, the IPCC reports tend to be conservative. They try to tell the truth, how inconvenient it might be.

The IPCC (see www.ipcc.ch) is organised into three working groups: the first one deals with the geophysics of the problem, the second with impacts, vulnerability, and adaptation, and the third deals with mitigation (reduction of greenhouse gas [GHG] emissions). I will now use the same structure in my remarks.

Climate change is happening now, mostly as a result of human activities

The first IPCC working group concluded in its AR4 contribution, that "warming of the climate system is unequivocal". Global mean surface temperature has increased by 0.74°C (1.3°F) over the last 100 years, with temperatures over land rising quicker than over oceans. The warming is widespread, with a maximum at higher northern latitudes. Most of the observed increase in temperature since 1950 is very likely (probability of occurrence: over 90%) due to the increasing GHG concentration as a result of human activities, mostly the burning of fossil fuels and deforestation. It is extremely unlikely that the global temperature change of the past 50 years can be explained by natural factors only. Indeed, during this time, the sum of solar and volcanic pressures would likely have produced a cooling down, not a warming up. Mountain glaciers and snow cover decline, while global average sea level increased recently by about 3 cm (a little over an inch) every 10 years.

Before the end of this century, (without particular emission reduction policies) global temperature is likely to increase by 1.1 to 2.9°C (2 to 5.2°F) if we follow the emission scenario B1, or 2.4 to 6.4°C (4.3 to 11.5°F) if we follow the fossil intensive scenario A1FI, i.e a total range of 1.1 to 6.4°C (2 to 11.5°F). The corresponding range for sea level increase is 18 to 59 cm (7 to 23 inches), but that is an underestimate because it does not take into account certain glacial processes. In the long term (centuries), the Greenland ice sheet might contribute up to 7 metres (23 feet) to sea level, and this is without the contribution from Antarctica. Heavy precipitation events are likely to increase (with the accompanying risks of floods, and I would like to stress that this needs to be better taken into account in rainwater management schemes in cities). Heat waves, such as the one which killed between 40 and 70 thousand persons in Europe in 2003, are very likely to become more frequent. Intense tropical cyclone activity is likely to increase.

Impacts will be felt everywhere, including cities, with most damage in developing countries

I will now turn to impacts, vulnerability and adaptation, the subject of the second volume of AR4. I will focus on what seems most relevant for cities.

With regard to observed impacts that have been attributed to climate change, the IPCC highlights the following: health impacts in Europe due to the heat wave of 2003, which was of unprecedented magnitude; changes in snow, ice, and frozen ground have increased the number and size of glacial lakes, increased ground instability in mountain and other permafrost regions; hydrological systems have been affected i.e. enhanced run-off and earlier spring peak discharge in many glacier and snow-fed rivers; warmer and drier conditions in the Sahel have led to a reduced length of growing season, with detrimental effects on crops.

Without mitigation, some of the projected impacts include:

- An increase in annual average run-off and water availability at high latitudes and in some wet tropical areas, and a decrease over some dry regions at mid-latitudes and in the dry tropics. Drought affected areas will likely increase in extent. In Africa alone, by 2020, between 75 and 250 million people are projected to be exposed to an increase in water stress due to climate change. Water security problems are also projected to intensify by 2030 in southern and eastern Australia.
- In the course of the century, water supplies stored in glaciers and snow cover are projected to decline, reducing water availability in regions supplied by meltwater from major mountain ranges (such as the Himalayas in Asia or the Andes in Latin America). In North America, the decreased snowpack in western mountains is projected to cause more winter flooding, and reduced summer flows, exacerbating competition for over-allocated water resources.
- Freshwater availability in Central, South, East and Southeast Asia, particularly in large river basins, is projected to decrease due to climate change, which could, in combination with other factors adversely affect more than a billion people by the 2050s.
- In Southern Europe, climate change is projected to worsen extreme heat and drought in a region already vulnerable to climate variability, reducing water supplies, hydropower potential, summer tourism, and crop productivity.
- In North America, cities that currently experience heat waves are expected to be further challenged by an increased number, intensity and duration of heat

waves during the course of the century, with potential for adverse health impacts.
- Coasts are projected to be exposed to increasing risks, including coastal erosion, due to climate change and sea-level rise. Many million more people are projected to be flooded every year due to sea-level rise by the 2080s. The numbers affected will be largest in the mega-deltas of Asia and Africa, while small islands are especially vulnerable. By 2050, ongoing coastal development and population growth in some areas of Australia and New Zealand are projected to exacerbate risks from sea level rise and increases in the severity and frequency of storms and coastal flooding.
- After the 21st century, very large sea-level rises (we are talking about 4-6 metres or more, that is at least 13 to 20 feet) that could result from widespread deglaciation of Greenland and West Antarctic ice sheets imply major changes in coastlines and ecosystems, and inundation of low-lying areas, with greatest effects in river deltas. Relocating populations, economic activity, and infrastructure would be costly and challenging.

In general, the net annual costs of the impacts of climate change are projected to increase over time as global temperatures increase. For example, while developing countries are expected to experience larger percentage losses, global mean losses due to climate change could be 1 to 5% of GDP for 4°C (7°F) of warming.

Adaptation measures can reduce some of the negative impacts, but they have limits and costs

Adaptation will be necessary to address impacts resulting from the warming which is already unavoidable due to past emissions. Adaptation is essential, particularly in addressing near-term impacts, because even the most stringent mitigation efforts cannot avoid further impacts of climate change in the next few decades. A wide array of adaptation options are available. One way of increasing adaptive capacity is by introducing the consideration of climate change impacts in standards and regulations, and in development planning, for example, by:
- including adaptation measures in land-use planning and infrastructure design (and let me add that this kind of measures, if well designed, can also have positive effects on emission reductions);
- ncluding measures to reduce vulnerability in existing disaster risk reduction strategies.

But adaptation alone is not expected to cope with all the projected effects of climate change, and especially not over the long term as most impacts increase in magnitude.

The picture emerging from the first two volumes of the IPCC AR4 is bleak, but the IPCC has a third working group, dealing with mitigation. It offers some reasons for optimism.

Together with lifestyle and behaviour changes, known technologies and policies can reduce GHG emissions at reasonable costs, but effective policies, including an effective carbon-price signal would be required

The WG3 observes first that global greenhouse gas (GHG) emissions have grown since pre-industrial times, with an increase of 70% between 1970 and 2004. Transport is a sector where emissions have grown even more: +120%. The buildings sector emissions have grown by 75% (including electricity-related emissions). And with current climate change mitigation policies and related sustainable development practices, global GHG emissions will continue to grow over the next few decades. The good news is that there is substantial economic potential for the mitigation of global GHG emissions over the coming decades that could offset the projected growth of global emissions or reduce emissions below current levels. All sectors and regions have the potential to contribute to the reductions (See Figure 1).

Economic mitigation potentials by sector in 2030 estimated from bottom-up studies

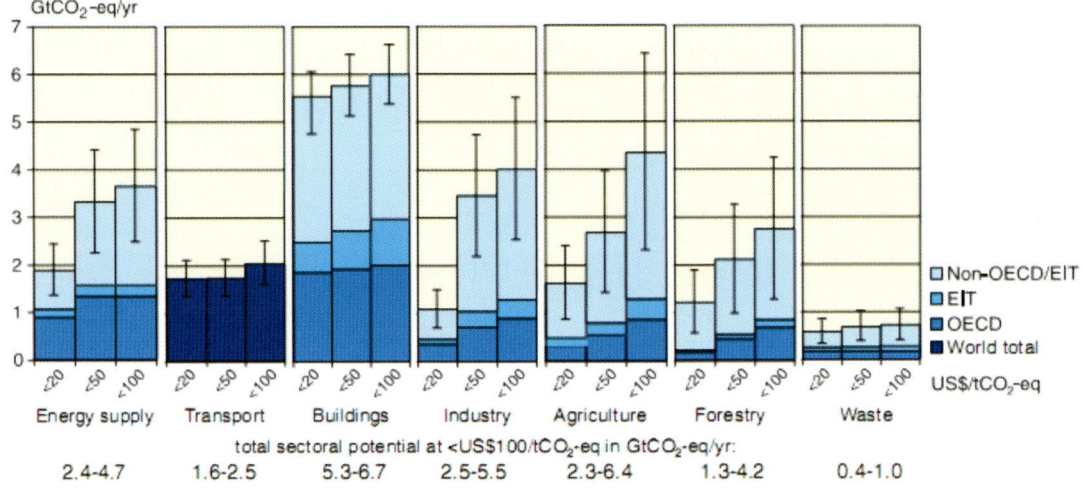

Figure 1[2] (=Figure SPM.10 from the IPCC AR4 Synthesis Report). Estimated economic mitigation potential by sector in 2030 from bottom-up studies, compared to the respective baselines assumed in the sector assessments. The potentials do not include non-technical options such as lifestyle changes.

Notes for Figure 1:

1. The ranges for global economic potentials as assessed in each sector are shown by vertical lines. The ranges are based on end-use allocations of emissions, meaning that emissions of electricity use are counted towards the end-use sectors and not to the energy supply sector.

2. The estimated potentials have been constrained by the availability of studies particularly at high carbon price levels.

3. Sectors used different baselines. For industry, the SRES B2 baseline was taken, for energy supply and transport, the World Energy Outlook (WEO) 2004 baseline was used; the building sector is based on a baseline in between SRES B2 and A1B; for waste, SRES A1B driving forces were used to construct a waste-specific baseline; agriculture and forestry used baselines that mostly used B2 driving forces.

4. Only global totals for transport are shown because international aviation is included.

5. Categories excluded are: non-CO_2 emissions in buildings and transport, part of material efficiency options, heat production and co-generation in energy supply, heavy duty vehicles, shipping and high-occupancy passenger transport, most high-cost options for buildings, wastewater treatment, emission reduction from coal mines and gas pipelines, and fluorinated gases from energy supply and transport. The underestimation of the total economic potential from these emissions is of the order of 10 to 15%

The largest potential is in the buildings sector. Some of the commercially available options assessed by IPCC are: efficient lighting and daylighting; more efficient electrical appliances and heating and cooling devices; improved cooking stoves, improved insulation ; passive and active solar design for heating and cooling; alternative refrigeration fluids, recovery and recycling of fluorinated gases. The IPCC estimates that by 2030, about 30% of the projected GGH emissions in the building sector can be avoided with net economic benefit. And there are also large co-benefits: e.g., improvements in indoor and outdoor air quality, improvement in social welfare. However, many barriers make it difficult to realize this potential.

Transport is important as well, with the following currently available options listed: more fuel efficient vehicles, hybrid vehicles, cleaner diesel vehicles, biofuels, modal shifts from road transport to rail and public transport systems, non-motorised transport (cycling, walking) and land-use and transport planning. The effect of mitigation options may be counteracted by growth in the sector. Market forces alone, including rising fuel costs, are therefore not expected to lead to significant emission reductions.

The waste sector can also positively contribute to GHG mitigation at low cost and promote sustainable development.

In order to stabilize the concentration of GHGs in the atmosphere, emissions would need to peak and decline thereafter. The lower the stabilization level, the more quickly this peak and decline would need to occur (the peak for CO_2 emissions is before 2015 if we want to achieve the lowest stabilization range assessed). Mitigation efforts over the next two to three decades will have a large impact on opportunities to achieve lower stabilization levels

The deployment of the portfolio of technologies that could achieve stabilization of GHG concentrations in the atmosphere assumes that appropriate and effective incentives are in place.

The IPCC concludes that an effective carbon-price signal could realize significant mitigation potential in all sectors, by making many mitigation options economically attractive.

What is the bottom line?
For the lowest range in concentration stabilization levels assessed, 445 to 535 ppm of CO_2-equivalent (which leads in the long term to a temperature increase between 1.5 and 2.3°C (2.7 to 4 °F), global CO_2 emissions need to peak before 2015, and the reduction of average annual GDP growth rate due to mitigation costs is less than 0.12 percentage points in 2050.

Knowing that climate change is threatening the livelihood, the water resources, the food security of hundreds of millions of people and knowing that 20-30% of plant and animal species assessed so far are likely to be at increased risk of extinction if increases in global temperature exceed 1.5 to 2.5°C above the 1990 temperature, is that price for mitigation (a reduction of average annual GDP growth rate of less than 0.12 percentage points) too expensive?

The IPCC will devote increasing attention in its next report to the regional aspects of climate change impacts, vulnerability and adaptation, as well as mitigation, and cities will form an important aspect of it.

The Fifth Assessment Report (AR5) is now under way. The outlines of the contributions of the three working groups were finalized in October 2009 (see www.ipcc.ch). Regional aspects will receive more attention in all working groups. For the first time, the WGII contribution will contain a separate volume on regional aspects, which will benefit from cross-working group collaboration. Infrastructure will also receive particular attention, both from the adaptation and the mitigation point of view. The 800+ authors of AR5 were selected in June 2010 out of more than 3000 nominations. The first volume (physical science aspects) will be finalized in September 2013, with the whole report completed one year later.

I hope many ISOCARP members will participate in the writing of the report, or as important, to its review, so that land use planning and issues related to cities can be covered even better in the IPCC AR5.

—

Sustainable Urbanism in Abu Dhabi

John P. Madden

This essay presents an overview of Abu Dhabi's efforts towards achieving improved levels of sustainability and high quality urbanism as a rapidly developing city through an integrated design approach. The formulation of the urban structure framework Plan 2030 with supporting regulations, guidelines and policies have been instrumental in shaping large- scale private and government led masterplans. The essay focuses on two key strategic projects - the Capital District as the embodiment of sustainable mixed use development primarily intended to house national government and commercial uses and the Masdar development as an ambitious effort to create a carbon neutral and zero waste development. The essay concludes with a summary of the lessons that can be drawn for other emerging developing cities.

Introduction

As one of the fastest growing emerging economies in the developing world, Abu Dhabi has been presented with unique challenges and opportunities from a spatial planning perspective. Abu Dhabi forms the capital city of the United Arab Emirates and sits approximately 24 degrees north of the equator in the north eastern part of the Arabian Peninsula. Over the past five years, Abu Dhabi has witnessed strong economic development, with a growth rate averaging 9 percent per year (UPC Real Estate Forecast Study, January 2010). Much of Abu Dhabi's historic growth has been linked to the exploitation of oil as it holds approximately 10 percent of the world's oil reserves and approximately 3 percent of the world's gas reserves. While its economy and resulting urban form have largely been driven and influenced by the fossil fuel era, the government's future agenda is focused on sustainability and transforming the capital city through the visionary Plan Abu Dhabi 2030 Urban Structure Framework Plan (Plan 2030). The growth of the city is expected to be largely driven by the Economic Vision Plan 2030 which seeks diversification into new sectors including education, finance, tourism, real estate, aerospace and industry with an emphasis on renewable energy. Unlike Dubai, its neighbour 90 kilometres up the coast, the emphasis has not been focused on the tallest, the biggest, the first, or the most expensive, but rather about getting back to the basics of defining the ingredients that make a great city. In the past two and half years Abu Dhabi has managed to formulate new plans, policies, and regulations to guide its own physical growth and that of its surrounding Emirate. In 2007, in order to help guide the implementation of those plans, the government of Abu Dhabi created the Urban Planning Council consisting of an interdisciplinary team of experts to govern and regulate private development as well as work with related government agencies to align policies, processes and regulations to achieve the vision of Plan 2030. This paper will highlight the approach and process in formulating its strategic planning efforts with an emphasis on sustainable urbanism and highlight how those efforts have manifested themselves in two strategic government projects: the Capital District and Masdar.

Governance Structure and Regulatory Framework to Implement Plan 2030

Years prior to the establishment of the Urban Planning Council in September 2007, decisions concerning development in the Emirate and city of Abu Dhabi were made directly by the Crown Prince through discussions with his advisors and proponents of major development proposals. The existing Abu Dhabi Comprehensive Plan (ADCP), formulated in the late 1980's began to lack the ability to address the scale, scope or complexity of current proposed and ongoing development. Major proposals were assessed on an individual basis using a plan whose conceptual limits, scope and mandate were becoming obsolete under unprecedented developmental pressure. Added to this, the year 2005 marked a surge in developmental growth when a governmental policy change allowed foreign property investment within Abu Dhabi, putting immense pressure on the existing Plan.

Figure 1: Expert Planners during the Plan 2030 Charette

The vision of His Highness Sheikh Mohamed Bin Zayed Al Nahyan, Crown Prince of Abu Dhabi and Chairman of the Abu Dhabi Executive Council, understood the importance of undertaking a more rational and systematic approach to planning. His advisors identified global experts in the field of urban design, planning, transportation and sustainability to undertake the ambitious job of establishing a planning framework to guide the growth of the Emirate in a more systematic and sustainable way.

The plan horizon was targeted to the year 2030 and would accommodate Abu Dhabi's population growth to increase from approximately 1 million to over 3 million people but had flexibility to accommodate up to 5 million people if needed. Plan Abu Dhabi 2030 was based on a set of overarching principles. These were formulated through an iterative charrette process which gathered local and international experts to collect data, conduct surveys, consult with stakeholders not only to understand the values of those that lived, worked and visited Abu Dhabi but also to understand some of the key environmental, social and physical assets that were to be protected and responded to through the planning process.

The creation of these principles provided a foundation to help guide the formulation of Plan 2030 and are now used to guide future policies and area plans. The overarching principles that helped guide Plan Abu Dhabi 2030 are:

- Abu Dhabi will be a contemporary expression of an Arab City, which has people living, working and recreating in healthy supportive proximity to each other;
- Abu Dhabi will continue its practice of measured growth reflecting a sustainable economy rather than uncontrolled growth;
- Abu Dhabi will respect, be scaled to, and shaped by the natural environment of sensitive coastal and desert ecologies;
- Abu Dhabi will manifest its role and stature as a capital city;
- Abu Dhabi's urban fabric and community infrastructure will enable the values, social arrangements, culture, and mores of this Arab community.

Formulating Abu Dhabi Plan 2030: An Integrative and Strategic Approach
Looking back at the creation of Abu Dhabi Plan 2030, a fundamental effort was made to understand the region's positive attributes and embrace them as central to the Plan's underlying principles. Preservation, enhancement, and stewardship of the natural environment were of key importance. An emphasis was placed on the protection and

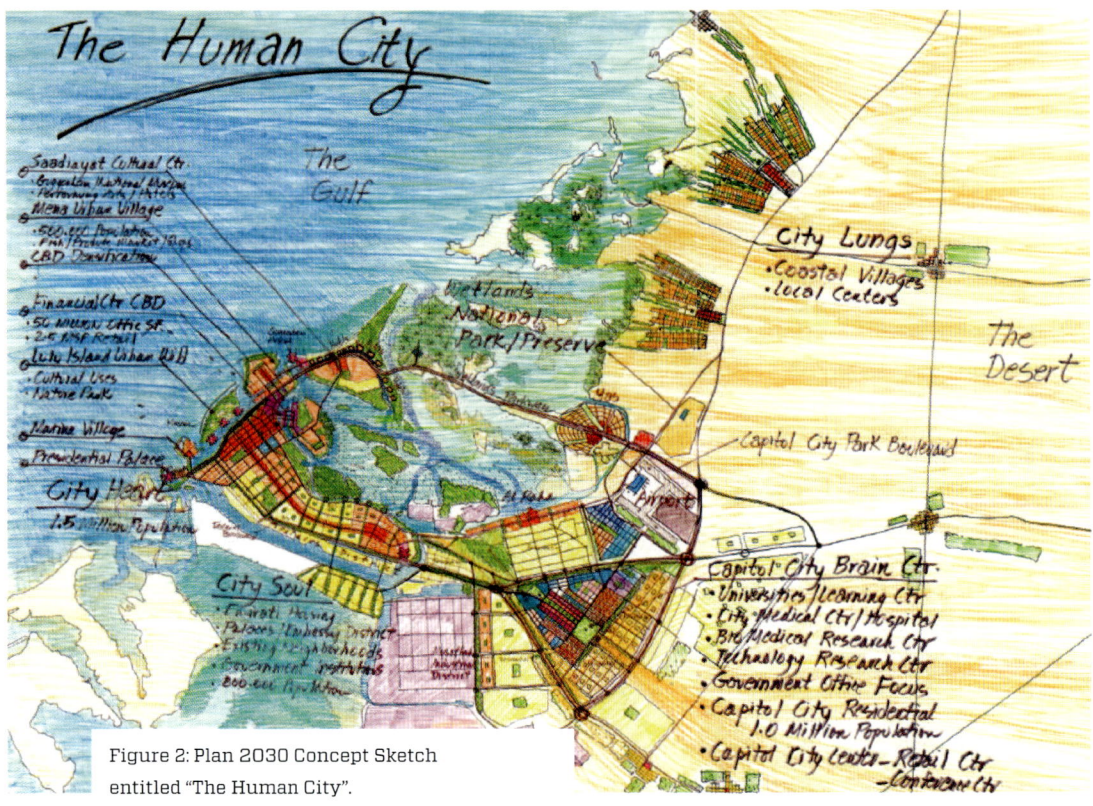

Figure 2: Plan 2030 Concept Sketch entitled "The Human City".

enhancement of the sensitive coastal and desert environments which still give Abu Dhabi its unique identity today.

The formulation of Abu Dhabi Plan 2030 was achieved by creating a series of maps and diagrams which identified environmentally sensitive areas, natural habitats, mangroves, cultural landscapes and historic buildings, transportation networks, land use patterns, built form (height) and figure ground diagrams, open space and park systems. These maps were used to provide a diagnostic on the existing conditions and to understand where future growth could be accommodated without threatening the natural ecology, cultural and historic assets. Economic forecasts were undertaken based on Economic Vision 2030 and equated these growth forecasts for each sector of the economy (leisure and tourism, retail, administration and management, manufacturing, light and heavy industry, etc) and derived a gross floor area projection to accommodate growth in each of those economic sectors to a planning horizon of 2030. The next step was to allocate a spatial and built form dimension to those gross floor areas and to map out a series of frameworks and basic structure plans for land use, transportation, environment, open space, parks, built form and density. Conceptual plans and schemes were formulated for key areas including the proposed expansion of the central business district, Capital District, Grand Mosque District and Lulu Island. To help articulate the principles of the plan, a series of more detailed studies were sketched illustrating potential designs for emirate neighbourhoods, revitalization of downtown blocks and new eco villages in selected desert and coastal areas.

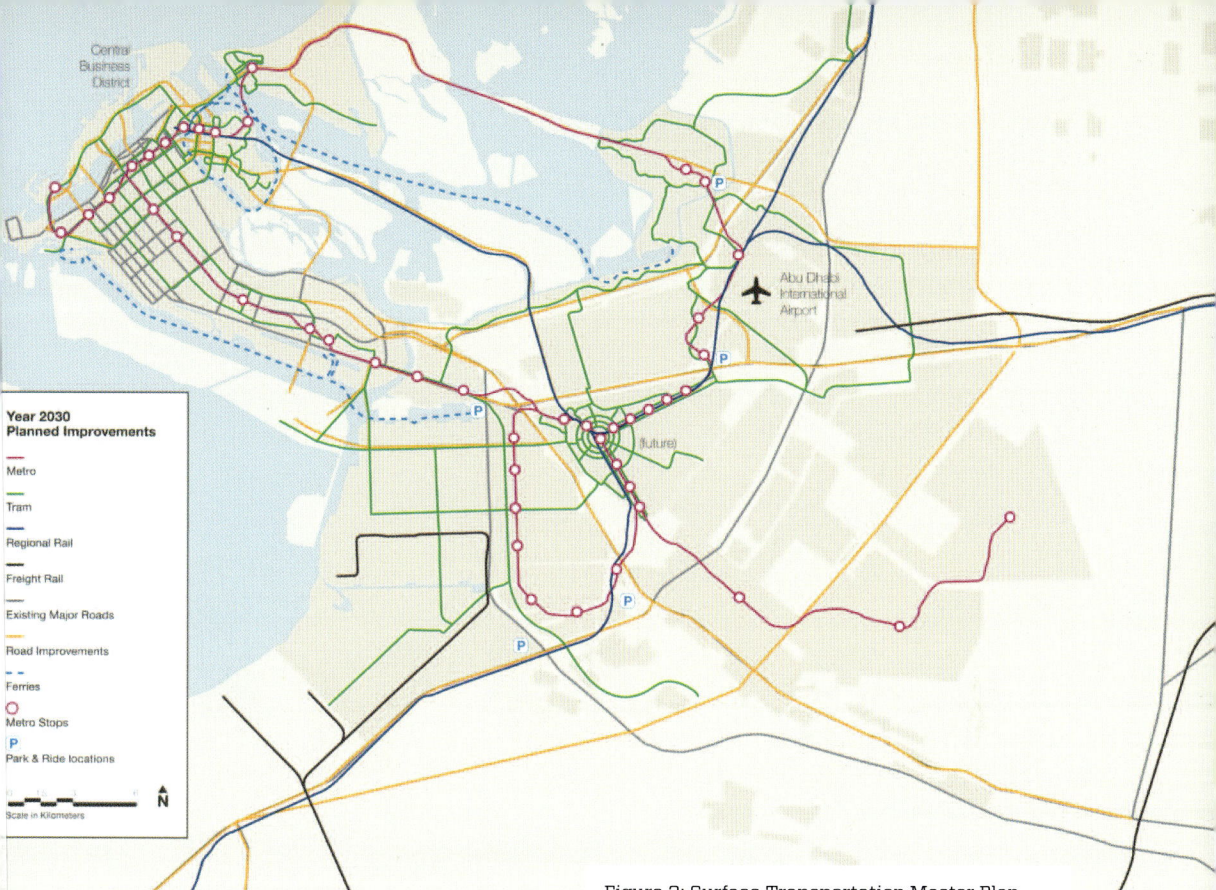

Figure 3: Surface Transportation Master Plan

Transportation Framework

In order to facilitate significant growth in Abu Dhabi, major emphasis has been given to the creation of a multi-modal transportation framework to guide transportation investments that serve land use patterns and densities outlined in the plan. The underlying premise of the plan starts by acknowledging that "the best transportation plan is a good land use plan" (Plan Abu Dhabi 2030). Coupled with a good land use plan, the transportation framework envisions a fine grained and integrated transport network that will provide regular and reliable service as a viable alternative to the private automobile. In the higher density urban areas, the plan aims to ensure that transit services are located within 300 metres to where people live or work. The layered network of transit services when built is estimated to carry 30 to 40% of the peak period volume of passenger trips. (STMP, June 2009).

The existing urban structure of Abu Dhabi is based on a super-grid of arterial streets and boulevards creating megablocks that can stretch almost a kilometer in length. The UPC has initiated a comprehensive planning effort to create a more regularized pattern of streets to maximize connectivity and improved mobility for all modes of transportation. A finer network of streets will allow for a better distribution of traffic while creating a more robust transportation system. If one segment of the system fails there are options for traffic to take alternative routes. The most important principle for the design of the street network is to maximize connectivity, providing the largest number of smaller options rather than the smallest amount of large options. The thrust of the framework moves away from the extension of highways into the downtown toward more human-scaled streets that are designed to move people rather than engineered to move vehicles. Expanding highways into the urban areas only serves to blight large swathes of land, devalue property, sever connectivity, increase latent demand to drive and create barriers to pedestrians.

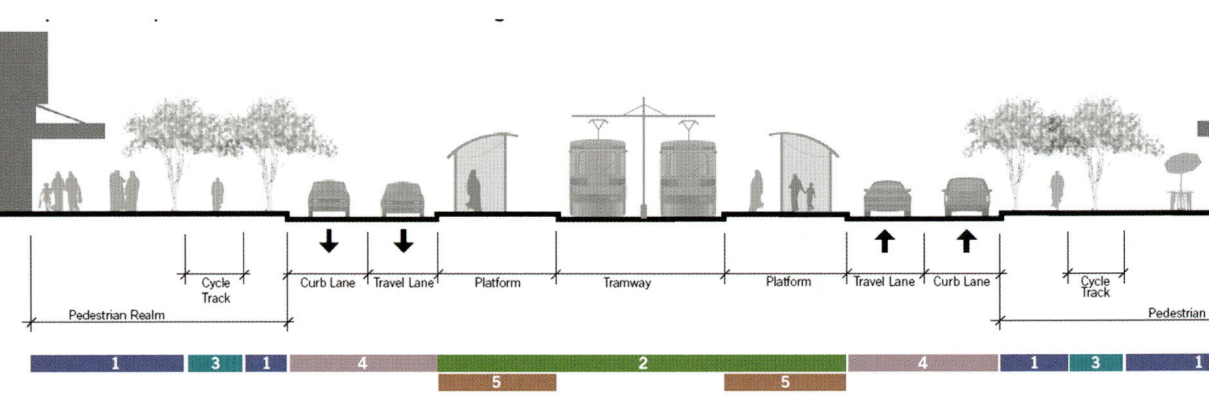

Figure 4: The Function of the Public Realm, Urban Street Design Manual.

To support this aim, the UPC has recently created an alternative urban street design manual that provides a hierarchy of street designs which responds more sensitively to land use context. The new street design manual responds to the types of activities and uses that are planned in the public realm as well as by capacity that is required to serve planned land use and density.

These principles are evident in the emerging revitalization plan for the inner city of Abu Dhabi called Wasat Al Madina, meaning the centre of the city. Connectivity is enhanced within the mega-blocks by connecting dead-end streets, and re-aligning streets to connect across blocks. This allows traffic to be distributed across a finer grid and reduces vehicle travel distances by increasing access.

As all trips begin and end as a pedestrian, plans place significant emphasis on improving the safety and comfort of pedestrians. This includes plans for constructing direct and universally accessible sidewalks, removing barriers, providing shading devices and providing investments in the public realm. Plans identify pedestrian priority areas with dedicated "shade-way" routes that connect between major activity nodes including transit stops.

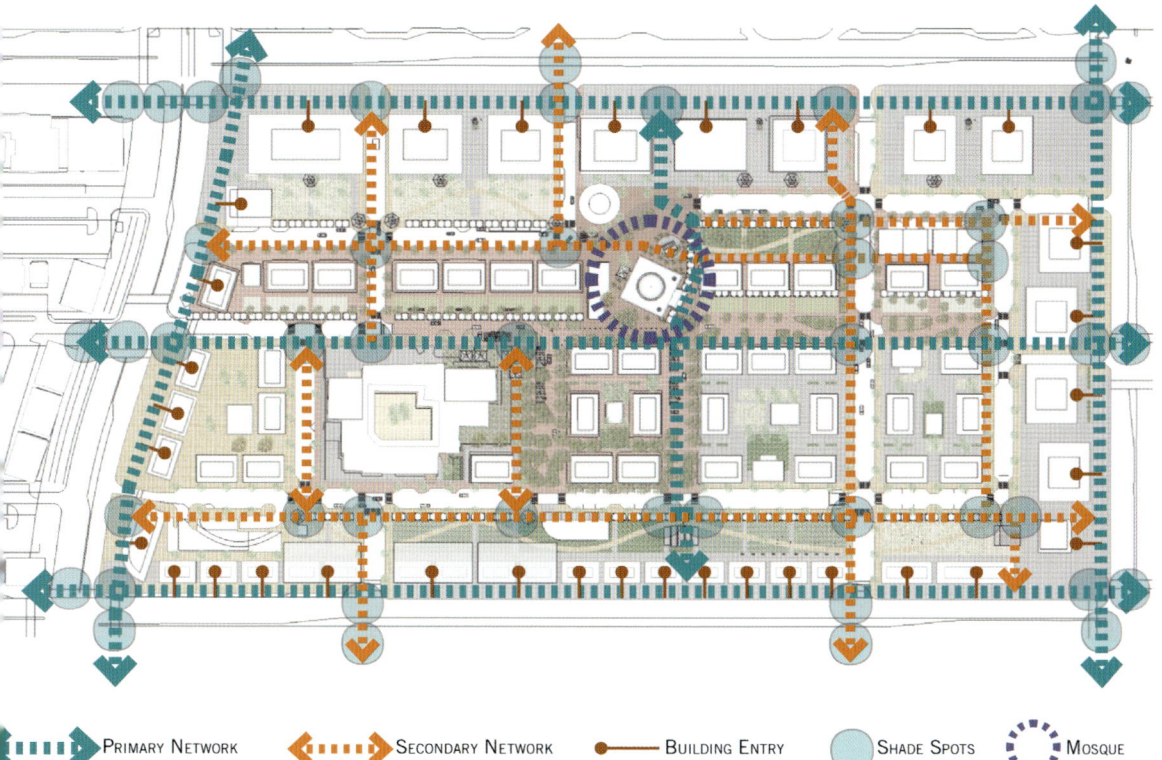

Figure 5: Identifying the Pedestrian Network, Wasat Al Madina

Land Use Framework

Rather than dispersion of growth, the plan outlines a pattern of two major growth areas: the expanded central business district on the north end of Abu Dhabi Island and the Capital District on the metropolitan mainland.

The planned expansion of the central business district will consolidate and expand the existing core to allow for the proposed financial hub to emerge on Al Sowwa Island. It will be surrounded by medium to high density mixed use and residential development to ensure it remains vibrant at all times of the day. The Capital District is the secondary core which will house government and knowledge based sectors. The two centres will be connected via a metro line which the plan envisions to extend to also connect Masdar, the international airport and eventually loop to connect Yas and Saadiyat Islands. The effect will be to improve the distribution of trips to these two centres helping to minimize congestion on Abu Dhabi Island, which is served by two bridges at the south end and the recently completed Saadiyat Bridge to the north.

The plan also defines limits to the growth of the city by creating an urban growth boundary. This is essential to preserving the sensitive ecology on the city's edge and for preventing urban sprawl through the desert. Development limits are also defined by a system of parks and desert fingers. These effectively help to consolidate growth in a more compact footprint making it more efficient and cost effective to deliver sustainable infrastructure.

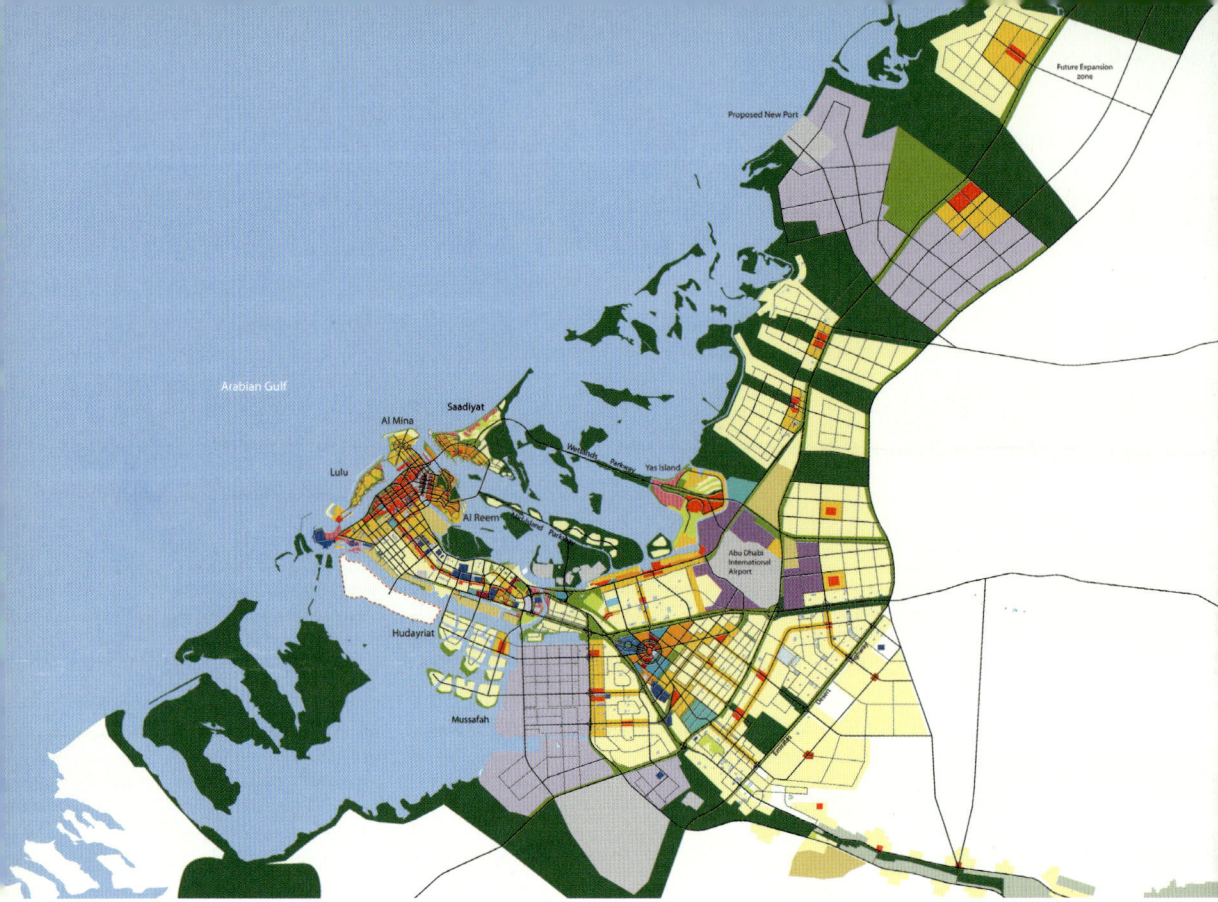

Figure 6: Land Use Framework Plan, Plan Abu Dhabi 2030

Sustainable Urban Infrastructure Planning

Infrastructure is a core building block to achieving sustainability. The UPC has initiated an infrastructure framework plan to address more efficient design and delivery of infrastructure to new development at a regional and building scale. The framework plan will address more efficient utilization of land for utility rights-of-way, provision of land for renewable energy production, and provision for smart grid and metering technologies. Additionally, the infrastructure plan will investigate the cost and benefits of centralized versus decentralized utility plants such as district cooling, desalination and sewage treatment to optimize the efficiency of the plants and their supporting networks.

Instead of planning large centralized systems, infrastructure components may be located closer to buildings, neighborhoods and renewable resources thereby reducing potential for network losses, inefficiencies and increased long term maintenance costs. For example, a district energy system can incorporate local energy sources such as geothermal energy or heating/cooling exchange from a water body. While large, centralized systems may be still be appropriate in many cases, an integrated approach will result in a network of more distributed and/or 'on-site' infrastructure systems, with shared elements, finely integrated into the fabric of the built

Figure 7: Photovoltaic Technologies as a Source of Alternative Energy

environment. Visible sustainable infrastructure that residents and businesses can see contributes to awareness and more efficient behavior, and acts as a catalyst for other sustainability projects.

More efficient land utilization for infrastructure corridors through vertical stacking, combined corridors and integrated design will reduce widths of rights of way which in turn increase development potential and create more compact community footprints. Other synergies of integrated sustainable infrastructure design allow for multiple uses of space for utility corridors. For example, replacing storm water drainage pipes with landscaped swales reduces costs (less pipe and paving) while creating a green amenity which also reduces urban heat island effect.

While Abu Dhabi has approximately 10% of the world's oil reserves, it has committed to diversifying away from its economic dependence on oil by placing a greater emphasis on renewable energy. By 2020, Abu Dhabi will generate at least 7% of its energy from renewable sources (Arabian Business, 2009). Renewable energy currently accounts for a small percentage of Abu Dhabi's energy profile at less than one percent. Abu Dhabi's geography and climate gives it a competitive advantage when it comes to solar energy potential. With an average of 10 hours of sunlight / day, it has considerable potential to capture significant amounts of the sun's radiation. As part of the Masdar development initiative, a 10MW solar photovoltaic power plant has been constructed to supply some of the city's energy demands. Other alternative energy facilities are being incorporated into a newly developed Plan 2030 for Al Gharbia, located in the western region of the emirate of Abu Dhabi.

The Development Review Process
The Abu Dhabi Urban Planning Council acts on two levels: first as an approval board to ensure the strategic long term development of the Emirate, and second as a guardian of Plan Abu Dhabi 2030's guiding principles. Key to achieving the plans was formulating a development review process that ensured the overarching vision of Plan 2030 would be implemented in a timely and coordinated manner.

   The Crown Prince directed that a new governance body be created to manage the development process and formulate policies, area plans and regulations to guide future development in the Emirate of Abu Dhabi. In September of 2007, by Emiri Decree, the Urban Planning Council was officially launched to perform these functions. As an immediate priority, a Development Review process was established to guide development proposals to comply with the principles of Plan 2030. The Development Review process was structured on an integrative design process. Key representatives of the proponent's design team (architects, engineers, cost consultants, developer and owner) met with the development review team which consisted of the Development Planner, transportation and environmental specialist to inform applicants of key policies, guidelines and regulations that will inform the design of the master plan.

   The Council's Development Review and Urban Design team now plays the lead role in reviewing and approving developments across the Emirate to ensure that new development responds to the cohesive planning frameworks for Plan 2030 in Abu Dhabi, Al Ain and Al Gharbia. As such, new development proposals within the Emirate of Abu Dhabi are subject to rigorous assessment to ensure that the approach to new development responds to its unique

Figure 8:
Establishment
of a Coherent
Development Review
Process

Estidama: A Program that Embeds Sustainability as a Way of Life

The Estidama Program was launched in May 2008 as one of the UPC's flagship programs to promote sustainable growth in the Emirate of Abu Dhabi. Estidama is the Arabic word for sustainability. Built on a 4-pillar philosophy (environmental, economic, social and cultural), Estidama is committing itself to supporting sustainable living and use of resources by working closely with communities, organizations, businesses and policy-makers to further encourage responsible decision making that moves Abu Dhabi towards global sustainability. Once fully articulated, Estidama is envisioned to touch upon every facet of daily life - the curriculum of schools, the type of investments made by the Sovereign Wealth Fund, the choice of products that companies procure, the type of food that is brought to the table and the focus on diversification of the economy to lessen its reliance on oil.

geographic location, context, and climate, as well as targeting market demographics in line with realistic economic projections.

Every development is assessed against how it complies with the framework plans and emerging policies. The process is set up to work in collaboration with external government agencies and utility providers so that development proposals address all the requirements in a coherent and logical way to ensure that we work towards stewarding growth that protects and enhances the unique desert and coastal environments.

The overall emphasis of the development review process is focused on two core elements: satisfaction of sustainability and urban design objectives. Key to achieving these objectives is taking a systems-based approach to designing communities more holistically rather than creating "gated islands" of development.

The Estidama Pearl Rating System for Communities, Buildings and Villas

Given the rapid growth that has been occurring in Abu Dhabi the initial focus of the Estidama program has been on the built environment. To that end, the Urban Planning Council created the Pearl Rating Systems (PRS) to guide all new physical development in becoming more environmentally sensitive and much more climatically responsive in its design and construction. Abu Dhabi Urban Planning Council established a clear vision for sustainability as the foundation of any new development occurring in the Emirate. More than just a sustainability program, Estidama is the symbol of an inspired vision for governance and community development.

Through implementation of the PRS it is estimated that a savings of approximately 11,000 GWh in the residential sector alone could be realized which equates to a financial savings to the

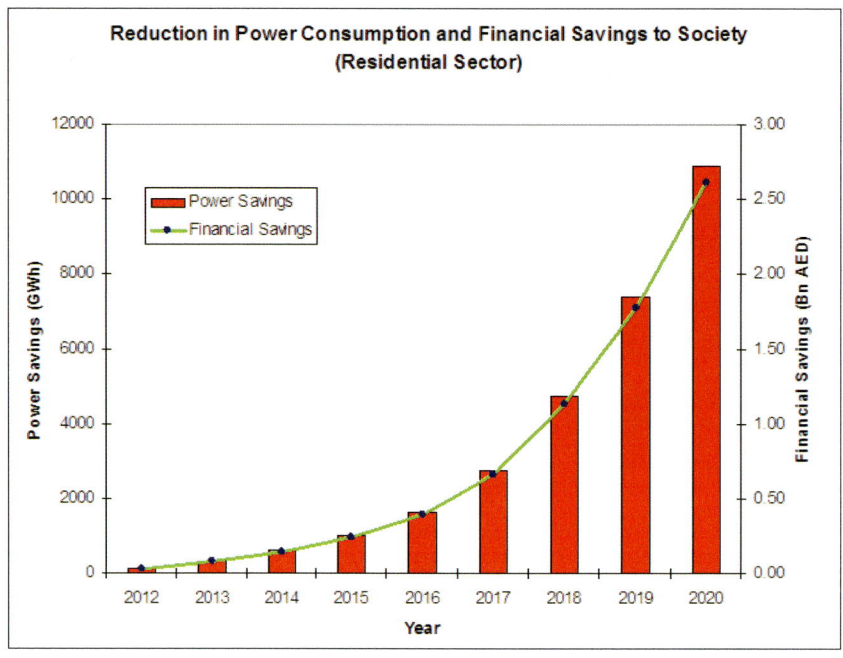

Figure 9: Reduction in Power Consumption and Financial Savings to Society (Residential Sector)

Figure 10: Impact of Estidama on CO2 Emissions Reduction in Residential Sector (2012 – 2020)

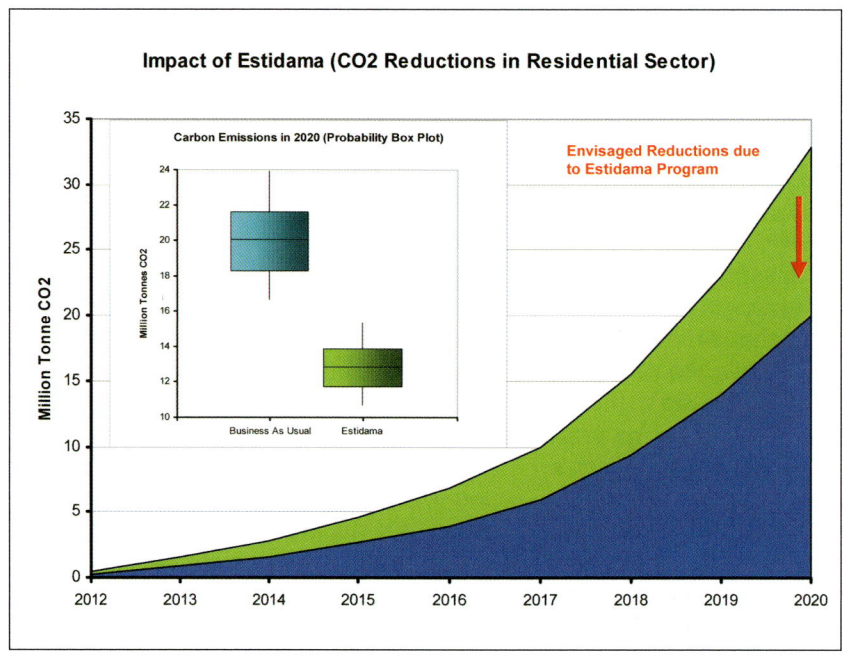

Source: Real Estate Market Forecasts, DR&UE, ADUPC; Energy and Water Savings and Pearl Rating System, ARUP; RSB Estimates for Cost of Electricity Generation; DR&UE Assumptions on Policy Penetration; US EPA eGRID for emissions from natural gas power plants in the US; Executive Affairs Authority, Abu Dhabi for maximum emissions in electricity sector factoring desalination (Consolidated number not decoupled for energy and water); DR&UE Analysis.

society in the order of AED 2.6 billion per annum at current cost (2010) of production of electricity (Figure 9). Similar outcomes would be anticipated for the commercial, retail, hotel and public sector buildings as well.

The PRS will not only result in significant operational savings for new buildings but it will also result in significant reduction in carbon emissions. With the potential energy savings that are achieved through the government mandated requirements towards energy efficiency, it is estimated that the Estidama Pearl Rating System has the potential to reduce carbon emissions by over 35 percent over a "business as usual" approach to new development over the next 10 years (Figure 10).

The Pearl Rating System takes an integrated approach by addressing sustainable design at all stages in the life of buildings and communities – planning, design, construction and operation. The UPC is one of the first planning authorities to formulate and administer a building and community rating system that addresses specific climate conditions, local culture and the regional context. The advantage is that the system is fully adapted and responds to the regulatory framework that is being developed by the UPC. At the same time, new building code and development regulations have also been developed which have enabled the alignment of multiple regulatory tools to address sustainability from buildings to large-scale master planned communities.

The Pearl Rating System is organized into seven categories that address performance and design metrics (Figure 11).

- Natural Systems: Conserving, preserving and restoring the region's critical natural environments and habitats.
- Livable Communities: Improving the quality and connectivity of outdoor and indoor spaces.
- Precious Water: Reducing water demand and encouraging efficient distribution and alternative water sources.
- Resourceful Energy: Targeting energy conservation through passive design measures, reduced demand, energy efficiency and renewable sources.
- Stewarding Materials: Ensuring consideration of the 'whole-of-life' cycle (from extraction and manufacturing to transportation, useful life, and disposal) when selecting and specifying materials.

Each of these sections contains both mandatory and voluntary credits intended to help the design team address the 4 pillars of the Estidama program. The PRS system places greater emphasis on

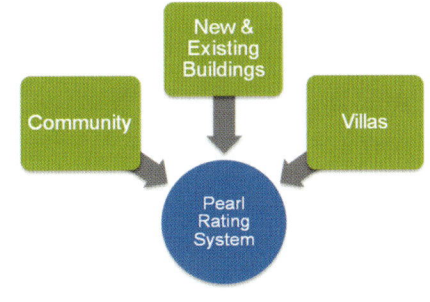

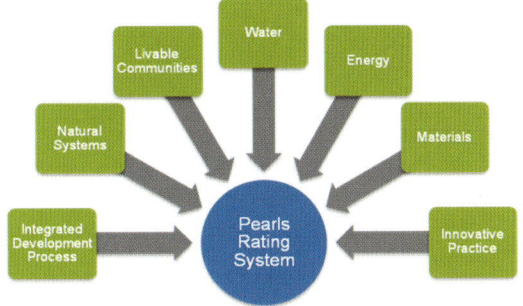

Figure 11: Performance & Design Matrix, Estidama

the credit weighting toward water and energy efficiency. The PRS has a monitoring and enforcement aspect which is also unique to other rating methods.

Most importantly, the PRS is context sensitive and focuses on how the built environment responds to the extreme heat and humidity of a coastal desert. A core mandate of the PRS requires that passive design strategies be undertaken throughout the planning and design stages of the application process. Key strategies include the orientation of the street grid and building plots to allow penetration of prevailing northwest coastal winds through the building site. The built form can also contribute positively to the local micro environment by orientation of buildings to provide shade on the public realm and providing variations in height to help direct winds downward to the pedestrian realm without creating a wind tunnel effect. Appropriately implemented, these factors will help realize immense benefits in the livability of the built environment. Credits also encourage the use of "grey water" or treated sewage effluent (TSE) for irrigation and district cooling systems. Abu Dhabi has commissioned the construction of a treated sewage effluent (TSE) plant which will have a capacity of converting 430,000 cubic metres of sewage per day and will use processes such as ultra filtration treatment and ultra violet light disinfection (The National, July 13, 2010).

Case Study: The Capital District

The Capital District forms the gateway to Abu Dhabi and is one of the major strategic initiatives of Plan 2030. The Capital District Masterplan provides a long term vision toward 2030 for the development of a global 21st Century capital based on sound planning principles, sustainable criteria toward environmental quality and energy consumption, and a desire to provide the highest quality of life possible for all its citizens.

The plan for this forty-five square kilometre site provides for a projected population of three hundred and seventy thousand residents. The Capital District is one of the most ambitious urban development projects being planned in the United Arab Emirates. In creating this new city, the Masterplan has capitalized on the site's physical assets - its centrality within the region and accessibility to both Abu Dhabi Island and to emerging developments on the mainland, its proximity to a well-connected highway network, coastal climate and breezes, and its adjacencies to existing residential neighbourhoods.

The site's triangular shape provided strong cues for organizing development around proposed high capacity transit lines through the site and in creating a series of symbolic and visual axes that link important civic spaces and landmarks, terminating at a central civic space that will represent the nation.

The Capital District is planned as a sustainable, compact, mixed use city, comprised of high-density transit-oriented communities, employment, major universities, hospitals and knowledge based employment sectors, as well as a lower density Emirati neighbourhood. A central driver behind the Masterplan vision is the symbiotic relationship between land use and transportation in the creation of high quality, attractive district and neighbourhood centres, vibrant streets and public spaces, and well-planned cultural and community

Figure 12 Capital District Plan & Context

Figure 13: Transit Orientated Communities

facilities, all served by a world-class public transportation system.

The Capital District will be the new seat of national government and house a diplomatic and embassy neighbourhood. It will also serve as the city of Abu Dhabi's second business district, providing over one hundred thousand jobs in a dynamic mixed-use urban core. In addition to a dense network of open spaces and community uses to support the local population, the Capital District will host an Olympic caliber 65,000 seat National Stadium as well as various sports venues and conference facilities. New universities and research facilities will position the city as a hub for education and research. The new city will also be a leader in environmental sustainability, with requirements for the use of highly energy efficient building structures, district cooling systems, water sensitive landscaping and irrigation and an overall urban design plan that promotes connectivity and pedestrian comfort.

Again, Abu Dhabi's desert and coast climate will pose significant challenges to maintaining human comfort in outside urban environments. The plan seeks to mitigate the negative impacts of thermal heat gain through comprehensive systems of shade and ventilation throughout the urban environment.

The fundamental principles guiding the geometry of the plan seek to naturally ventilate the city by having roadways, block orientation, landscape and building form oriented to capture the prevailing winds as a cooling source. Throughout the planning process, modeled design scenarios were tested in order to understand the implications from a wind and cooling standpoint.

Based on results from these studies and additional scientific research, strategies were developed to guide

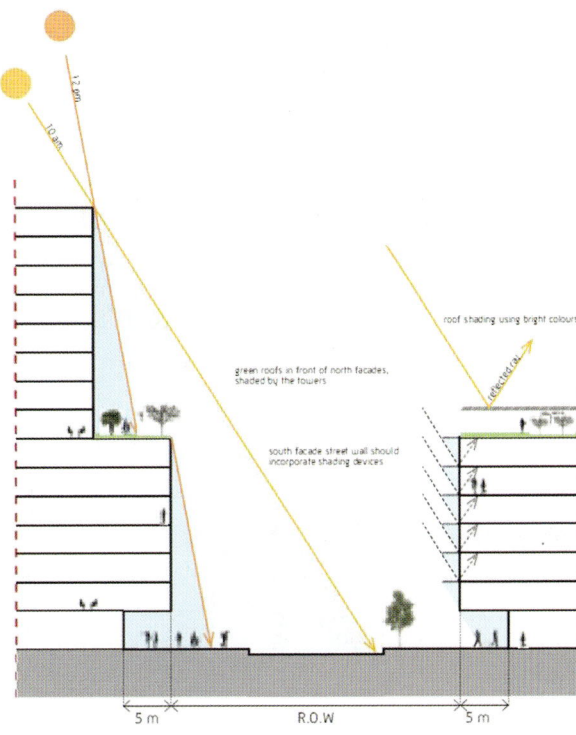

Figure 14: Solar Shading from street-wall setbacks

decision-making with regard to the orientation of streets and the positioning and dimensioning of buildings in order to best take advantage of the wind. Also, shading devices such as arcades, trellis and landscaped canopies are planned as a complex network of places that allow pedestrian movement, solar protection and refuge from the harsh climatic conditions of Abu Dhabi.

Sustainable practices towards conservation of energy and water are key priorities of the Capital District Plan. The plan optimizes building energy use and water consumption through the application of "green building" practices as defined by the government's Estidama Program. The design of the public realm and open space systems will incorporate xeriscaping strategies which use drought resistant plantings and materials which significantly reduces the consumption of potable water. Recycling centers will be located within the ground floor of public parking facilities and encourage individuals and households to recycle.

In addition to enhancing urban fabric and community infrastructure which will enable the values, social arrangements and culture of the Emirati communities to be preserved, Capital District clearly aims to manifest Abu Dhabi's role and stature as a capital city.

Figure 15: Integration of Built Form into the Public Realm, Capital District

Figure 16: Oblique view of Masdar development proposal

Case Study: Masdar

Masdar is planned to be a mixed-use development strategically located on the metropolitan mainland of Abu Dhabi between the international airport, Capital District and approximately 17km from the existing central business district at the north end of Abu Dhabi Island. The plan aspires to create a carbon neutral and zero waste city which will become a model for demonstrating traditional and high tech approaches to sustainability in the region. The 640 hectare site of Masdar will accommodate 40,000 residents and approximately 50,000 employees when fully built (Masdar City Development, UPC Review Panel Report, 2008).

The focus of the development is centred on the Masdar Institute of Science and Technology (MIST) and the headquarters of the International Renewable Energy Agency (IRENA). The first phase of the development will have an academic and research focus on sustainable technologies and alternative energies. In addition to the educational facilities, the mix of land uses include commercial, community and residential uses which help to create a job-housing balance which in turn reduces the potential number of commuter trips. The planned mix of land uses will also help create a more vital community and sense of place.

The master plan for Masdar incorporates traditional Islamic-Arabic design with advanced sustainability techniques into a contemporary architectural expression. The spatial footprint of the development is very compact but is relatively low in scale with predominate building heights ranging from 4 to 7 stories. Studies have shown that the optimal densities to support a basic provision of commercial services and

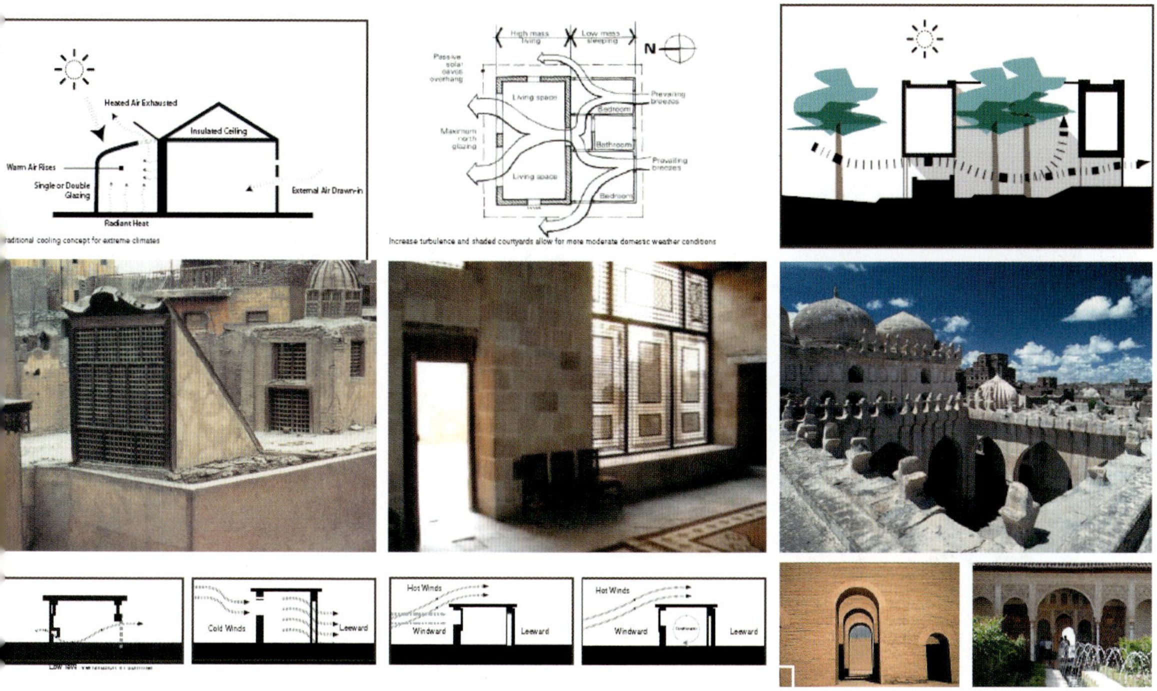

Figure 17: Traditional Passive Design Techniques in Islamic Architecture

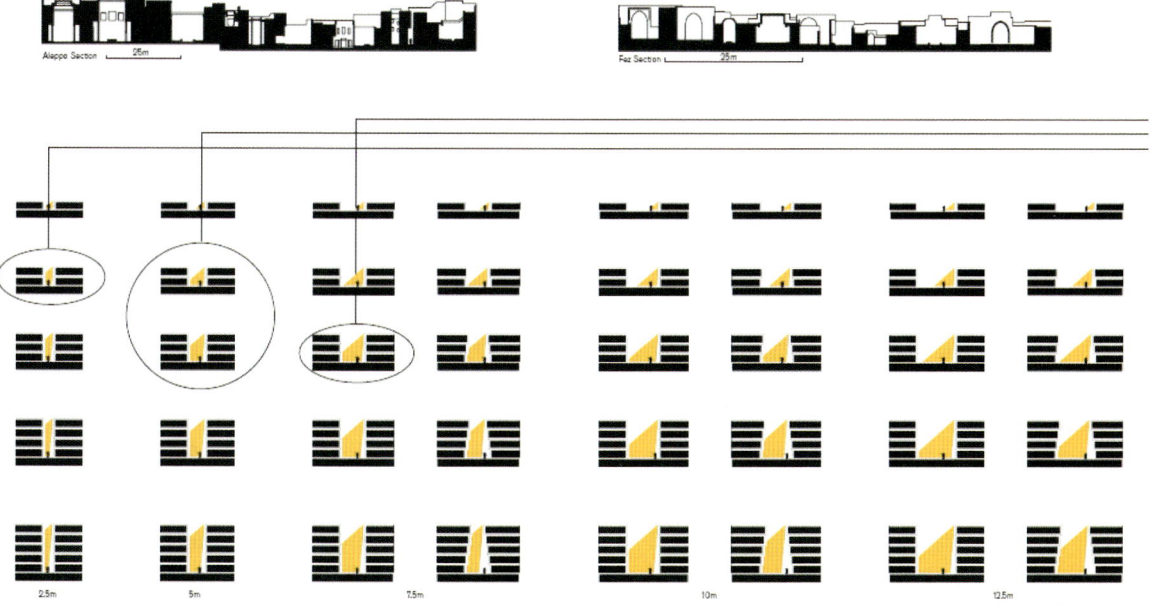

Figure 18: Solar shading analysis - street widths to building height ratios

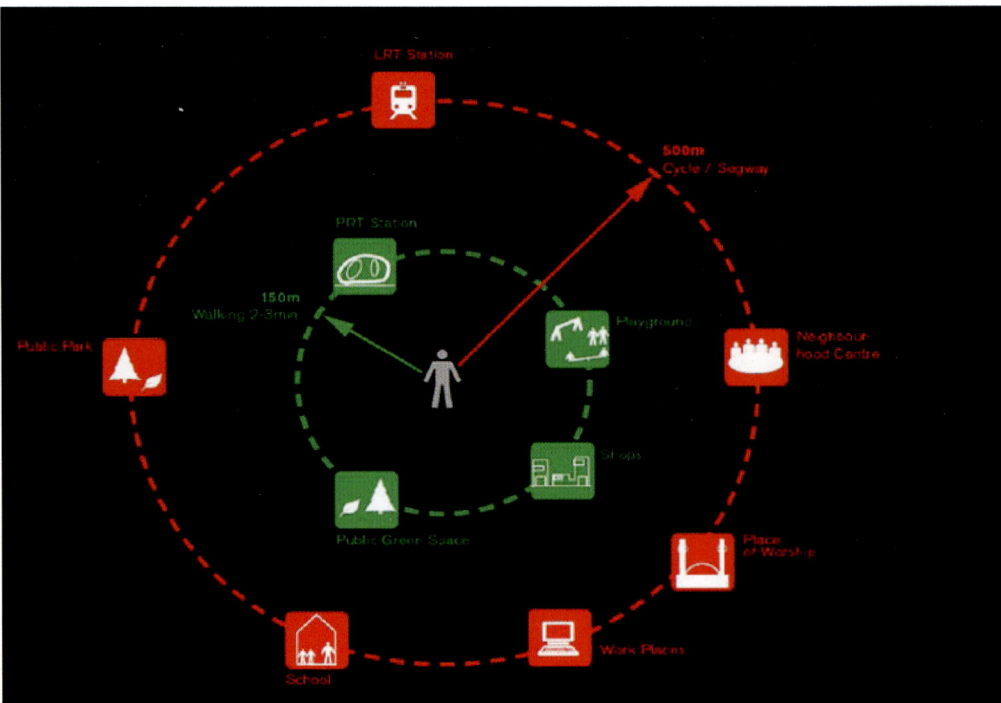

Figure 19: Transportation Strategy, Masdar

public transport is about 5000 people within a catchment area of 300 metres walking radius. This equates to a design population density of 200 people per hectare. To induce greater pedestrian trips, the Masdar plan proposes densities of 245 people per hectare, which reduces the effective pedestrian catchment areas to nearly 150 metres (Figure19).

The transportation strategy is premised entirely on alternative modes to the private automobile. All trips within the Masdar development will be either by transit, walking or cycling. To achieve this, the plan proposes a hierarchy of transit systems including a personal rapid transit system (PRT) and a network of bicycle and pedestrian routes that are seamlessly interconnected. A compact development footprint, a comprehensive alternative transportation network and strategically clustered public facilities and amenities induce a greater number of pedestrian trips. The transportation strategy alone will reduce carbon dioxide emissions by 7 percent. (Masdar, 2010)

The planned orientation and layout of the development responds to climate and its geographic location. Through solar analysis and thermal dynamic modeling, the design strategy of Masdar evolved to minimize solar radiation and thermal heat gain. The entire city's street orientation and urban structure were rotated by 45 degrees to the northwest to minimize solar gain within the public realm and along building facades thereby reducing the potential cooling load of buildings and improving overall microclimate and outdoor thermal comfort. Building height to street width ratios help to maximize solar shading.

Figure 20: Pedestrian routes with passive and active solar shading

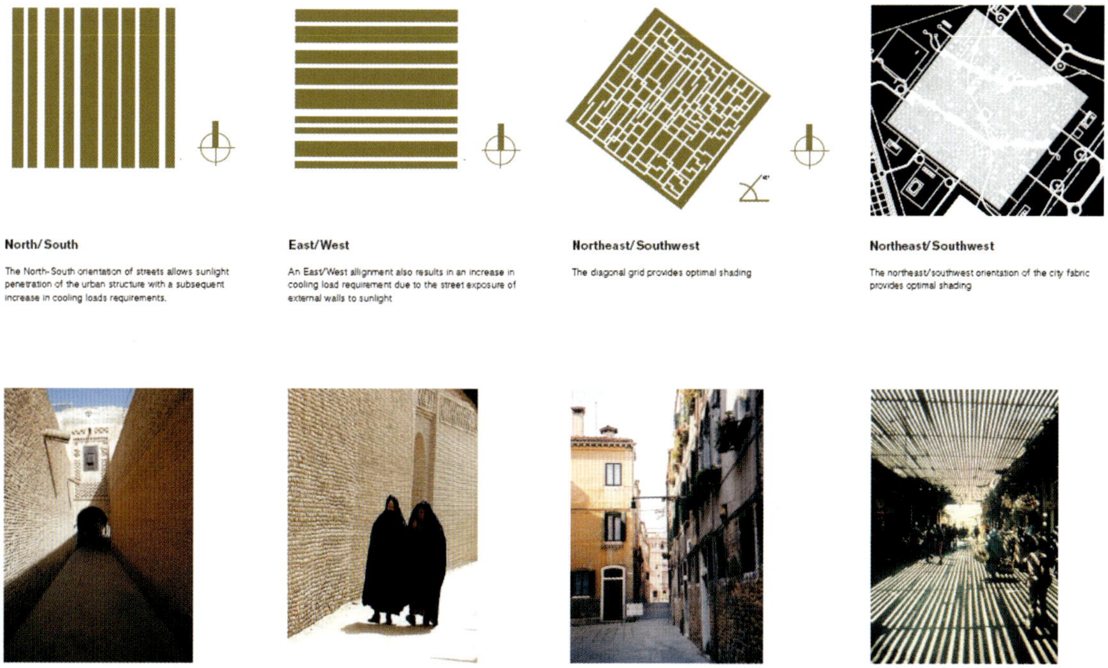

North/South
The North-South orientation of streets allows sunlight penetration of the urban structure with a subsequent increase in cooling loads requirements.

East/West
An East/West allignment also results in an increase in cooling load requirement due to the street exposure of external walls to sunlight

Northeast/Southwest
The diagonal grid provides optimal shading

Northeast/Southwest
The northeast/southwest orientation of the city fabric provides optimal shading

Figure 21 Grid Orientation & Built Form, Masdar

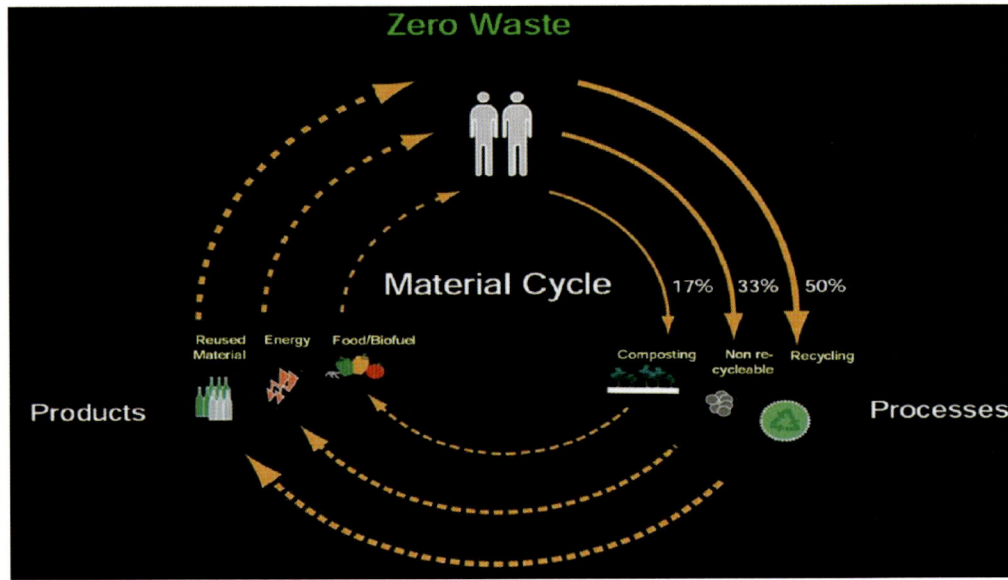

Figure 22: Zero Waste and Material Reuse Strategy

The combined passive solar strategies with the improvement in building energy efficiencies (i.e. high efficiency building envelopes, ventilation and air conditioning systems, improved shading devices, etc.) is estimated to help to reduce CO2 emissions by up to 56% (Masdar, 2010).

Masdar plans that all of the energy to be used within Masdar City will be generated through renewable sources including:

- 8 % waste to energy
- 16% evacuated tube collectors
- 36% concentrated solar power (CSP)
- 42% photovoltaic

The utilization of renewable energy is estimated to reduce carbon emissions by approximately 24% compared to "business as usual". The development of Shams 1, a 100MW concentrated solar plant (CSP) in the Western Region of Abu Dhabi will contribute significantly to the renewable energy supporting the operations of the development. Apart from the CSP plant, the alternative energy generation, waste management, wind farms, bio-remediation fields, and grey water recycling are almost entirely integrated within the site.

The Masdar project has also targeted the development to be zero waste. In the initial stages it has already implemented this strategy by diverting construction waste generated on site as well as using residual concrete and wood waste from surrounding construction sites to be incorporated into the initial phase of development. Scrap wood waste is converted into wood chips to place over landscaped areas and footpaths. This material helps to reduce evaporation of irrigation water in landscaped areas as well as replacing asphalt or concrete for footpaths which helps reduce embodied carbon and heat island effect. Masdar has targeted 50% of the materials that are used on site to be either reused or recycled with 33% of non-recycled waste being converted to energy. Plans include systems for 17% of all organic materials to be composted or converted into bio-fuels (Masdar, 2010, Figure 22).

Education and awareness will be a critical component to shifting behavior to meet its sustainability targets. To help assess the success of the Masdar sustainability initiative, an intelligent metering and building control system has been planned to monitor water, energy and waste. These systems are intended to help inform and educate occupants as to how they rank against the established targets. Ongoing monitoring to assess progress will play an important role in ensuring compliance with such targets.

The Masdar plan will be integrated with regional transportation infrastructure with an emphasis on accommodating the planned metro and tram network. Further, its immediate proximity to the international airport will create an easy and efficient public transit link between Masdar and the International Airport, Capital City, Raha and the existing central business district on the north edge of Abu Dhabi Island.

Conclusion

Abu Dhabi has experienced remarkable growth and change since the discovery of oil transformed it from a small pearl fishing village into a modern metropolis. With projected growth expected to treble the city's population growth over the next quarter century, Abu Dhabi is presented with some unique challenges and opportunities. The UPC has focused its attention on the rapidly changing built environment as part of its Estidama Program and has developed plans that will help guide future growth in areas earmarked for growth based on sound sustainability principles that seek to protect the environmental assets and restore the natural systems that give Abu Dhabi its unique identity.

The most resilient cities will be those that respond to challenges through innovation. Both the Capital District and Masdar have been highlighted for their innovations in urban design, built form to sustainable technologies which are intended to improve the overall efficiency within the city. The success of the planning efforts is also dependent on establishing strategic partners that are committed to realizing its success. This includes the development and construction industry, government agencies including transportation, and environment. Utility and infrastructure providers must be willing partners to adapt to innovative approaches to more integrated infrastructure design and delivery. Ultimately, planning must capture the minds and build the capacity of the citizens that use the city. It is not enough to build sustainable buildings and communities if the broader population is not empowered to act in a more sustainable manner.

—

References

Hartley, Joanna. Abu Dhabi pledges 7% renewable energy by 2020. Arabian Business Magazine, January 19, 2009.

Abu Dhabi Urban Planning Council. Abu Dhabi Plan 2030 Urban Structure Framework Plan. September 2007.

Abu Dhabi Urban Planning Council. Abu Dhabi Urban Streetscape Design Manual. January 2010.

Department of Transport. Surface Transport Master Plan (STMP): A Vision for Connecting Abu Dhabi. June 2009.

Abu Dhabi Urban Planning Council. Estidama. January 2010

Abu Dhabi Urban Planning Council. Capital District Master Plan Summary. April 2009

Masdar Master Plan Submittal to the Abu Dhabi Urban Planning Council, UPC Urban Design Review Panel, 2008.

Masdar City Corporate Website 2010

http://www.masdarcity.ae/en/index.aspx

Todorova, Vesela. Treated Sewage will reduce Gulf Water Use. The National, July 12, 2010.

Energy Saving and Emission Reduction:

Chinese Low Carbon Strategy in 11th Five Year Plan Period

SHI Nan & YU Taofang

With the rapid urbanization of China, the strategy of Energy Saving and Emission Reduction (ESER) has been the inevitable choice as a result of its high economic growth during the last 30 years. China is highly deficient in energy and resources. Residual reserves of petroleum and natural gas per capita are only 7.7% and 7.1% respectively of the average world level, while its rich reserves of coal are no more than 58.6% of the world average level.

In the early 1980s, the Chinese Central Government developed the policy of energy development where 'emphasis is attached to both development and saving, and saving has the highest priority in the short-term', and in the middle of that decade it put forward an energy development and utilization strategy emphasizing efficiency and an energy consumption adjustment strategy focusing on electricity. In the 1990s, the Government's policy was

1. 11th Five-Year ESER Objective and Latest Development

1.1. ESER Objective

The 11th Five Year Plan[1] puts forward well-defined rules relating to ESER: i.e. maintain rapid and stable economic development; accelerate the transformation of economic growth, that is, saving energy; develop a circular economy (with greater re-use of resources); protect the ecological environment; and, insist on development in an economic, clean and safe manner. For this purpose, the following detailed goals of ESER apply for social and economic development:

- China should limit its total population to 1.36 billion;
- The energy intensity should be reduced by 20%;
- Water use per 'industrial added value' should be reduced by 30%;
- The 'efficient use coefficient' of agricultural irrigation should be improved by 0.5;
- On waste recycling, the 'comprehensive utilization ratio' of industrial solid waste should be improved by 60%;
- The quantity of arable land should be maintained at more than 120 million hectares;
- Total emissions of sulphur dioxide, and chemical oxygen demand (COD, a measure of water pollution) should each be reduced by 10%;
- The ratio of forest coverage should be 20%.

to pursue energy development and saving in tandem, with priority being given to the latter. Entering the 21st century, China has seen continuous rapid urbanization and industrialization, and with global climatic change and the financial and economic crisis of recent years, ESER not only means shouldering international responsibility, but also the responsibilities of national energy security and the health of the Chinese people.

1.2. Progress
1.2.1. Approaching the Set Goals

The major ESER goals set by the 11th Five Year Plan will be hopefully achieved in accordance with the trends observed in the past few years (Table 1). But it can also be seen that, in the provinces, municipalities and autonomous regions in ESER, the energy intensity and the concentrations of the main pollutants vary largely in different regions (Figures 1 and 2).

Index	Situation in 2005	2010 target	Growth target	Actual data in the end of 2009
Water use per industrial added value	166	116.2	- 30%	116.40
Effective utilization coefficient of water use for agricultural irrigation	0.45	0.5	0.05	
Comprehensive utilization ratio of industrial solid waste (%)	55.8	60	4.2	64.95 (2008)
Total emission amount of main pollutants			- 10%	
National COD[2] (10,000 tons)	1414.2	1272.8	-10%	1277.5
Total emission of SO_2 (10,000 tons)	2549.4	2294.4	-10%	2214.40
Forest coverage ratio (%)	18.2	20	1.8	20.36 (in 2008)

Table 1: Realization of 11th Five Year Plan goals with reference to the population, resources and environment since 2005 *(Source: 11th Five Year Plan of the People's Republic of China for the National Economy and Social Development; Statistical Report of the National Economy and Social Development in 2009; China Statistical Yearbook 2009)*

1.2.2. Strategic Regions for ESER

From the energy intensity in different regions of China, it can be seen that in 2008, this was the lowest in Beijing, Guangdong, Shanghai, Zhejiang, Jiangsu and Tianjin, which are actually the main components of or are influenced by the city zones of the Pearl River Delta, the Beijing-Tianjin-Hebei region and the Yangtze River Delta. This conclusion has been basically proven after analysis of the correlation between energy consumption (Figure 3) and the emission of the main pollutants (Figure 4) with their economic development levels. Starting from this point and promoting ESER, the major urban agglomerations in East China are to remain the foci of economic activities, urbanization and industrialization.

Figure 1: Energy intensity of provinces, municipalities and autonomous regions in 2008 (excluding the data for Hong Kong, Macau, Taiwan, and Tibet) *(Source: China Statistical Yearbook 2009)*

Figure 2: Emission of COD & SO_2 per GDP in 2008 (Ton per Million Yuan) *(Source: China Statistical Yearbook 2009)*

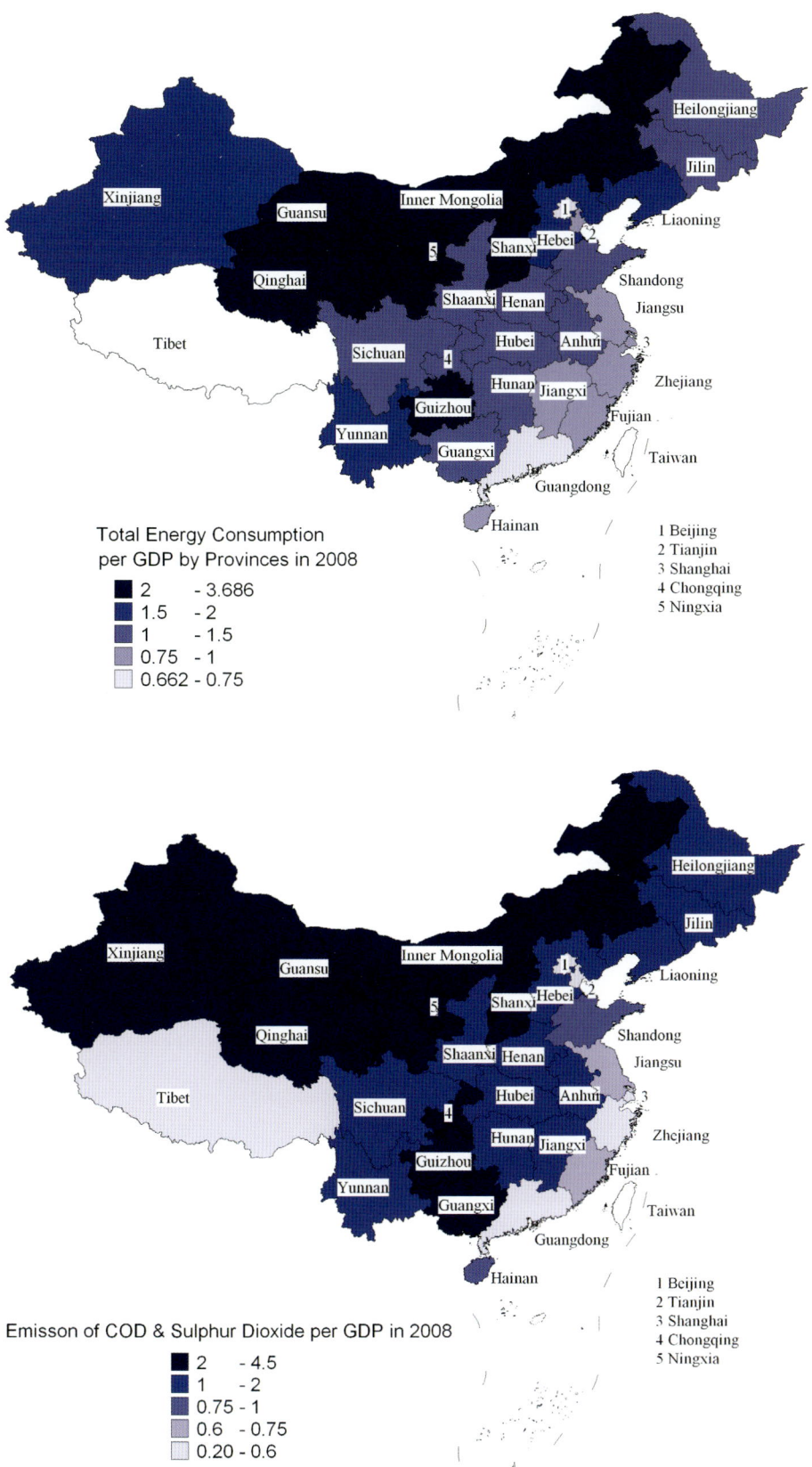

Region		2005			2008		
		Energy consumption			Energy consumption		
		Per GDP (ton coal equivalent/ 10,000 Yuan)	Per industrial added value (ton coal equivalent/10,000 Yuan)	Emission of main pollutants (10,000 tons)	Per GDP (ton coal equivalent/10,000 Yuan)	Per industrial added value in 2008 (ton coal equivalent/10,000 Yuan)	Emission of main pollutants (10,000 Yuan)
Economic zone	East China	1.05	1.84	1567.63	0.93	1.44	1385.81
	Central China	1.61	4.09	1123.37	1.42	3.05	1047.83
	West China	1.88	3.62	908.38	1.69	2.83	863.38
	Northeast China	1.67	2.86	364.19	1.48	2.18	344.91
Main urban agglomerations	Beijing - Tianjin - Hebei	1.42	3.13	287.48	1.24	2.37	254.76
	Yangtze River Delta	0.90	1.51	461.12	0.80	1.18	397.37
	Pearl River Delta	0.79	1.08	235.21	0.72	0.87	209.96

Table 2: ESER in typical regions and main urban agglomerations 2005-2008
(Source: Source: National Bureau of Statistics of China)
http://www.stats.gov.cn/tjgb/qttjgb/qgqttjgb/t20090630_402568721.htm
http://www.stats.gov.cn/tjgb/qttjgb/qgqttjgb/t20060801_402341575.htm)

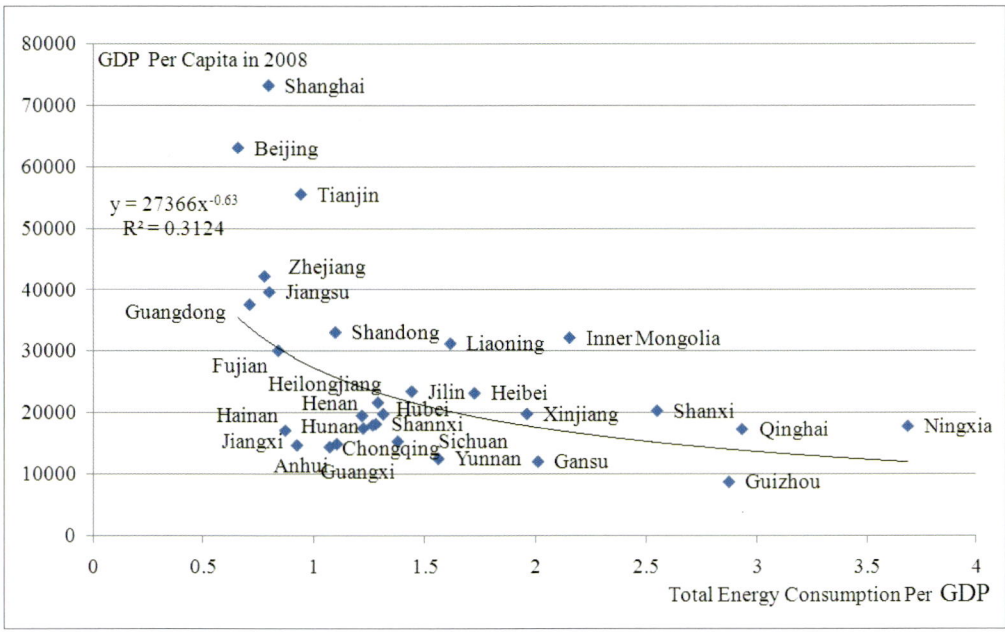

Figure 3: Regression analysis on energy intensity by provinces and economic development level in 2008 (excluding the data for Hong Kong, Macau, Taiwan, and Tibet). Units are: vertical axis- RMB Yuan per capita; horizontal axis- ton coal equivalent per 10,000 Yuan *(Source: China Statistical Yearbook 2009)*

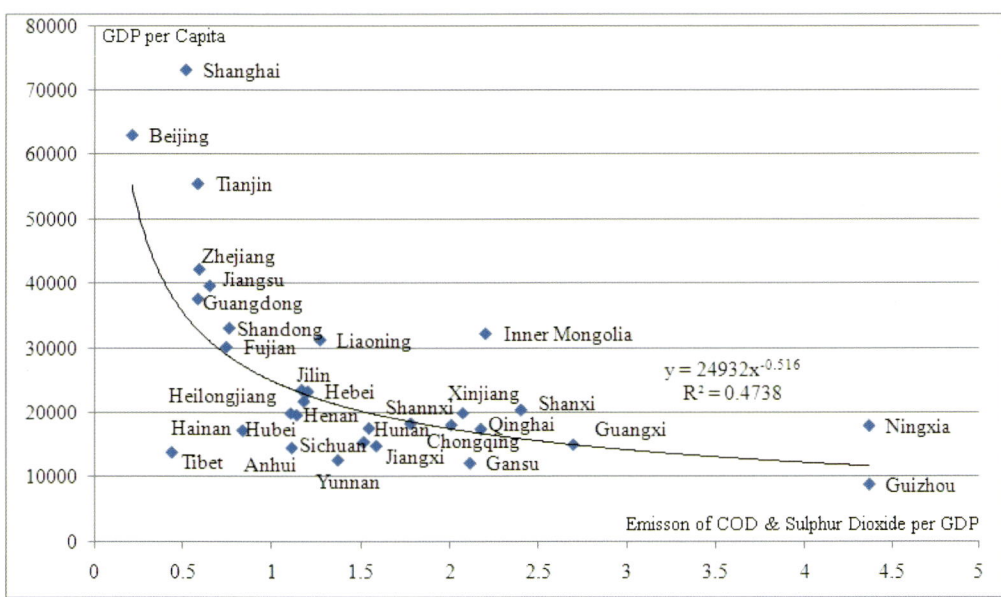

Figure 4: Regression analysis on emission of main pollutants per GDP by provinces and economic development level in 2008 (excluding the data for Hong Kong, Macau, Taiwan, and Tibet) Units are: vertical axis – RMB Yuan per capita; horizontal axis- ton coal equivalent per 10,000 Yuan *(Source: China Statistical Yearbook 2009)*

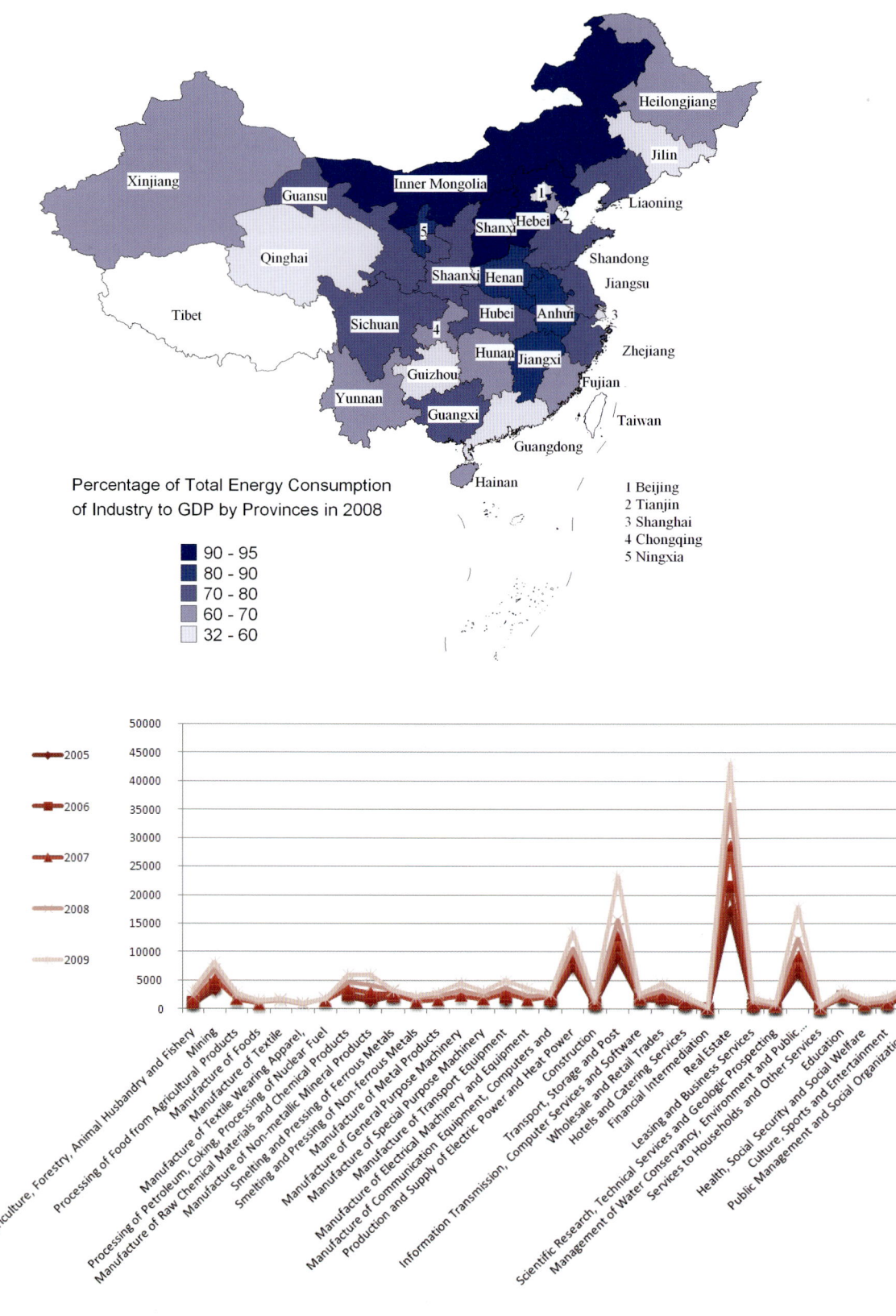

1.2.3. Major Challenges

The difficulty of reducing industrial energy consumption has been regarded as an obstacle to realizing the goal of ESER. It can be seen that consumption by this sector accounts for a considerable proportion of GDP energy consumption in China, and even for more than 90% in Inner Mongolia, Shanxi Province and Hebei Province (Figure 5). In addition, heavy industry, traffic and transportation, real estate industry and power account for a considerable proportion of industrial investment (Figure 6), while all these industries are characterized by high energy consumption, pollution and emissions. These developments have brought pressure for environmental and ecological protection.

Since the third quarter of 2009, reflecting a brisk demand for products with high energy consumption, energy consumption levels and emissions related to those industrial sectors have grown rapidly, slowing down the previous trend towards a lower energy intensity . Indeed, in the first quarter of 2010, a large upsurge was seen in the power, iron & steel, nonferrous metal, building materials, petrochemical, and chemical sectors.

According to the National Development and Reform Commission (NDRC), the energy consumption level per GDP in 12 regions of China (which include Shanghai Municipality) has moved from decreasing to increasing. Indeed, in the six sectors comprising power, iron & steel, nonferrous metal, building materials, petrochemical, and chemical industries, that figure is currently 17.3% greater than in the same period last year. Moreover, the accounting work of NDRC shows that, overall in China, energy intensity increased by 3.2% by comparison with last year. This reverse will make the achievement of China's energy goals more difficult. Indeed, the ESER is very challenging, particularly in terms of energy saving, because there is a relatively large gap between the completion of the goal and the goal of about 20% in the 11th Five Year Plan.

There is also a regional imbalance for ESER (Figures 7 and 8). Though the total emissions of the main pollutants since 2005 (per unit of GDP) have been significantly reduced, there are many provinces and cities where there has been an increase. For example, during the period 2005 -2008, they increased by 4.7% in Hainan, by 10.5% in Tibet, by 12.89% in Qinghai, and by 18.68% in Xinjiang, these being regions with sensitive ecological conditions and a low environmental capacity. At the same time, energy consumption in such places continued to increase rapidly, driven primarily by the exploitation of their mineral and other resources. In Inner Mongolia, Ningxia, Qinghai and Shaanxi, total energy consumption during the period 2005-2008 increased by more than 60%.

The environmental quality of water has been considered as another challenge to realizing the ESER goals. According to the China Environmental Bulletin 2009, surface water pollution is still serious in China (Figure 9). The seven water systems in Zhejiang, Fujian,and the northwestern region are relatively clean , and the rivers in the southwestern region have good water quality, but the quality of the remaining rivers is usually below Grade III and down to Grade V in places.[3]. There is also a serious problem of eutrophication in

Figure 5: Percentage of energy intensity by provinces in 2008 (excluding the data for Hong Kong, Macau, Taiwan, and Tibet)
(Source: China Statistical Yearbook 2009)

Figure 6: Change of investment in various industries since 2005 (units are 100 million yuan)
(Source: China Statistical Yearbook 2009)

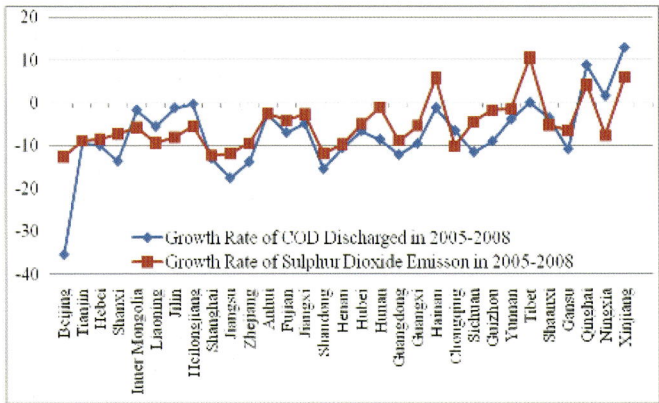

Figure 7: Change of emission of main pollutants by provinces in 2005-2008 *(Source: China Statistical Yearbook 2009)*

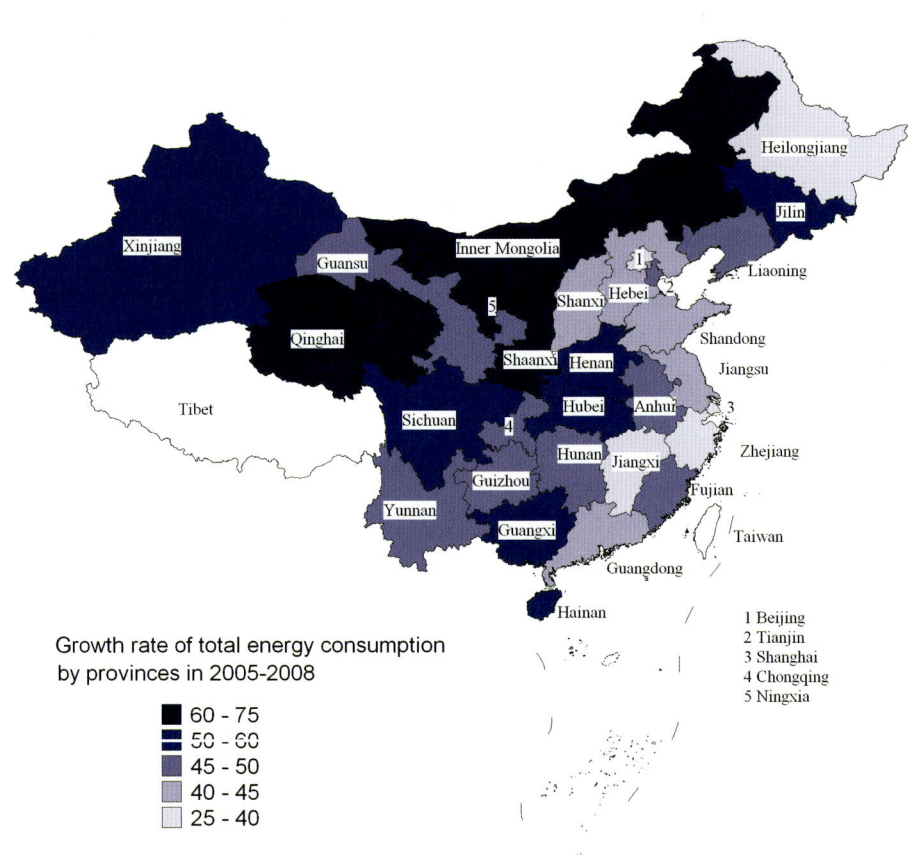

Figure 8: Growth rate of total energy consumption by provinces in 2005-2008 (excluding the data for Hong Kong, Macau, Taiwan, and Tibet)
(Source: National Bureau of Statistics of China)
http://www.stats.gov.cn/tjgb/qttjgb/qgqttjgb/t20090630_402568721.htm
http://www.stats.gov.cn/tjgb/qttjgb/qgqttjgb/t20060801_402341575.htm

certain lakes and reservoirs.

The water in the offshore areas generally is lightly polluted (Figure 10). In 2009, the monitored offshore area was 279,940 km2, in which the Grade I and II seawater area is 213,208 km2, the Grade III area is 18,834 km2, and the Grade IV and the worse than Grade IV area is 47,898 km2. According to the water monitoring, Grade I and II seawater accounts for 72.9%, 2.5% above that in 2008, Grade II seawater accounts for 6.0%, 5.3% lower than that in 2008 and Grade IV and the worse than Grade IV seawater accounts for 21.1%, 2.8% above that in 2008.

However, some offshore areas, those associated with certain urban agglomerations have extremely poor water quality. Thus the Yangtze and Pearl River estuaries have worse than Grade IV seawater over more than 40% of their defined areas, while, in the case of Hangzhou Gulf, the entire seawater area is of worse than Grade IV quality. Seawater quality is also poor adjacent to several other urban agglomerations, the affected areas being Bohai Gulf, Liaodong Gulf and Jiaozhou Gulf in the pan-Bohai Sea area, and the estuary of the Minjiang River adjacent to the Haixi urban agglomeration.

It is also argued that the structural problem of energy consumption has not been adequately addressed. In April, 2007, the NDRC issued the 11th Five Year Plan for Energy Development, which stated that to 2010, the control target for total consumption of primary energies in China was about 2.7 billion ton coal equivalent, with an annual increase rate of 4%. Coal, petroleum, natural gas, nuclear power, hydropower and other renewable energies account for 66.1%, 20.5%, 5.3%, 0.9%, 6.8% and 0.4% respectively of total consumption of primary energies. While natural gas, nuclear power, hydropower and other renewable energies have increased their percentage share of this mix, in 2008, total consumption of primary energy in China was 2.85 billion ton coal equivalent, far more than the 2.7 billion ton coal equivalent control goal, and the absolute consumption of coal increased by 405 million tons.

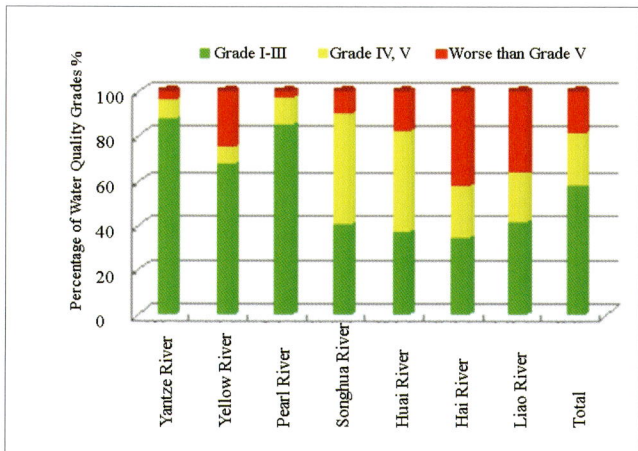

Figure 9: Water quality of major rivers in 2009
(Source: China Environmental Bulletin 2009)

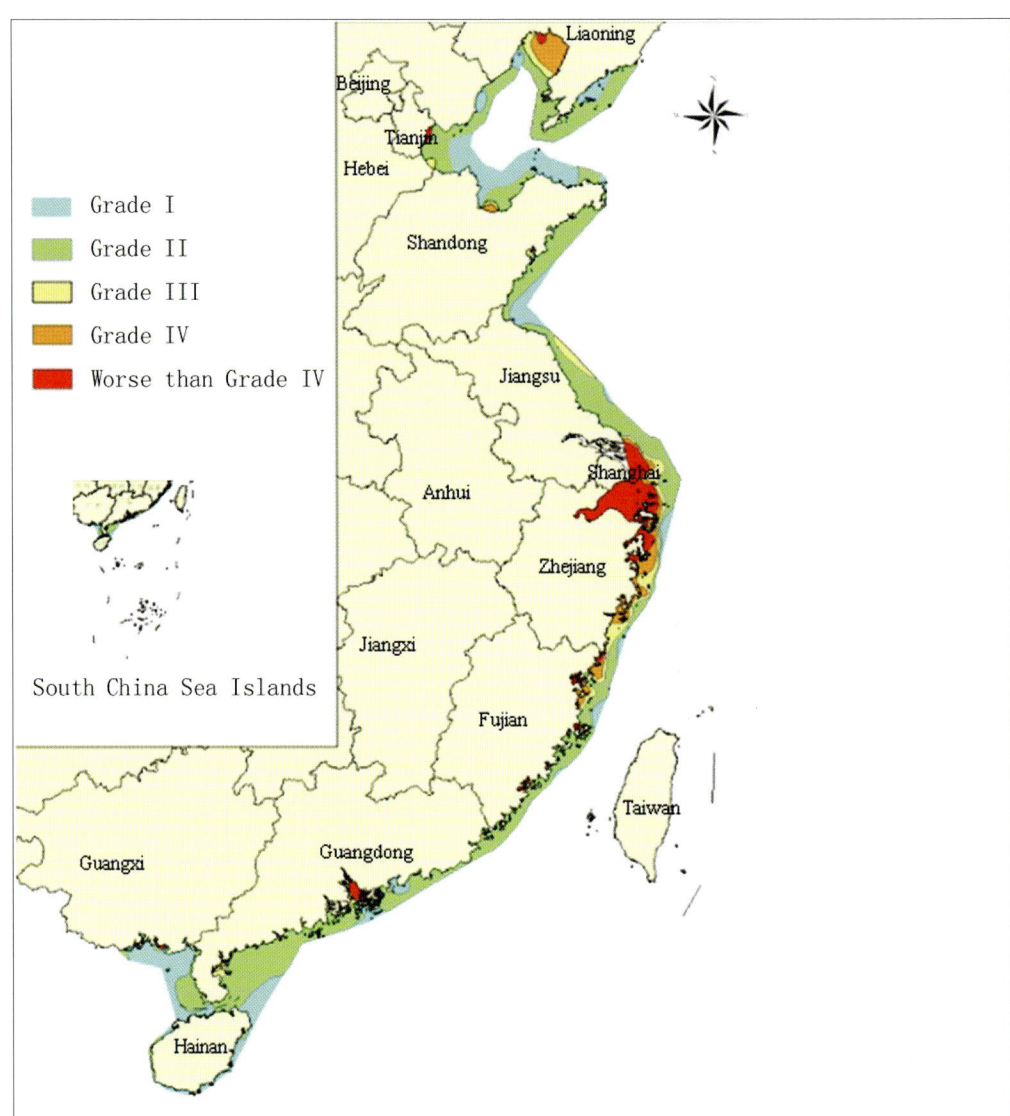

Figure 10: Water quality distribution of offshore areas in 2009
(Source: China Environmental Bulletin 2009)

2. Main Approaches of ESER

Since 2005, the strategic design and action plan for ESER in China has been made from a standpoint which is mainly related to industry, traffic and the building industry.

2.1. Transformation of Economic Development Mode

The Chinese Government encourages the development of a circular economy, which means saving energy, water, land resources and raw material etc, thereby creating an energy-saving and environmentally-friendly society. To that end, in January 2007, the NDRC issued Guidelines on the Comprehensive Utilization of Energies during the 11th Five Year Plan Period, which required that by 2010, the total 'exploitation ratio' of mineral resources and that of associated minerals should be increased by 5% compared with that in 2005, reaching 35% and 40% respectively. The 'comprehensive utilization ratio' of industrial solid waste should reach an overall 60%, with the percentages for the re-use of fly ash and coal mining residues reaching 70% and 75% respectively. The 'recycling and utilization ratio' of the main renewable resources was increased to 65%, and the percentage of secondary copper, aluminum and lead now accounts for 35%, 25% and 30% of production.

Low carbon industry and a green economy are becoming popular bases for planning strategies at city and town level. Allied to this, in 2010, more effort will be made to eliminate 'lagging production'[4], which involves shutting down 10 million KVA small fossil-fired generator units, 25 million tons of iron production, 6 million tons of steel production, 50 million tons of cement, 330 thousand tons of electrolytic aluminum, 530 thousand tons of papermaking capacity, and much glass production.

Many cities in China are trying to upgrade their industrial structure by accelerating the development of service industries and promoting hi-tech industries through independent innovation. In February, 2006, the State Council issued *Several Supporting Policies in the Outline of the Medium and Long-term Plan on Science and Technology Development in China (2006-2020)*. To implement this important document, the relevant departments of the State Council made and gradually released more than 70 implementation rules. The aim of the new policies is to stimulate independent innovation. Since 2005, investment in R&D has been significantly increased in the provinces, autonomous regions and municipalities (Figure 11).

In the superlarge cities[5] and city regions such as Beijing, Shanghai and Guangzhou, the action plans for independent innovation provide the framework for a new emphasis on implementation.. In March, 2009, the State Council approved Zhongguancun National Independent Innovation Demonstration Zone, to promote Zhongguancun[6] as the source of strategic emerging industry, so as to constantly form an emerging industry cluster with low energy consumption, high added value and high motivation, the objective being to drive the science and technology development as well as the transformation of the urban and economic growth pattern in Beijing and even the whole of China.

Transformation has also been seen in the foreign trade related areas. The Government attaches priority to guiding foreign capital to the hi-tech, high-end manufacturing and service industry sectors, to infrastructure development and ecological/ environmental protection, and to the old industrial bases in

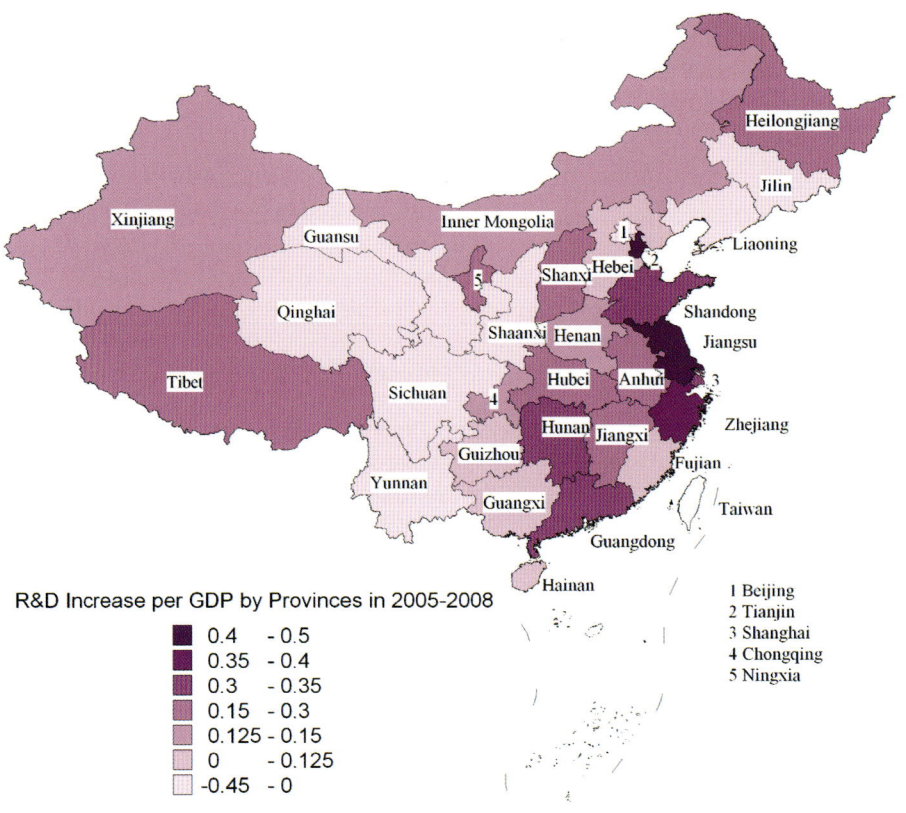

Figure 11: Change of investment in R&D by provinces in 2005-2008 (units are 100 million yuan)
(Source: National statistical bulletin of science and technology expense in 2006 and 2009)

the central, western and northeastern regions. The aim is to encourage transnational companies to set up headquarters, as well as R&D, purchasing and training centers in China. It is also to encourage foreign enterprises to carry out technological innovation, increase supporting capacity and create industrial linkages. The regions and development zones with the capacity to attract foreign capital are to concentrate on raising their manufacturing levels, expanding their R&D and modern logistics capacities and bringing their motivation and enterprise into full play.

2.2. Energy-saving Traffic

Traffic and transportation are large energy consumers, and also a significant field for ESER in China. In 2006, energy consumption in both road and domestic water transportation together in China accounted for 7.6% of total energy consumed. That consumption had grown by 10.8% and 12.2% respectively compared with that in 2000. With a view to the future, central government and the local authorities have established energy consumption and emission standards for vehicles, as well as systems for the certification and monitoring of performance. They are also setting policies to encourage the development of low-carbon traffic, with large subsidies to encourage electric vehicles. In March, 2010, the Ministry of Transport of the People's Republic of China issued Important Work for ESER in the Traffic and Transportation Industry in 2010. It is now required that general arrangements for ESER are made in the traffic and transportation industry during

FDI	2005	2009	Growth %
Agriculture, forestry, husbandry, fishery	7.2	14.3	98.6
Mining	3.5	5	42.9
Manufacturing	424.5	467.7	10.2
Production and supply of power, natural gas and water	13.9	21.1	51.8
Building industry	4.9	6.9	40.8
Traffic, transportation, warehousing and postal service	18.1	25.3	39.8
Information transmission, computer service and software industry	10.1	22.5	122.8
Wholesale and retail industry	10.4	53.9	418.3
Lodging and catering	5.6	8.4	50.0
Finance	2.2	4.6	109.1
Real estate industry	54.2	168	210.0
Leasing and business service	37.5	60.8	62.1
Scientific research, technical service and geological surveying	3.4	16.7	391.2
Water conservancy, environment and public facility management	1.4	5.6	300.0
Resident service and other services industries	2.6	15.9	511.5
Education	0.2	0.1	-50.0
Health, social security and social welfare	0.4	0.4	0.0
Culture, sport and entertainment	3.1	3.2	3.2
Service industry	149.2	385.4	158.3
Total	603.2	900.3	49.3

Table 3: Distribution of actual utilization of foreign capital in 2005-2009 (units for 2005 and 2009 are $100 million)
(Source: China Statistical Yearbook 2006 and 2009)

2010 and that plans are developed for the 12th Five-Year Plan period.

City traffic in China has the largest potential and opportunity for ESER, and presents its greatest challenge. . At present, public traffic is heavily promoted in many cities, e.g. bus rapid transit (BRT) or rail transit system. BRT has been operational in Beijing, Guangzhou, Hangzhou, Kunming, Changzhou, Jinan, Xiamen and Zhengzhou, and in superlarge cities such as Beijing and Shanghai; the construction of rail transit is now proceeding at a very intensive rate.

The document Key Points of ESER in the Traffic Industry 2010 issued by the Minister of Transport stressed the importance of further developing public transport; it also promoted A National Regulation Regarding Urban Public Traffic. Important measures to realize ESER in urban traffic have been adopted which include increasing the share of public transport, reducing the use of private cars, encouraging the use of energy-saving and environmentally-friendly public vehicles etc.

Local policies and measures to encourage bicycle traffic have been adopted by municipalities and cities in their transportation plans. Cities like Hangzhou, the Capital of Zhejiang Province, also introduced a 'public bike service', which provides free or rental service to both local residents and tourists.

In January, 2010, the Minister of Transport said that, in 2010 and during the 12th Five-Year Plan period, further measures will be implemented in both structural and technological ESER, to form a permanent mechanism for ESER with regard to traffic and transportation.

Energy-saving Buildings

The Guideline on the Development of Energy Saving and Land Saving for Housing and Public Buildings issued by the Ministry of Construction in May, 2005 requested that by 2020, the consumption of energy and resources used for the construction of housing and public buildings in China should reach the level of the moderately developed countries. The actual goals are that by 2010: new buildings in towns should realize energy saving of 50%; the renovation of existing buildings should be gradually carried out, with the big cities improving 20% of the area designated for renovation, the medium-sized 15% and the small 10%; a maximum of 15% of the land needed for new buildings should be arable farming land; water should be saved during the construction and use of the buildings, the saving to be at least 20% compared to the current basis, and; new buildings should reduce the total energy consumption of nonrenewable energies by 10% compared with the current level.

In certain areas, more stringent goals are being set[1]. By 2020, in Northern China and the developed zones in the coastal area and in the superlarge cities: new buildings should realize the goal of energy saving of 65%; the renovation of most of the existing buildings should have been completed; the percentage of arable land taken for new buildings in rural and urban areas should be greatly reduced in 2010; efforts should be made to increase the water saving ratio during construction and utilization by 10% in 2010 and; the total consumption of nonrenewable energies in new buildings should be reduced by 20% on the basis of the level in 2010.

In addition, several other key documents have been issued[2].

New and Renewable Energies

Since the 1950s, hydropower has flourished in China. From the 1980s, technological R&D, and the application and demonstration of wind power, solar energy and modern biomass have achieved stable development through government support (Figure 12). Chinese industry is now first in the world with respect to renewable energy technologies such as small hydropower stations, solar energy water heating, methane (biogas) in rural areas, and small wind power plants. In the new century, renewable energies have become one of the important areas for development and they will play a significant role in the alternative energy strategies of the future.

In January, 2006 the Renewable Energy Law was formally implemented. Its supporting polices are being issued; in the Outline of the Medium and Long-term Plan on Science and Technology Development in China; these recognize the key part to be played by technological innovation in respect of new and renewable energies. In 2007, the 17th CPC National Congress determined that by 2020, renewable energies should play a significantly greater role in China as a new requirement for the building of a well rounded, prosperous society. Another milestone was the issue by the State Council of National Middle and Long-term Planning Specifics for Renewable Energy, This emphasis the development of renewable energy as one of the significant national tasks of ESER and of the national action program, to address global climatic change.

In terms of immediate targets, NDRC's 11th Five Year Plan for Energy Development stated that by 2010, natural gas, nuclear power, hydropower and other renewable energies will increase by 2.5%, 0.1%, 0.6% and 0.3% respectively. It can be seen that since 2005, nuclear power, hydropower and other renewable energies increased by 1.78% (Figure 12).

The details of the Government's measures to encourage renewable energy development include:

A levy upon every kWh electricity to establish the Renewable Energy Development Foundation, which is used together with budget money from the Ministry of Finance, and support through the Golden Sun[9] and other demonstration projects as government subsidy for the utilization of biomass and geothermal energy, This support funding will amount to more than 20 billion Yuan every year.

Access to bank loans and capital market support (both at home and abroad) is encouraged.

The use of private equity funding is encouraged.

Possible access to international aid through the Clean Development Mechanism (CDM).[10]

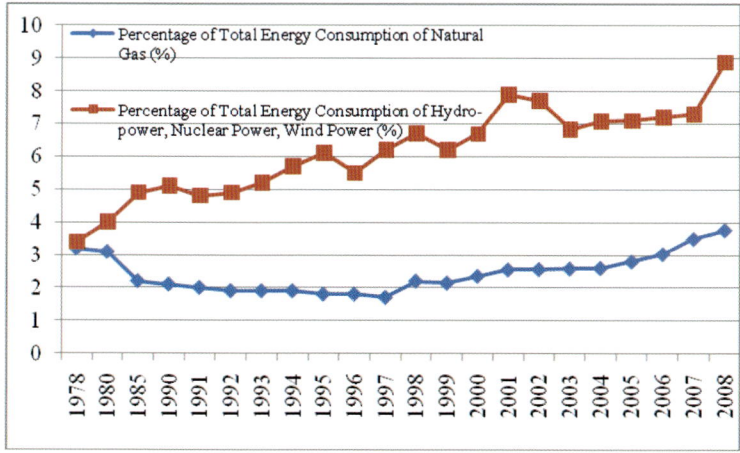

Figure 12: Growth Rate of Renewable Energy in 1978-2008
(Source: China Statistical Yearbook 2009)

2.3. The Low-carbon Eco-city

Traditionally, Chinese cities are relatively compact. The population density in the medium and large-sized cities[11] of China is regularly 10,000 persons per km2. The low-carbon eco-city model not only conforms to the current international trend and the requirements of the Kyoto Protocol, but it is also well suited to China's development needs generally (Qiu Baoxing, 2009). In fact, in recent years, low-carbon, energy saving and ecological preservation policies have been given priority at city or new district scale (Table 4,).

Table 4: Some Examples of low-carbon eco-cities in China

March, 2009	The construction of Caofedian International Eco-City was formally started
May, 2009	International competition for Master Planning of Sino-Singapore Tianjin Eco-City is finished
October, 2009	Grand Canal International Eco-City Project was launched in Xianhe, Hebei
October, 2009	Sino-Swedish Eco-City in Wuxi initiated
January, 2010	Ministry of Housing and Urban-Rural Development signed with Shenzhen City Government a framework agreement of Low-carbon Ecological Demonstration City
January, 2010	The first low-carbon tourism experiment zone was established in Miyun District, Beijing
January, 2010	Construction of modern ecological island of Chongming County, Shanghai started

Figures 13: Location and General Layout of Caofeidian Eco-City in Tangshan, Hebei Province

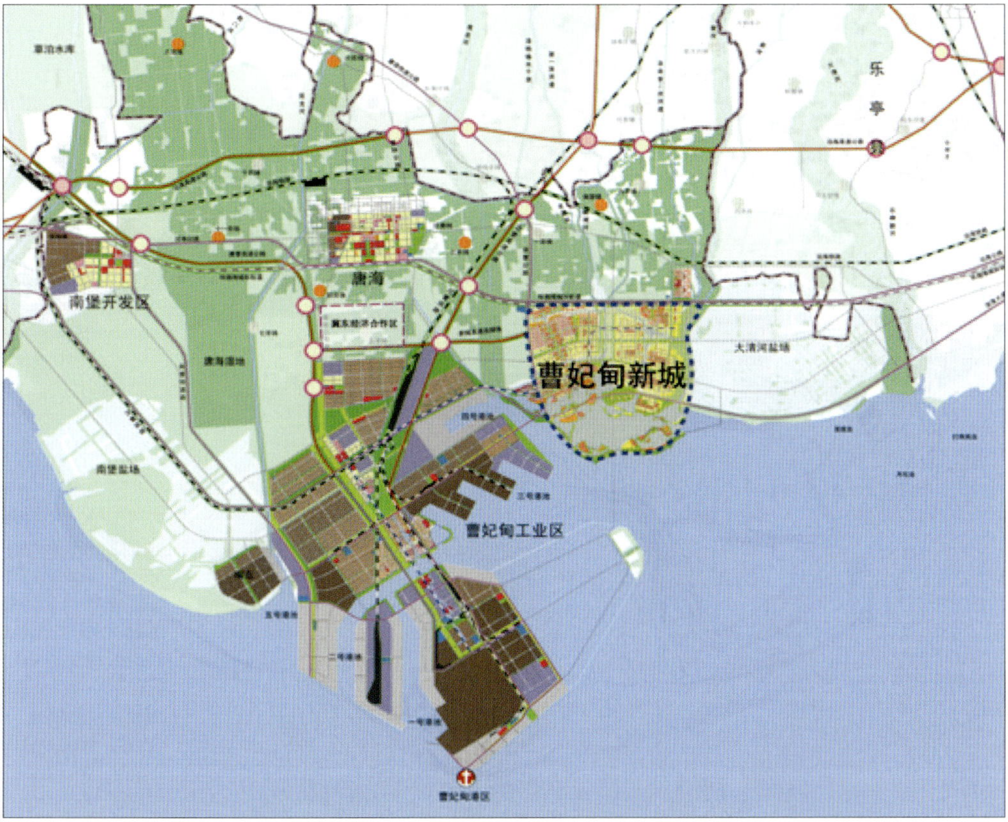
唐海
南堡开发区
曹妃甸新城
曹妃甸工业区
乐
亭

北
图 例

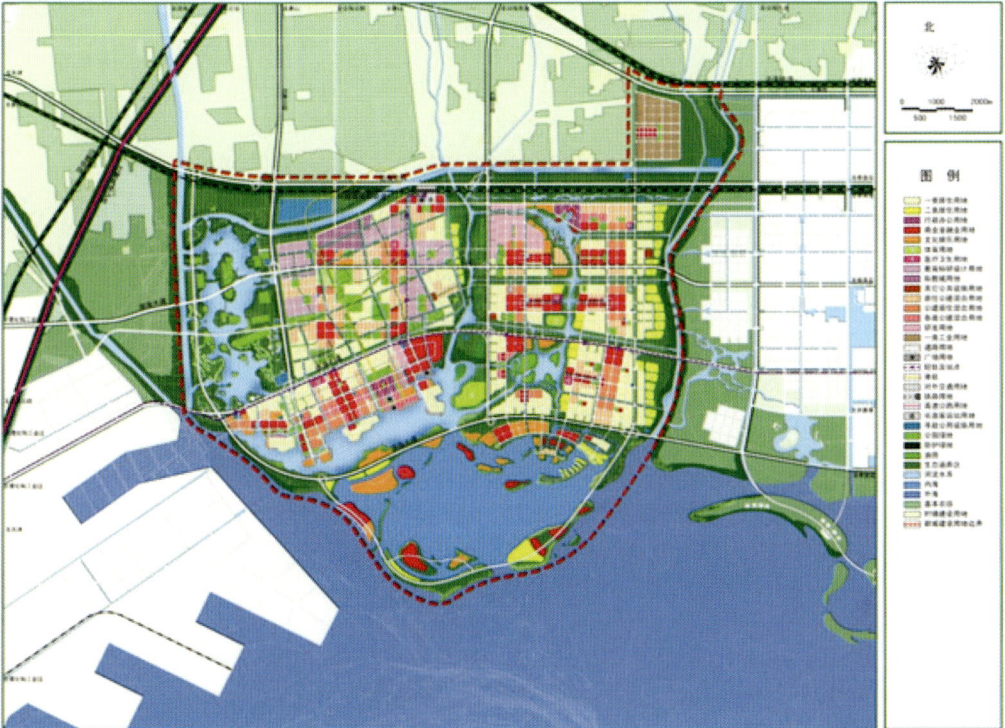

Figure 14: Land Use Planning of Sino-Singapore
Tianjin Ecological Science and Technology City

3. Institutional Innovation and Market Mechanisms

Since 2005, cities at varying scales and the related enterprises have sought to pursue institutional innovations in respect of ESER (Table 5) and to promote the use of market mechanisms.

3.1. Institutional Innovation

Legal initiatives have been very important in promoting ESER. A new version of the Energy Saving Law was issued in October, 2007, consisting of general rules, energy-saving management, energy-saving technology, incentive measures, etc. This new law clearly defines energy saving as a basic national policy in China and stipulates a series of basic systems on energy saving management, such as a responsibility system, an examination and evaluation system, etc. The State Council and the local governments above county-level are required to report to the CPC National Congress or its Standing Committee with the corresponding energy saving level achieved every year; the lower tiers of government report their performance annually to the State Council.

The inauguration of the National Energy Committee in January 2010 is a major initiative by the Central Government to address the energy challenge. The State Council determined that this new national agency should be responsible for studying and developing national energy development strategies, reviewing significant issues in energy security and energy development, planning and coordinating significant matters for national and international energy cooperation. Premier Wen Jiabao serves as the Director of the Committee and Vice Premier Li Keqiang as the Vice Director. The constitution of this high profile Committee demonstrates great awareness of the complexity of energy policies and this body will have the authority to improve national energy management.

Financial subsidy and favorable tax policy also play a critically important role in strengthening energy saving and ecological/environmental protection. These tax initiatives include tax reductions and exemptions, incentives and rewards, as well as transfer payments.

In 2008, the national government issued more than 30 favorable taxation policies to encourage ESER, and NDRC issued the *Medium and Long-term Development Plan for Renewable Energies*, which required greater commitments to the development and utilization of renewable energy, through greater financial investment and favorable tax policies.

In May, 2010, the State Bank released *A Guideline for Credit to Support ESER,* which established and promotes a Green Credit system. This imposes strict control over the credit supply to industries with 'two-highs (high pollution and high energy consumption)', increases the rapid growth of credit business for ESER and attaches great importance to the support of clean energy and energy-saving and environmentally-friendly projects.

With regard to renewable energy, the central and local finance authorities have set up a specific fund for the development of renewable energies under the *Renewable Energy Law*; support is provided through tax and other economic policies. NDRC, the State Electricity Regulatory Commission (SERC) and the China National Energy Bureau regulate electricity prices, alleviate the enterprise burden, provide financial subsidy to encourage consumers to purchase smaller more energy-efficient vehicles and promote new technologies such as solar energy.

Direct investment by government and the formulation of an industry plan have proved a successful method of promoting ESER. In 2008-2009, the Chinese Government issued two economic incentive plans, in which 23 billion Yuan were contributed to energy saving projects, emission reduction, ecological construction and environmental protection, accounting for 10% of total added investment by central government for the economic incentive plans. In addition, central government issued 10 industry adjustment and revitalization plans to encourage the iron/steel and automobile industries to adapt their structure, eliminate energy inefficient production and improve the efficient utilization of energy and resources.

The adoption of an energy manager system provides another system guarantee. The national *Energy-Saving Law*

Table 5: Significant ESER national legislation published by Central Government since 2005

February, 2005	Renewable Energy Law
May, 2005	Guideline on the Development of Energy-Saving and Land-Saving Housing and Public Buildings
July, 2005	Notice of the State Council on Accelerating the Development of the Circular Economy
July, 2005	Notice on the Building of Energy-Saving Society in the short-term
January, 2006	Regulations on the Management of Energy-Saving in Private Housing (revision)
January, 2007	Guideline on the Comprehensive Utilization of Resources in the 11th Five Year Plan
April, 2007	11th Five Year Plan for Energy Development
June, 2007	Notice of the State Council on the Comprehensive Work Proposal for ESER
October, 2007	Energy Saving Law (Revised)
December, 2007	Provisional Measures on Financial Subsidy and Funding Management for the Promotion of High-Efficiency Lighting Products
January, 2008	Medium and Long-term Development Plan for Renewable Energies
March, 2010	Notice on ESER for the Traffic Industry in 2010
April, 2010	Notice on Accelerating the Promotion of Contract-Based Energy Management and Promoting the Development of the Energy-Saving Service Industry
May, 2010	Notice of the State Council on Further Strengthening the Work Efforts to Realize the Goal of ESER in the 11th Five Year Plan Period
May, 2010	Decree on Accelerating the Contract-Based Energy Management and Promoting the Development of the Energy-Saving Service Industry
May, 2010	Guideline for Credit to Support ESER
June, 2010	Provisional Measures on Supervision and Administration of ESER for State-Owned Central Enterprises
June, 2010	Guidelines to Promote the ESER in the Tourism Industry

requires that significant energy consuming enterprises establish energy manager positions. An extensive pilot operation is currently under way. This has progressed smoothly and has been extended.

3.2. Market Mechanisms

Both central and local governments have recognized that market mechanisms play a significant role in ESER through the rational allocation of resources. The role of government is to encourage market based ESER and to provide policy direction.

Energy price reform has been characterized by adjustments to the natural gas price, promoting a cascade price system for electricity for private use, differential electricity pricing for the high energy consumption industries, imposing wastewater and garbage treatment fees and so on.

Emission trading is becoming increasingly important as a means of promoting ESER in China. Under emission trading, those enterprises with low emissions may benefit from the sales of surplus allowances, while enterprises with high emissions may purchase the allowances to reduce the emission reduction cost, comply with the requirements and minimize the total cost of social pollution. As an independent initiative, Tianjin Energy Efficiency Market is the first emission trading system in China to be based on a compulsory energy efficiency index. It was launched in Tianjin Climate Exchange and completed its first trading in December, 2008. In September, 2009, the Exchange launched a new initiative, aimed at voluntary emission reduction by businesses, winning positive responses from 36 enterprises from home and abroad. As another initiative, the China Everbright Bank has put into operation the concept of a 'carbon neutral bank' to promote carbon trading and related activities.

International exchange and cooperation are other important approaches to promoting the use of market mechanisms. China has been engaged in fruitful exchange and cooperation with many countries and international organizations in the energy and environmental fields, particularly in renewable energy, in order to promote innovation, technological improvement and the industrial development of ESER. Thus, forums and symposiums have been held, there has been training, cooperation and research on projects of mutual interest, research facilities and demonstration projects have been jointly established and there has been cooperation in terms of investment and financing (Han Qide, 2010).

4. Discussion and Conclusion

ESER not only plays a significant role in energy development and saving, but more importantly it aims to seek a new road for energy development and economic development, where. it has a significant role to play in improving national competitiveness. ESER represents no less than a revolution which requires fundamental change in the economic system, legal and finance and taxation policies, consumption modes, technical innovation, and city development strategy.

However, there is a long way to go for ESER. China is undergoing a period of swift growth in energy demand with its rapid industrialization, urbanization and modernization. In 2009, the urbanization percentage was more than 45%, and the urban population is increasing by about 15 million each year (15.19 million in 2008-2009), with a one percent annual average increase in urbanization. In the following years, China will continue its rapid development and the situation with regard to resources and the environment will become very challenging. Although the average energy consumption per capita for the Chinese people is low, the population base is large, and therefore total energy consumption will maintain its strong rising trend.

Basically speaking, therefore, the absolute scale of energy consumption and carbon emission in China will continue for a considerable time. The resource conditions of 'rich in coal, lacking in gas, deficient in petroleum' have determined that energy structure in China will continue to be be mainly based on coal... The overall level of independent innovation lags behind, and technological R&D capacity and input is limited. In 2010, the likely expenditure on research and experimental development will amount to some 1.66% of GDP, thus below 2% of the expected target for 2010. These are fundamental obstacles to ESER that will need to be addressed.

The Chinese-road to urbanization provides a potential opportunity for ESER and the starting point for solving the problems. As urbanization enters the medium and long term phases it will face increasing constraints from environmental pollution and in terms of energy supply, and there will be growing pressures to lower carbon emissions. For these reasons, the superlarge city regions and city agglomerations, particularly those in the eastern coastal regions, will not lose their position in the future, but their significance as urban centres will be gradually highlighted.

Their planning should continue to pursue compact forms of urbanization, so as to improve the quality of urbanization, and it should seek to counter the present emphasis on the extension of cities. If not controlled, such expansion would bring with it all the potential dangers of American-type suburbanization, possibly arising from the overlapping of mechanization, motorization and urbanization (Qiu Baoxing, 2009). In this regard, city planners and decision makers should study and use various advanced technologies, improvement mechanisms and systems, so as to create a low-carbon and ecologically friendly urbanization path to ESER. (Qiu Baoxing, 2010; Gu Chaolin et al., 2009).

Therefore, China's urbanization will provide a major opportunity to promote ESER. The city is the key to emission reduction, and the research suggests that an 80% emission reduction should be achievable over time (WWF, 2010). Thus the potential is there, and planners and other decision makers now face the challenge of delivering ESER and the low carbon cities upon which our long term future depends[12].

Endnotes

1. The Chinese Central Government has established a five-year plan for the national economy and social development, mainly to guide stable development of the economy and social affairs. Compared with previous five-year plans, the 11th Five Year Plan (2006-2010) not only places special emphasis on the development of different regions and areas but, importantly, defines indicators that relate to the implementation of ESER policies. The targets cited relate to the five year period 2006-2010.

2. Editor's Note - Chemical Oxygen Demand (COD) is an indirect measure of the amount of organic pollutants in water, and thus a measure of water quality.

3. The surface water quality is classified into 5 grades in China, Grade I is the best quality, which can be used for drinking after simple sterilization, while the Grade V water is not suitable for drinking, and can only be used on the land etc.

Bibliography

Dai Xingyi, Research on the Policy System for the Low-Carbon and Ecological City. China Low-Carbon and Ecological City Development Report. Beijing: China Architecture & Building Press, 2010.

Gu Chaolin, Tan Zongbo et al., Climatic Change and Low-Carbon City Planning. Nanjing: Southeast University Press, 2009.

Han Qide, How to Develop Low-carbon Technology, and Promote Green Building Development: The Low Carbon and Ecological City. 2010 (3): 35-36.

Qiu Baoxing, A Discussion on Urbanization from the Chinese Standpoint. City Development Research. First Issue, 2009.

Qiu Baoxing, Challenges and Opportunities- New Dynamics in City Planning during Middle and Later Periods in China. The Low-Carbon Ecological City. 2010 (3): 2-10.

Shi Dingyuan, 2010. The Present Situation and Prospect for Renewable Energy in China. Sino-Europe Round Table Meeting on Accelerating the Building of the Green Economy.

Yu Cong, 2009. How? to? Enhance ESER and Cope with the Economic Crisis.

WWF. Reinventing the City: Three Prerequisites for Greening the Urban Infrastructure. http://assets.panda.org/downloads/wwf_reinventing_the_city_final_3_low_resolution.pdf. 2010

---

4. A government phrase that refers to inefficient, wasteful production.

5. Superlarge city refers city with over 1 million inhabitants by household registration.

6. Part of the Haidian District in Beijing Municipality, where universities, research institutions and hi-tech industry companies are concentrated.

7. These reflect the fact that the cities in the north of China consume more energy than elsewhere because of their winter heating needs, while the cities in the developed coastal regions have readier access to new technology and financial resources.

8. Notice to Further Promote the Renovation of Walling Materials and the Energy Saving Building, Notice to Further Strengthen the Implementation and Monitoring of Energy Saving Standards for Buildings, Notice about a Special Check on Energy Saving Buildings, Notice about Organizing the Survey Related to Energy Saving in Buildings. Decree on the Administration of Civic Building Energy Saving (Ministry of Construction, 2006).

9. A government initiated pioneer project for photovoltaic (PV) power development. The power company with PV technology is entitled to receive subsidies from government up to 50% of its total construction costs, and even up to 70% in remote areas.

10. According to the statistics of the PEW Research Center, global investment in clean energies in 2009 was 162.0 billion USD; China has 34.6 billion USD of this, accounting for 21.3%, and takes the number one position in clean energy investment worldwide for the first time. (Shi Dinghuan, 2010).

11. Medium sized city refers to a city with a population of 200,000 to 500,000, and large-sized with over 500,000.

12. The authors wish to express their sincere gratitude to the editor and proof reader for their diligent work in making the text more readily understandable to international readers

Low Carbon Kunshan: Towards a Sustainable Future

Zhang Quan

1. The Epitome of the "China Miracle"

1.1. Profile of Kunshan

Kunshan is located in the central area of the Yangtze River Delta, adjacent to China's economic center Shanghai. Its administrative area measures 928 km2, of which 19% are rivers and lakes including Yangcheng Lake in the northwest, Dianshanhu Lake in the south and Chenghu Lake in the southwest. With a time-honored history and a rich cultural legacy, Kunshan is the cradle of Kunqu Opera which has been listed by UNESCO as a Masterpiece of the Oral and Intangible Heritage of Humanity. In addition, there are a group of well-known towns such as Zhouzhuang, Jinxi and Qiandeng, which are examples of ancient Chinese watertowns. Zhouzhuang has been crowned as China's foremost watertown and is one of the most beautiful such towns in the world.

By the end of 2008, the Kunshan area had a resident population of 1.64 million, a total GDP of RMB 150 billion and a per capita GDP of RMB 91,223.

Kunshan is ahead of all comparable cities in China in terms of the extent to which it has pursued reform and opened itself up. It is a wonderful example of the Chinese miracle.

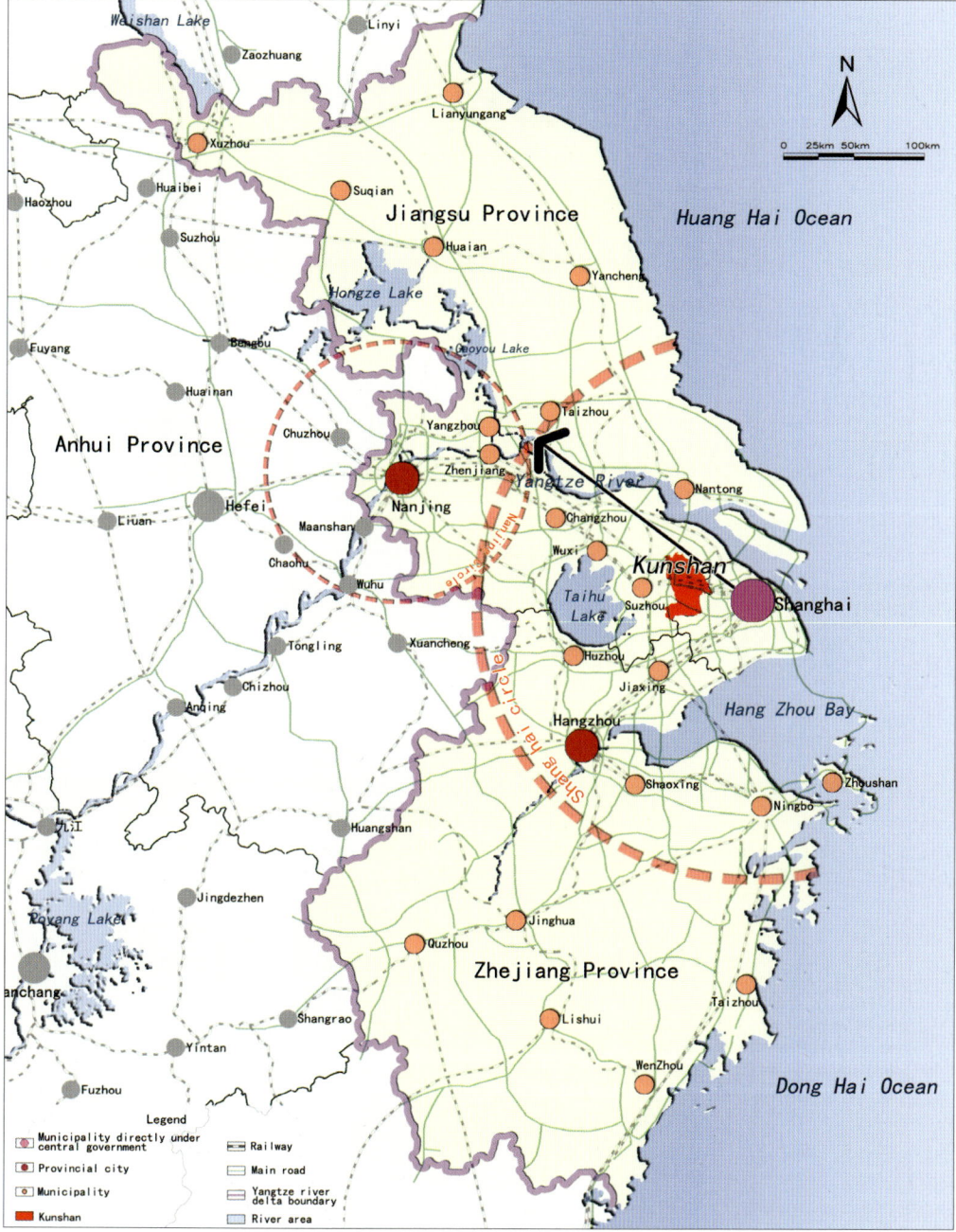

Figure 1: Location of Kunshan

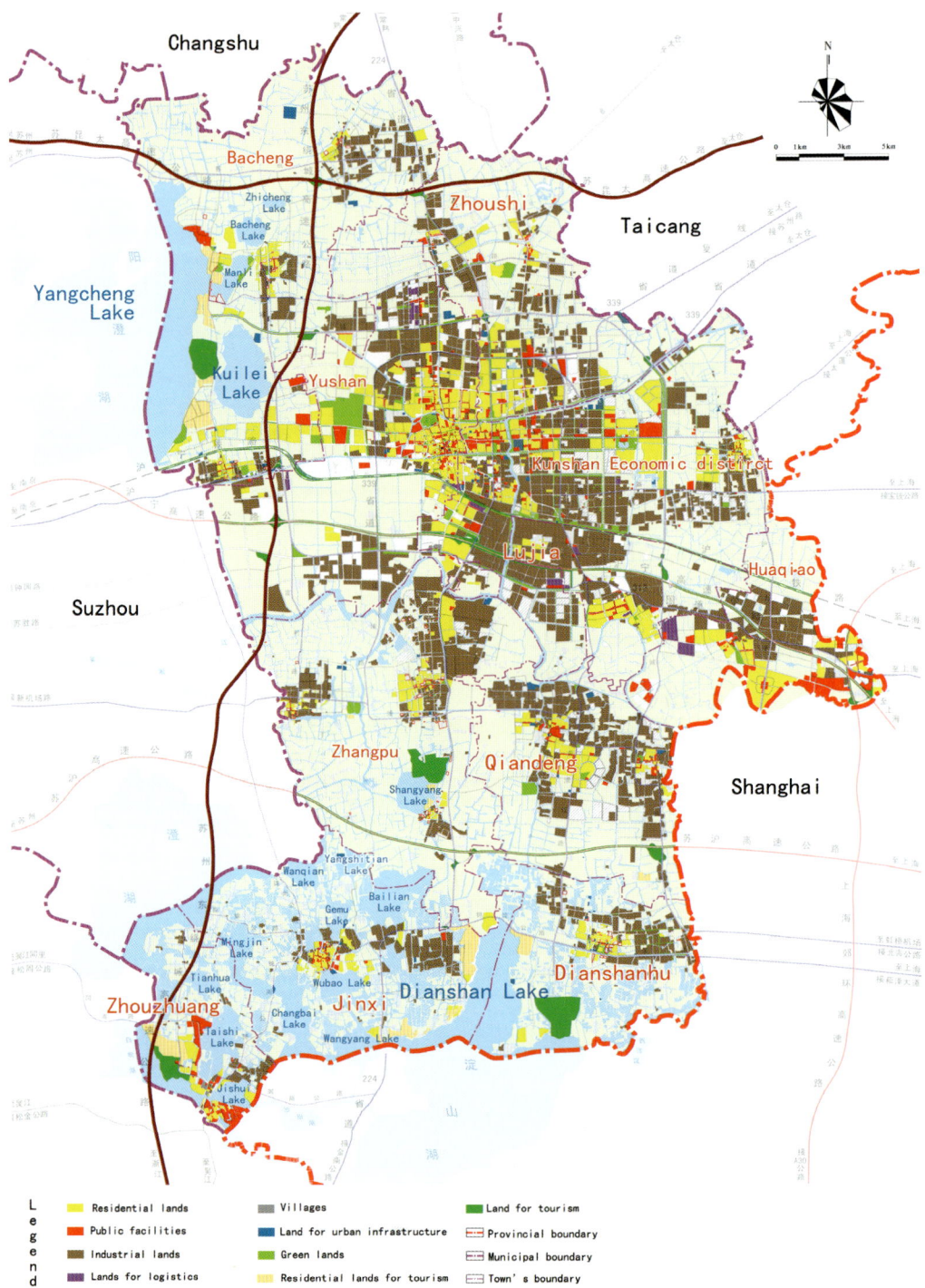

Figure 2: Current land use of Kunshan

Figure 3: Kunqu Opera, UNESCO Masterpiece of the Oral and Intangible Heritage of Humanity
Figure 4: Historic Zhouzhuang, China's foremost water town
Figure 5: Jinxi, the folk museum town of China
Figure 6: Qiandeng, the most charming town in China

1.2. From a small town to a big city

The core settlement of Kunshan has achieved the leap from a small town to a big city over the past 30 years. At the beginning of the 1980s, it was just a small town with a population of less than 80,000 and a land coverage of 4.25 km². Its urban functions then were agriculturally-oriented, its appearance run-down and the town lagged behind with regard to its infrastructure. What about today's Kunshan? It is progressing towards becoming a big city with an urban population[1] of 1.2 million and an expanded urban area of 180 km² in 2008.

Manufacturing industry and modern services have been developing rapidly along with improved urban functions. Continued progress has been made in social programs. Science and technology, education, culture, health, sports and other undertakings have developed in an all-round way. Moreover, the city has taken on a brand new look. Infrastructure is getting better and better. Highways radiate in all directions and the high-speed rail is under construction and will be open to the public very soon. It will then take only 30 minutes to reach the center of Shanghai. In addition, Kunshan is taking the lead in improving its drinking water supplies. A truly modern city has taken shape.

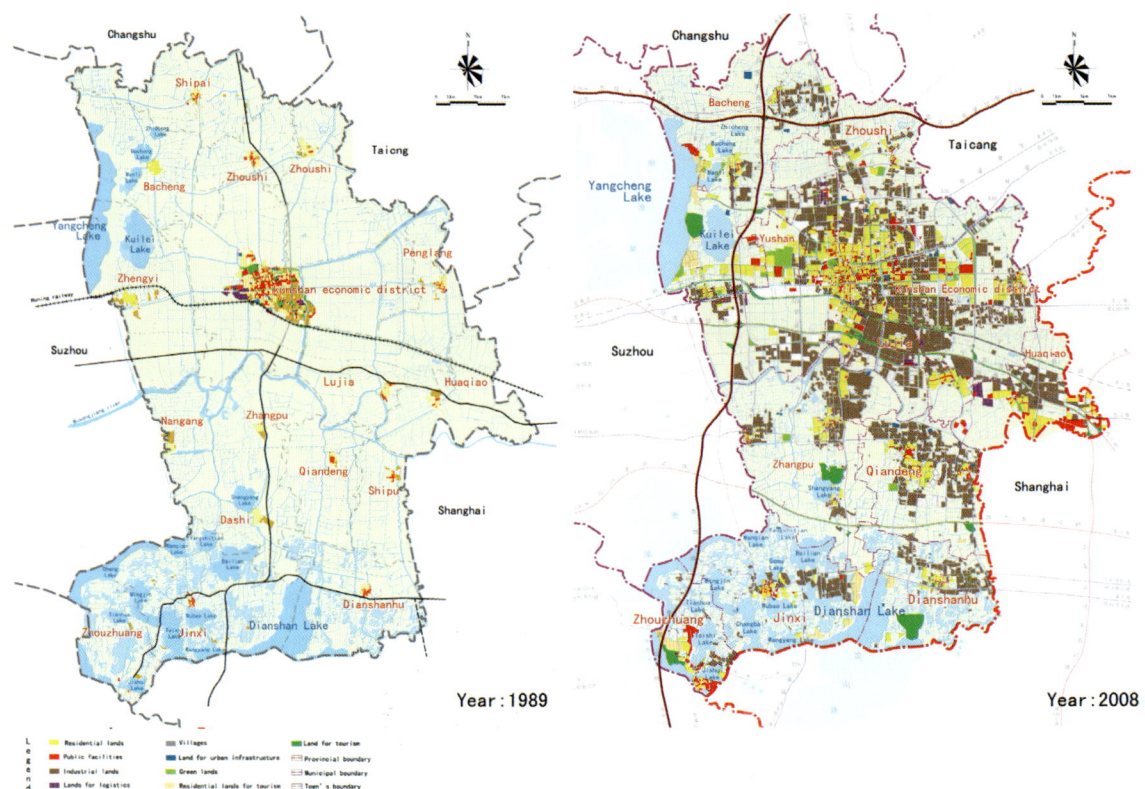

Figure 7: Contrast in urban construction in 1989 and 2008

1.3. From an agriculturally-oriented town to a renowned manufacturing city

In the early period of reform and opening up, Kunshan was a typical agricultural town and its ratio of industrial structure[1] was 51.4:28.9:19.7. In 2008 the ratio was adjusted to 0.8:65.3:33.9. Secondary industries contributed significantly to economic growth and boosted economic growth together with tertiary industries. In addition, Kunshan is one of the newest high-tech industrial bases in the world and has formed a cluster of electronics and communications companies with an output of more than RMB 100 billion. In particular, the output of laptops in 2009 increased to 65 million, accounting for half of the world's output.

Figure 8: Kunshan – the recent past and the present

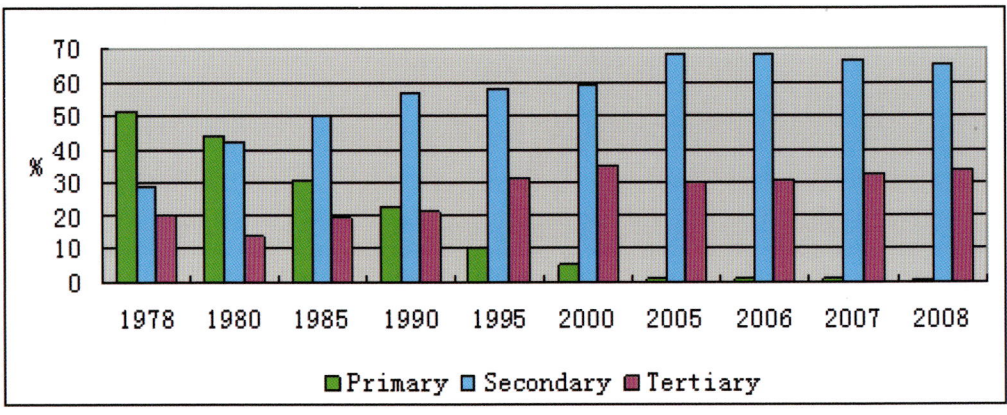

Chart 1: Analysis of industrial structure from 1978-2008

1.4. From a closed town to an open city

Kunshan's open economy began with the economic district initiated by the government in 1984. During the past 20 years, Kunshan has developed from a comparatively closed town to an open city, with the foreign investment ratio up by 264%. It approved over 347 foreign investment projects in 2008 compared with 2 in 1985, and achieved $3.099 billion of contractual foreign capital[4] whereas it was $1.51 million in 1985. Moreover, foreign capital increased from $3.08 million in 1990 to $1.603 billion in 2008 and the foreign trade dependence ratio[5] increased from 10.1% to 280.9%. 55 out of the Fortune 500 companies have invested in Kunshan. Although the global financial crisis broke out in 2008, the import and export volume has kept growing and totaled $618.6 billion.

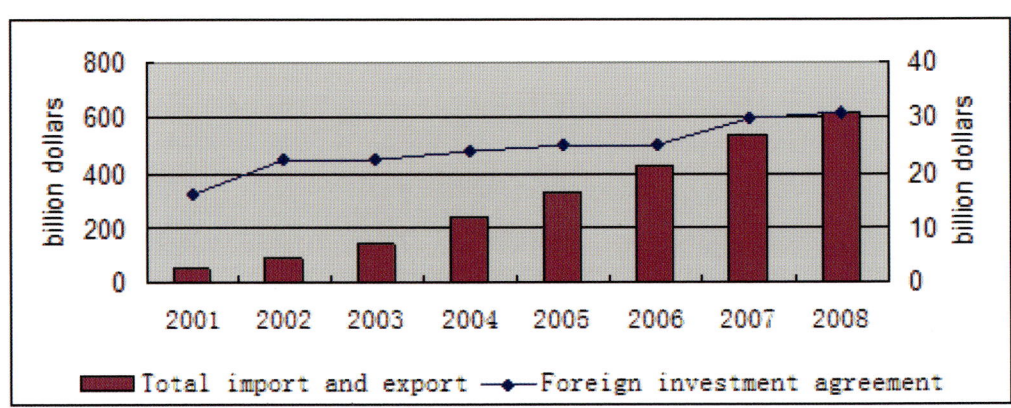

Chart 2: Analysis of paid-in foreign capital during 2001-2008[5]

2. The Cost of the Development Process

1.5. From poverty to a relatively wealthy and comfortable life

Over the 30 years since the policy of reform and opening up, significant changes have taken place in urban and rural society. People's lives have continued to improve. Urban per capita disposable income rose from 813 yuan in 1985 to 24,808 yuan in 2008, with an increase of 16% per year. Rural per capita net income grew from 201 yuan in 1985 to 11,934 yuan in 2008, with an increase of 19% per year. The gap between urban and rural income declined from 4:1 to 2:1.

Moreover, living conditions have improved greatly. On average, in 2008, there were 357 telephones, 71 computers and 31 cars per hundred households. In terms of relative incomes, the urban Gini coefficient[6] was about 0.3, the same as for the rural areas and poverty has been eliminated generally. Average life expectancy has increased to 80.24 years, and the degree of satisfaction with the quality of life[7] has increased by 73.2% and the degree of satisfaction with social security[8] by 96 %.

2.1. A limited supply of land with a decrease in rural land

With the development of manufacturing and the extension of urbanization, much of Kunshan's rural land has been turned into urban construction land, especially over the past eight years. Over that period, rural land decreased by 23 km^2 per year whereas urban and rural construction land rose from 168 km^2 to 343km^2, with an increase of 22 km^2 per year.

In accordance with the policy of strictly protecting basic farmland[9], Kunshan must conserve at least an area of 280 km^2 of this type of land, which is a compulsory index announced by China State. However, deducting an area of 176km^2 for lakes and rivers and an area of 343 km^2 for construction land there is only 129km^2 left. If Kunshan continues to expand at the current rate, the construction land would last only 5-6 years, so there is no doubt that the land resource will be the main obstacle limiting the sustainable development of Kunshan.

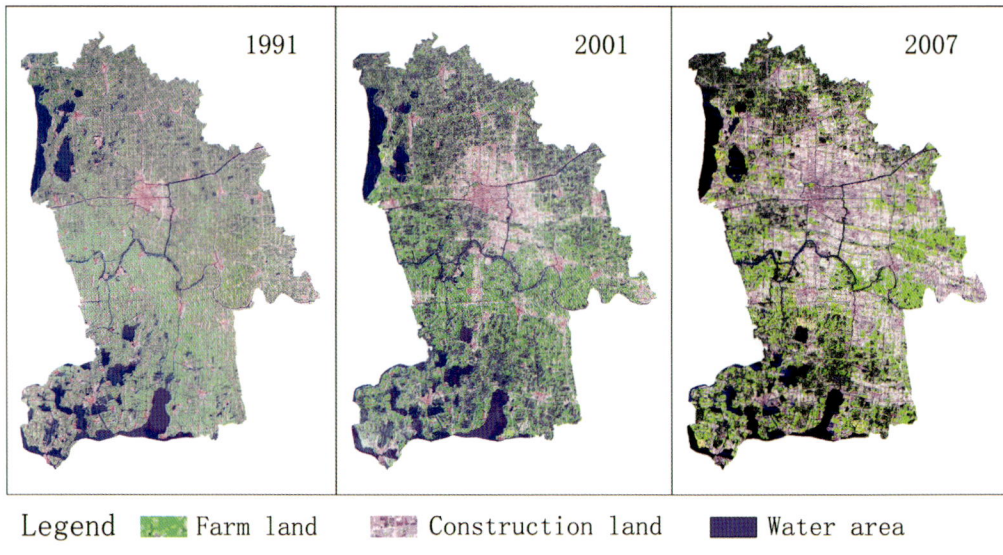

Legend ▇ Farm land ▇ Construction land ▇ Water area

Figure 9: Analysis of various land use in 1991, 2000, 2007

2.2. A considerable emphasis on environmental protection due to increasing pollution

Kunshan has a landscape which is typical of the south of Yangtze River, and water is the most important element. However, water and air pollution have increased gradually in the process of industrialization. Indeed, water quality has declined greatly, with many rivers reduced to the 'most polluted' minus V category. Fortunately, things changed for the better after the implementation of mandatory requirements for pollution control. The sewage treatment system has improved, with enhanced handling capacity. What's more, pollution has been under effective control by eliminating large quantities of old equipment and obsolete technology.

As a result, the Chemical Oxygen Demand (COD), which is an indirect measure of the amount of organic material in water, and hence pollution, has decreased. However, there is no room for complacency in the quality of water. As for the rivers, pollutants are mainly organics while in the case of the lakes, eutrophication is a particular challenge with nitrogen and phosphates being the main pollutants. Consequently, environmental protection is still a heavy responsibility.

Kunshan's overall air quality at present basically meets China's second grade[10] and the total amount of sulphur dioxide emissions has declined to 12,600 tons, accomplishing the objective put forward in the Eleventh Five-Year Plan ahead of schedule （14,000 tons）.In addition, sulphur dioxide emissions per unit GDP amount to 0.084 gram per yuan, better than the national average. However, the maximum daily amount of NOx and of inhalable particles, which comes mainly from the combustion of coal, exceeded the standards by 13% and 45% respectively. Moreover, with the growth of motor vehicles, the influence of automobile air pollution becomes more and more significant.

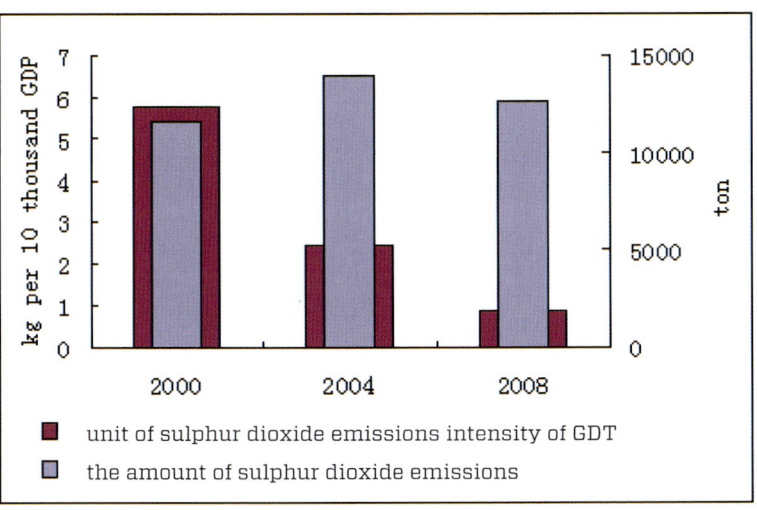

Chart 3: Analysis of sulphur dioxide emissions

2.3. The intense pressure to conserve energy and reduce emissions against the background of increasing energy consumption

In 2008, energy consumption per unit GDP was 0.61 tons of coal equivalent (tce) per 10^4 yuan, approaching the average level of developed countries. But the total energy consumption increased to 9.152 million tce. The energy supply of Kunshan depends on imports from other areas, and the utilization of clean energy and renewable energy is at a preliminary stage - and is a very low proportion of total energy consumption. Though energy conservation with regard to buildings and transportation is limited, there has been great progress in industrial energy conservation. Nowadays the amount of carbon dioxide per unit GDP is 0.48 ton per 10^4 yuan - much lower than the national average of 2.2 tons per 10^4 yuan - but still falling far behind the level of developed countries.

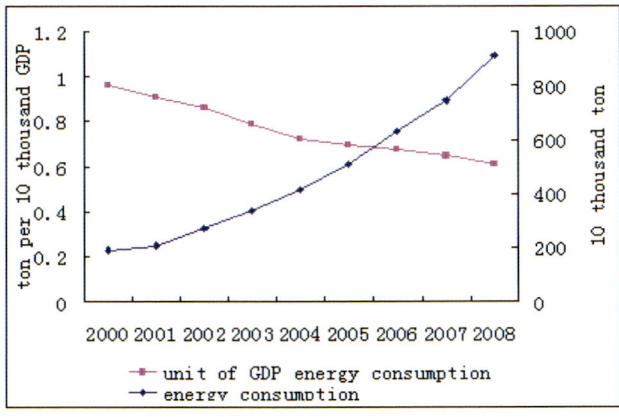

Chart 4: Analysis of energy consumption

3. Changing the Pattern of Economic Growth for Sustainable Development

Since the reform initiative and opening up, Kunshan has achieved remarkable success in economic and social development; this forms the "Kunshan Way". However, problems and conflicts have emerged gradually. If Kunshan continues to develop as now with the present land reserves, output efficiency and energy consumption, the city will not be able to catch up with the low carbon trend and sustain a steady or even rapid development. Therefore, as pointed out in the master plan[11], it is only by changing the development mode that the city can maintain sustainable development in the context of world climate change and resource scarcity.

3.1 Optimizing the industrial structure to promote the green economy

Following international experience, tertiary industry has come to occupy the dominant position, with primary industry having the lowest share. Related to that, the city master plan provides for several industry policies to be followed:

Firstly, the service sector should be expanded in order to boost the transformation of the economic growth mode. Following the trend of industrial transformation in the Yangtze River delta, productive service industry should be developed based on current manufacturing advantages, such as modern logistics, finance, insurance and service outsourcings. Meanwhile, by taking advantage of this area's outstanding tourism resource, the traditional service industries, including leisure, catering and hotel accommodation in both urban and rural areas, could be promoted, and the overall service function for the main city could also be improved.

Secondly, by building relevant centers covering R&D, technical services and industrial development, the leading position of the IT industry should continue to be strengthened. Also, through preferential policy concerning tax, funding and land assembly, industries with a rising demand from foreign and domestic markets could be fostered, e.g. for railway equipment, personalized electronic products, equipment for port operations, environmentally-friendly energy technology and new materials. On the other hand, the application of strict standards will lead to a phasing out of industries associated with high energy consumption, high contamination and low efficiency, while the traditional industries that are still needed could gradually be upgraded with the help of modern technology.

Thirdly, in parallel with the continuing growth of Kunshan, urban agriculture could be developed to exploit the geographical advantages of proximity to Shanghai. We should explore centralized, large scale approaches to agricultural development, while recreational agriculture and village tourism should be vigorously facilitated.

By implementing the above industrial policies, the following outcomes are expected. In the short term, secondary industry will be given a prominent role, while tertiary industry will be accelerated, towards an industrial structure of 0.5:59.5:40. In the long run, the core competitiveness of secondary industry will be enhanced and tertiary industry strengthened, leading to an industrial structure of 0.4:49.6:50.

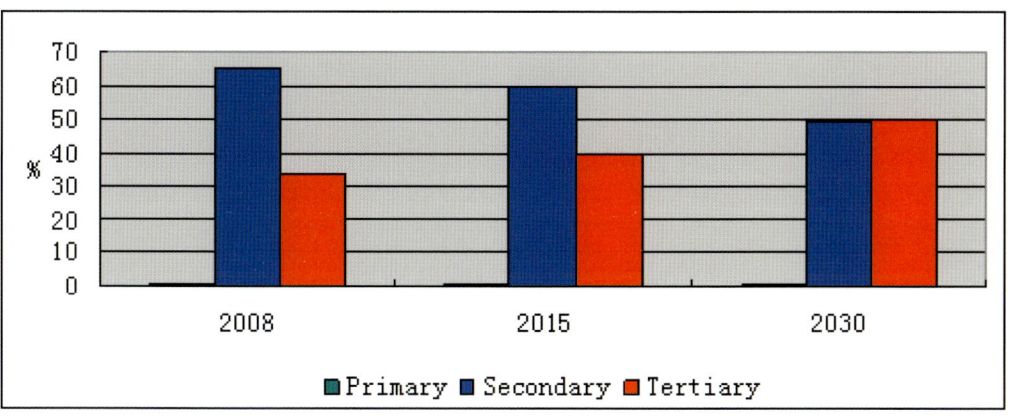

Chart 5: Analysis of industrial restructuring

3.2 Optimizing energy structure to reduce greenhouse gas emissions

Utilization of renewable energy like solar power, geothermal energy and biomass based on the local situation in Kunshan should be promoted, with the aim of raising the proportion of renewable energy relative to total energy consumption to 20% in the long term. According to the degree of utilization of solar energy, Kunshan is classified as fourth grade, mainly focusing on the integrated development of solar power and building. In the urban area, photovoltaic power generation and heating systems will be boosted in public and residential buildings, with a view to reducing dependence on public heating and power grids. In the rural areas, solar heating systems including solar water heating and greenhouses will be developed in local residences and courtyards, in order to improve living conditions.

As a low-grade renewable energy, geothermal energy is widely distributed in constant temperature zones near the land surface. It is easily utilized in different places and seasons because of its resistance to geographical and seasonal changes. By establishing a geothermal heat pump system through the availability of surface and ground water, the city is capable of providing heat and cooling to buildings. Biomass energy is mainly used in rural areas where marsh gas, fermented products from straw and animal manure provides energy for cooking and heating.

Clean energy is widely encouraged in light of the high consumption rate of non-clean energy with a negative impact on the eco-environment, such as coal, gasoline and oil. The plan is aimed at reducing sulphur dioxide, NO_x and dust emission and increasing the proportion of clean energy to 80% or so[12]. Therefore, we will intensify efforts to eliminate existing industrial coal-fired boilers and to reduce the coal consumption rate through centralized heating and to encourage the building of high-efficiency boilers. Moreover, according to the national industrial policy, vehicles with alternative sources of power, such as electricity and natural gas will be encouraged in order to reduce oil consumption.

Figure 10: Utilization of solar energy

Figure 11: Utilization of geothermal energy

3.3 Optimizing spatial structure to save land resources

Transport-oriented land use patterns which are more compact, can promote effective integration between the use of land and the mode of travel. Consequently, the whole region is divided into three areas according to the master plan, the southern, the central and the northern - in order to closely combine the urban and regional railway systems and influence spatial concentration in the urban areas. In the southern and northern areas ecological spaces must be protected and the sprawl of the construction land should be avoided.

By contrast, in the central area (including the town of Kunshan and its environs), development should be intensive, so that the best use can be made of the land in conjunction with its public transportation corridors, with the aim of giving priority to the development of public transport. In parallel, outdated industrial and storage uses could be replaced gradually in order to promote new concentrations of commercial, residential and mixed use development.

New transportation hubs are envisaged, allowing passengers to transfer between different transport modes, including the subway, conventional bus routes and the high speed railway. The hubs would provide excellent accessibility and they would be ideal places for the clustering of public facilities at regional and city level. Development would be

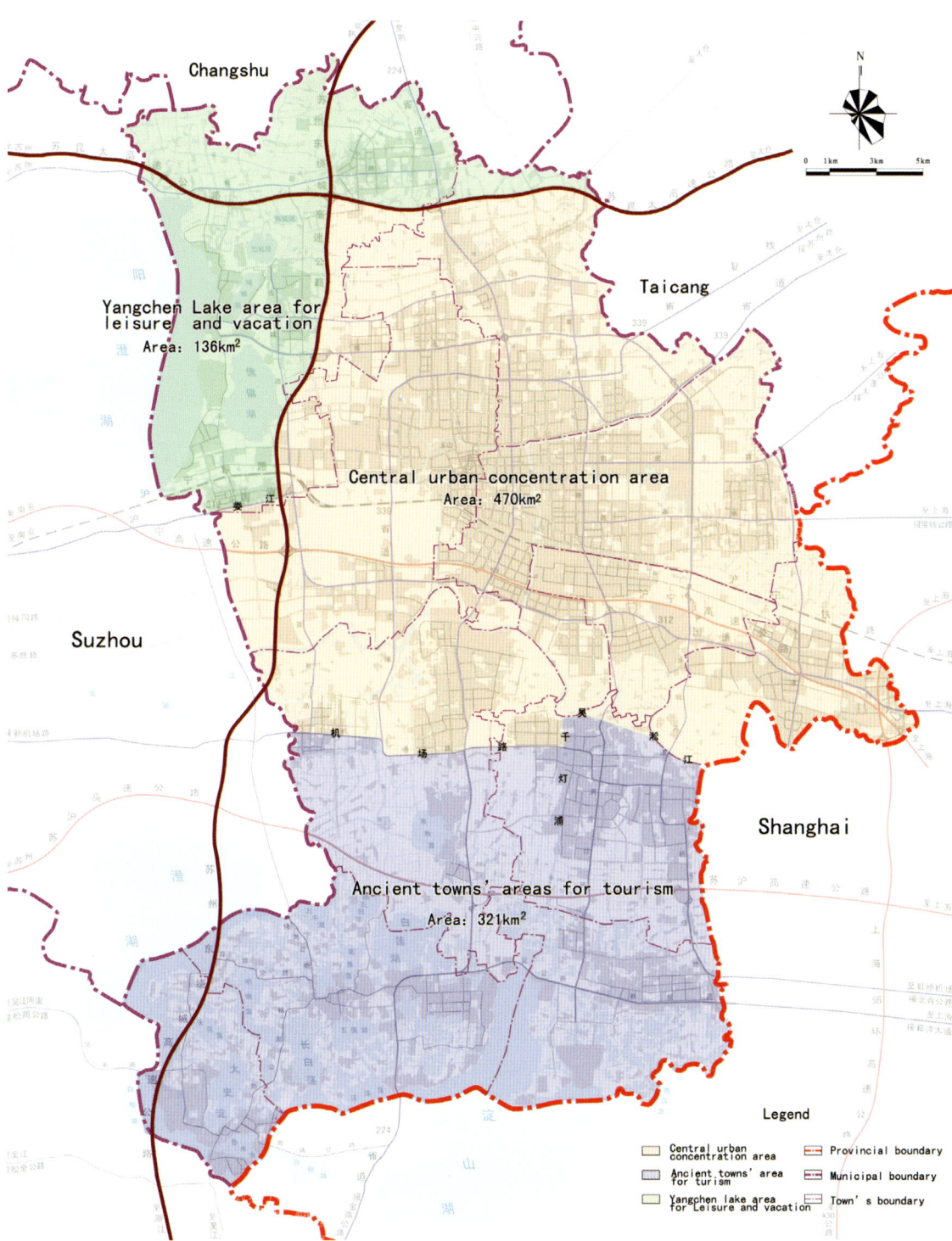

Figure 12: Master plan divisions of Kunshan

intensive, making full and efficient use of the land, both above and below ground. New road systems would come later and they would serve less intensively developed areas. In terms of its overall aims, the master plan seeks to:

- promote diversity through an appropriate mixture of functions
- shorten commuting distances, reducing both motor traffic congestion and energy consumption.
- create a multi-center system, to avoid the traffic jams of a single center.
- replace inefficient factories and make efficient, integrated use of brown field land.
- improve the Floor Area Ratio of industrial land through measures such as increasing the density of building and the number of floors.
- make more efficient use of all available land.
- change the method of development from one of dependence on the provision of land resources, to one of strict control over the scale of construction land in order to achieve the expected economic growth.

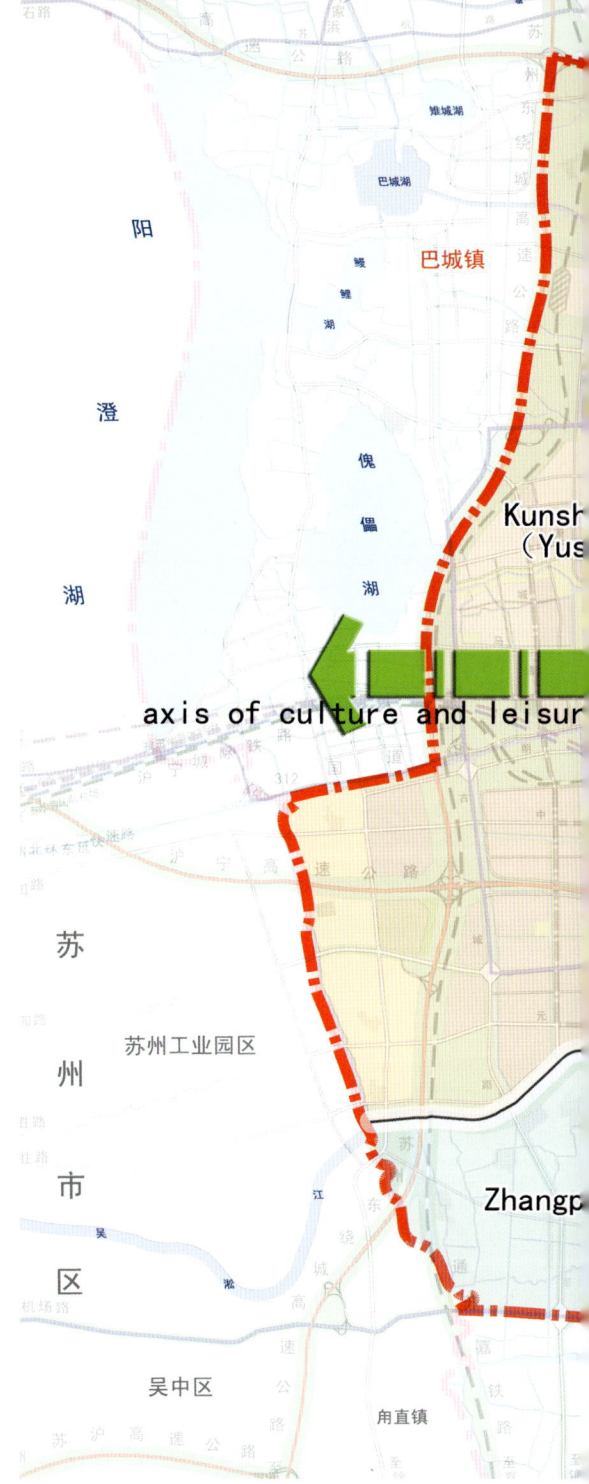

Figure 13: Planning structure of the city center

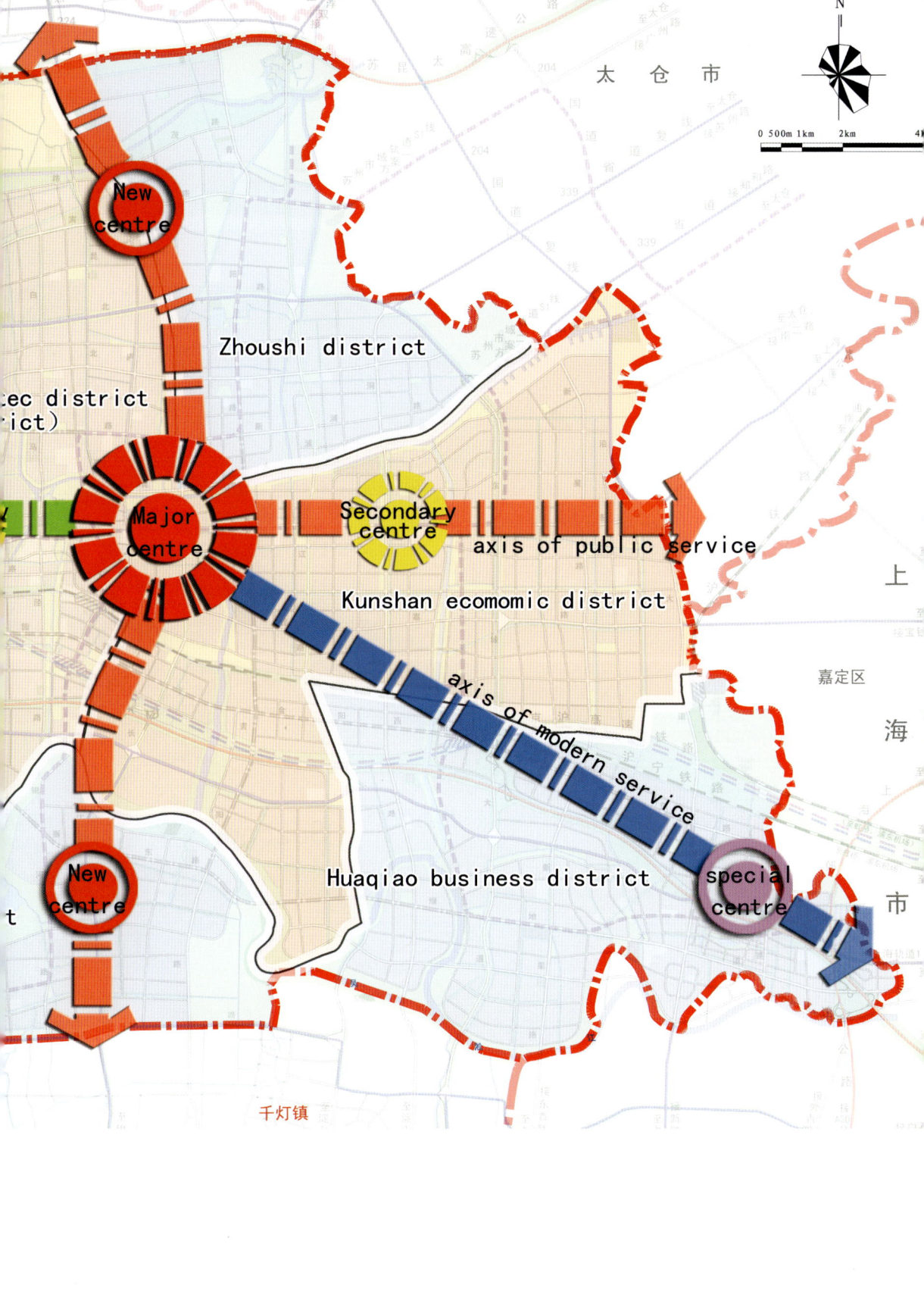

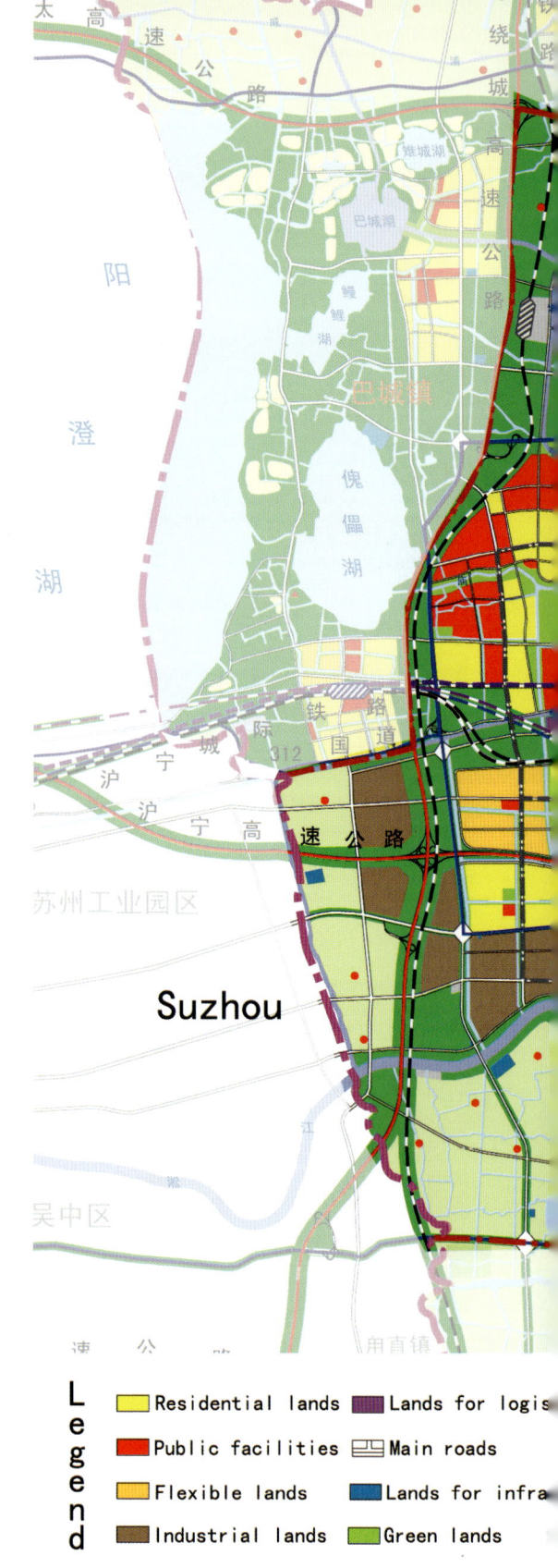

Figure 14: Overall land use planning of the city centre

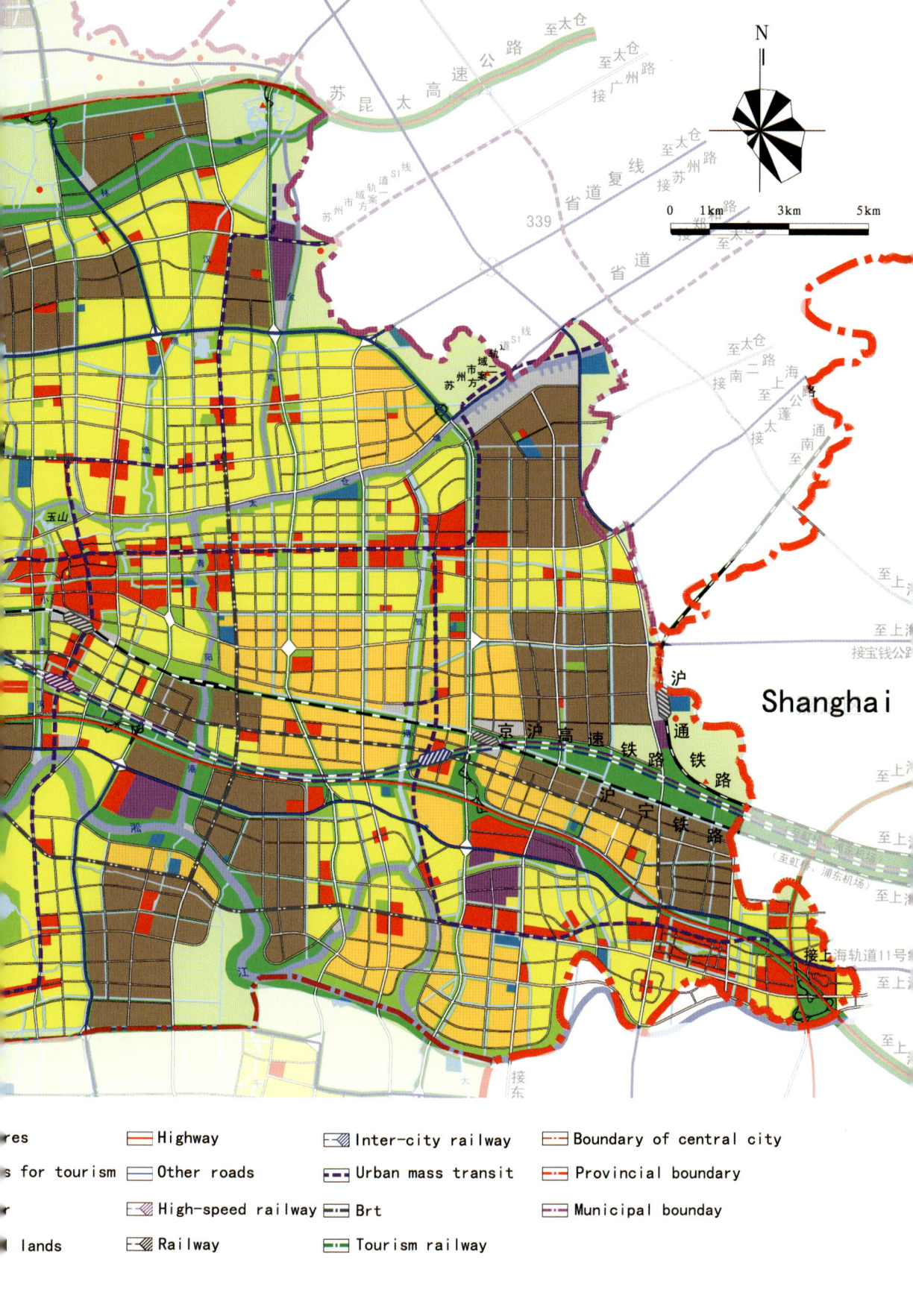

3.4 Optimizing transportation structure for green travel

As a result of the various travel needs, land use functions, development expectations and the need to protect resources, the city of Kunshan is divided into four main types of transport area as defined by the city master plan (see figure 15). One gives priority to the development of the city bus; another balances the demands of travel by bus and private car; the third area allows unrestricted use of the private car; and the fourth limits the of motor vehicles. Different policies are in force in these areas in terms of road network density, public transport development level, parking limits and freight transportation management, with the aim of altering the distribution of demand and optimizing the transportation environment.

The creation of these divisions has resulted in a user-friendly transport system, geared to the needs of the public, has been achieved by means of:

- the strict policy control of parking, for example, to reduce parking provision in the city centers and other congested areas
- increasing parking fees for private cars in congested areas
- advocating the use of bus priority areas
- restrictions on the use of private cars in certain areas
- the introduction of speed limits in certain areas

Figure 15: Plan of traffic distribution

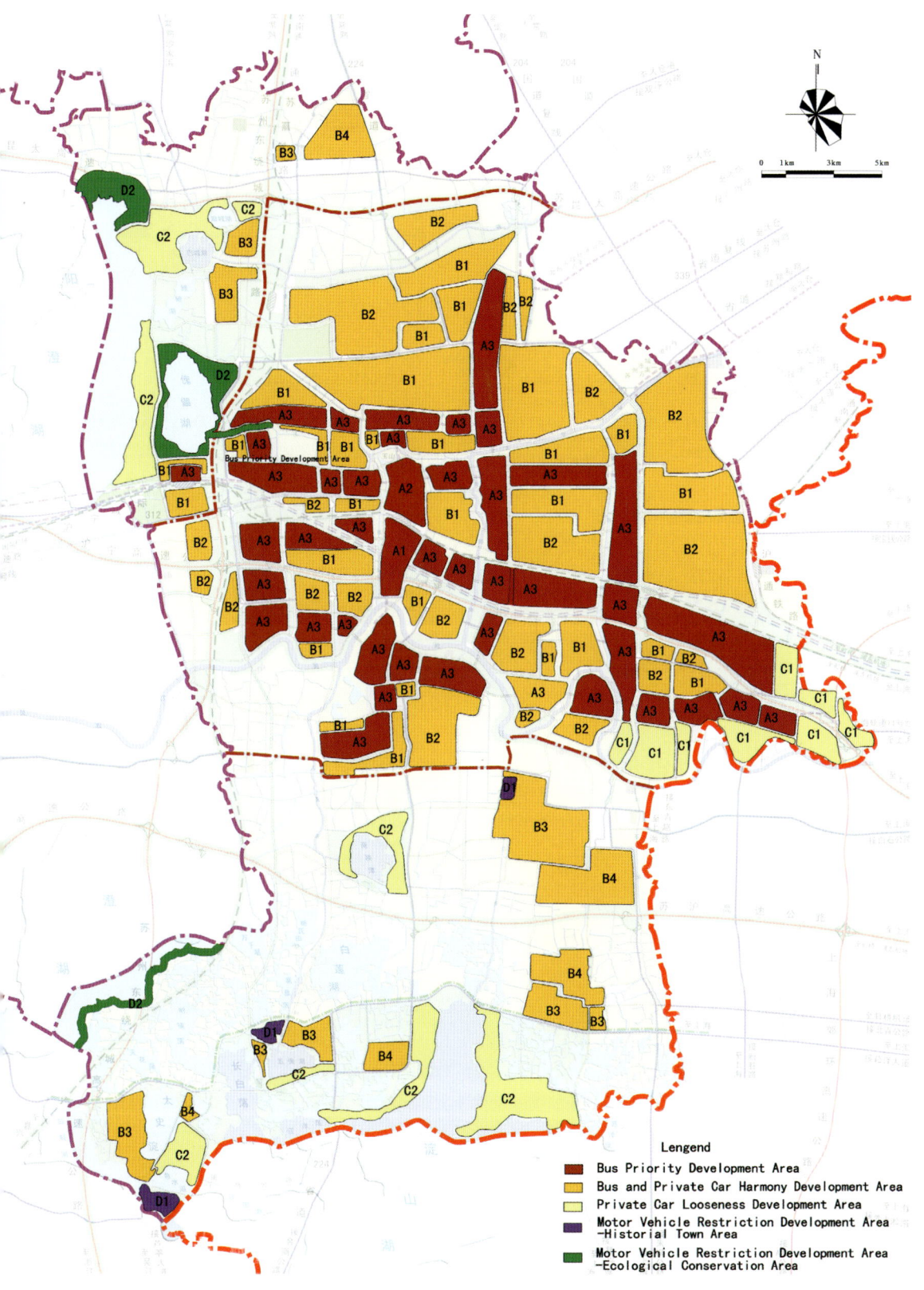

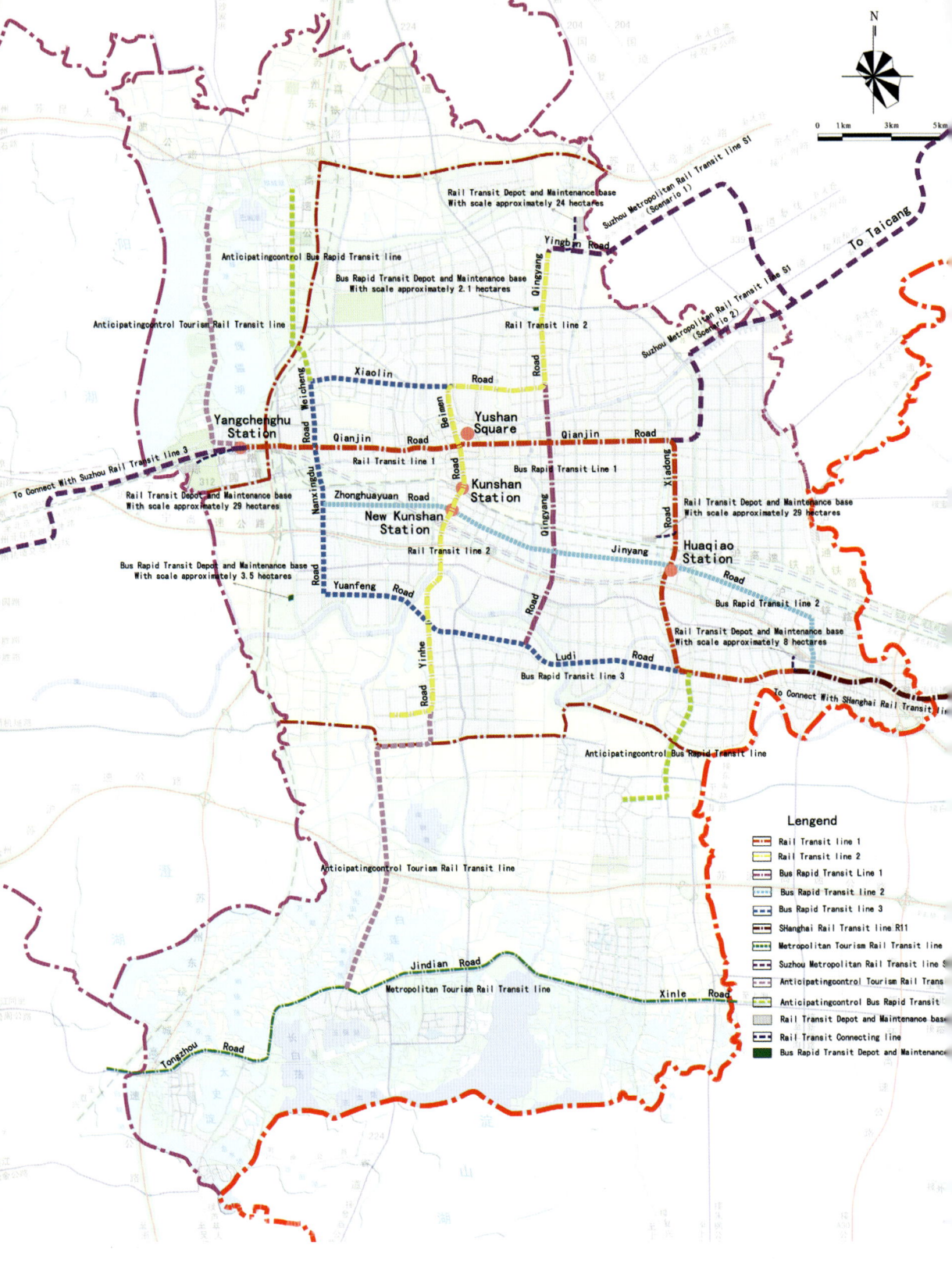

Figure 16: Plan of public transportation

4. Prospects

It is expected that under the influence of the master plan, Kunshan will take the lead in achieving modernization by 2030 and that economic development and living standards will catch up with developed countries and regions. Average GDP per person will increase to $50,000, with urban per capita disposable income up to $30,000. Meanwhile, the consumption level of resources, together with energy and polluting emissions will decline greatly. The energy consumption per unit GDP will drop to 1.71tce per 10^4 US dollars and water consumption per unit GDP 47.8 cubic meters per 10^4 US dollars. Moreover, the amount of carbon-dioxide emissions per unit GDP will drop to $2.05 tons per 10^4 dollar, the forest coverage rate will increase to 26% and the ecological environment will be improved. This will make Kunshan a truly sustainable city.

5. Conclusion

The rapid development of Kunshan over the last thirty years is a typical example of the China Miracle. Although the development opportunities and development path are unique, problems in the development process, the way we think and the approaches to solving the problems will no doubt provide a common reference point for other cities in China which are experiencing or will experience rapid development, and for other developing countries in the world.

—

Endnotes

1. The population living in the built up area of the city

2. The ratio of primary industry (which includes agriculture) to secondary industry (manufacturing) to tertiary industry (services).

3. Contractual foreign capital means the amount of foreign investments which have already assigned in the contracts.

4. The foreign trade dependence ratio represents the ratio of total export-import volume to the GDP.

5. The left hand axis measures the volume of total import and export, and the right hand axis measures the volume of foreign investment agreement.

6. The Gini coefficient is an international measurement of income disparity, a zero Gini coefficient represents perfect equality and 1 indicates a complete monopoly of wealth by the privileged.

7. The index is an official statistic which comes out from sampling survey.

8. The social security includes social insurance and social welfare.

9. In order to guarantee the food supply, China's government made a national policy to preserve the necessary farmland with the total amount of 1,200,000 km2, and at county level, Kunshan must preserve a slice of 280 km2 farmland of the whole national cake.

10. This grade refers to "Integrated emission standard of air pollutants" published by the Ministry of Environmental Protection of China.

11. This represents the City master plan for Kunshan city (2009-2030), which is a comprehensive and programmatic document for Kunshan city. Many aspects such as economic growth, land use and environment problems were taken into account.

12. At present, clean energy consists 54% of the total energy in Kunshan city, which are 50% proportion of electricity, 4% proportion of natural gas. In the future 2030, clean energy provides 80% of the total energy, while electricity makes the contribution of 50%, natural gas of 10%, and other reproducible energy such as solar power, salinity gradient power of 20%.

03 New Methods and Strategies

The Carbon Footprint of UK Cities:

4M: Measurement, Modelling, Mapping and Management

Kevin J Lomas

Bell MC
Firth SK
Gaston KJ
Goodman P
Leake JR
Namdeo A

Rylatt M
Allinson D
Davies ZG
Edmondson JL
Galatioto F
Brake JA

Guo L
Hill G
Irvine KN
Taylor SC
Tiwary A

The City of Leicester

Introduction
The planet is threatened by the emission of human-made greenhouse gasses, and in particular carbon dioxide (CO_2) from the combustion of fossil fuels. In 2009, average annual CO_2 emissions were 4.1 t CO_2 per person worldwide, although in developed countries this was substantially higher at 11.5 t CO_2 per person (IEA, 2009). Atmospheric CO_2 concentration has reached 380 ppm globally, with levels increasing by 1.9 ppm annually between 1995 and 2005 (IPCC, 2007). The world's population currently stands at 6.8 billion and is set to rise to c.8 billion by 2050 (PRB, 2009). In 2008, for the first time, over half of all people lived in cities and by 2030 this is expected to rise to nearly two-thirds (UNFPA, 2007). The high density of people in cities, who use energy for transport, food, and consumer goods and services, make them major contributors to global greenhouse gas emissions. The need to reduce CO_2 emissions from cities is clear.

International negotiations to curb emissions have had mixed outcomes, but notwithstanding, national and sub-national initiatives proliferate. Policies and economic instruments to cut CO_2 emissions need to operate in a manner that preserves, or even enhances, cities' functioning and environment.

Transport emissions have to be curbed without impinging on necessary travel, building energy use needs to be controlled without rendering them inoperable, and emission reduction practices need to impact as little as possible on key ecosystem services[1]. Importantly, emissions reduction in all of these areas can go hand-in-hand with improvements to lifestyles and well-being: reduced traffic improves air quality and therefore human health, more energy efficient buildings lower fuel costs to occupants, and green spaces can sequester carbon whilst improving the aesthetic environment and human health and well-being. Thus, a low carbon city can be a cleaner, quieter, healthier and more enjoyable city.

The 4M project is examining these issues by estimating key components of the carbon footprint (Wiedmann & Minx, 2008) of the city of Leicester in the UK. The project adopts a multi-disciplinary perspective and is being progressed through collaboration between researchers from five UK universities and Leicester City Council. This enables a rounded view of proposed carbon reduction initiatives to be evaluated in the real social and economic context of a functioning and dynamic city. The project has four activities, measuring, modelling, mapping and managing carbon emissions - hence 4M.

The project team are measuring the carbon emissions from buildings and transport, as well as biological carbon storage and sequestration in soil and vegetation. The aim is to establish a strategy by which city authorities can measure the changes in carbon emissions and sinks over time, and to create a workable, bottom-up, methodology for urban carbon foot-printing. Models underpinned by the measurements enable the relationships between emissions and human activity to be understood and mapped. The models also enable the likely impact of carbon management practices to be predicted. Although the effect of individual management interventions can be small, added together and over time many small additive interventions can deliver deep cuts in carbon emissions.

The 4M Aims and Objectives

Aims
- Provide a methodology, data sources, models, data collection techniques, analysis methods and validation approaches, that can be used to benchmark and manage the carbon sources and sinks in UK cities;
- Produce ways of representing carbon sources and sinks in a form suitable for visualisation and interpretation by policy makers and other stakeholders;
- Generate key components of the direct carbon footprint for the City of Leicester and assess the likely impact on it of some municipal building energy, ecosystems and traffic management strategies.

Objectives
- Map the actual carbon produced by both domestic and non-domestic buildings in the City of Leicester through the acquisition of existing data, the collection of new data and the development of people-sensitive models of energy use;
- Predict the likely impact on the carbon footprint of proposed (and other) deployments of a district combined heat and power scheme, domestic micro-generators and non-domestic energy efficiency measures;
- Map the carbon emissions due to vehicles travelling in the City of Leicester road network;
- Predict the effects of driver behaviour, new vehicle technologies, intelligent transport systems and novel policy interventions on urban transport-related carbon;
- Map the carbon pools associated with green spaces in the City of Leicester;
- Determine the impact of alternative building, traffic and green-space management practices on the urban carbon pools;
- Explore the implications of different carbon emissions reduction initiatives targeted at households from different socio-economic groups;
- Assess the scope and impact of local policy initiatives and thus gain an insight into the rate at which carbon emissions could plausibly be reduced.

Funding
The four year project began in March 2008 and is supported by the UK Engineering and Physical Sciences research Council (EPSRC) through grant EP/F007604/1 'Measurement, Modelling, Mapping and Management 4M: an Evidence Based Methodology for Understanding and Shrinking the Urban Carbon Footprint'. The 4M consortium has 5 UK partners: Loughborough University (lead), De Montfort University, Newcastle University, the University of Sheffield, and the University of Leeds. The project has 8 active academics, 10 funded research assistants and 7 contributing higher degree students. It is actively supported by Leicester City Council and an international advisory panel who help to steer the direction of the research.

UK Carbon Emissions and Policies

The UK currently has a population just over 61 million (ONS, 2009), with approximately 58% living in cities and 80% in urban areas, the latter of which comprises 11% of land cover. Around 56 km² of countryside is urbanised each year (Schoon, 2001). The population is expected to rise to about 73 million by 2033 (ONS, 2009). In 2006, the UK was the 8th largest gross emitting nation, at 9.2 t CO_2 per person (UN, 2010). Of these emissions, business, homes and transport account for about 89%: 34% from business, 28% from homes, and 27% from surface transport (DECC, 2010a), but road traffic is increasing at around 2% per year (SDC, 2010).

The UK government, through the Department of Energy and Climate Change (DECC), has set a target of 80% reduction in UK greenhouse gas emissions on 1990 levels by 2050 (Great Britain, 2008). This puts energy demand reduction and low-carbon energy supply at the forefront of managing future urban environments. The Committee on Climate Change (CCC) has now set legally binding carbon budgets for the first three five-yearly periods up to 2022 (CCC 2008), and produced its first report on progress against these budgets (CCC, 2009). Decreasing dependency on centrally supplied energy to heat, cool and light buildings and moving towards less polluting transport systems are key components of the CCC carbon reduction pathway. Recognising the need for comprehensive data by which local authorities and others might monitor emissions, the government, through DECC, has begun to publish measurements of the carbon emissions from buildings and transport (DECC, 2009a)[2].

The buildings sector has been the target of a number of recent policy initiatives. The building regulations that set minimum carbon emissions standards will be radically tightened such that, by 2016, all new homes must be zero-carbon (CLG, 2006). However, the existing 25 million homes are the important target for emissions cuts and the great British refurbishment aims to retrofit 7 million homes by 2020 (DECC, 2009b), a truly mammoth task. It is planned that the initial cost can be met by pay-as-you-save (PAYS) grants, tied to each house, which will be paid off by successive occupants of that property through their fuel bill (HM Government, 2010). To encourage the installation of new and renewable energy technologies, from April 2010, feed-in tariffs (FITs) have guaranteed householders income from each unit of electricity exported to the grid (DECC, 2010c). The roll out of smart meters[3], such that all homes will have them by 2020 (DECC, 2009c), will enable such a scheme. The renewable heat incentive (RHI), intended to begin in April 2011, will, if it proceeds, credit households for the installation of new heating technologies such as solar water heating (DECC, 2010d). However, very little work has been done to determine the likely uptake of such schemes, what might be done to promote them (there is a valuable role here for local authorities) and, importantly, the true impact they might have on carbon emissions.

There is an ambition that all new non-domestic buildings should be zero carbon from 2019 (HM Treasury, 2008). Whether one imagines this to be possible or not, delivering carbon reductions of 80% by 2050 requires radical improvement to the energy efficiency of the UK's existing c1.8million non-domestic buildings. The EU Energy Performance of Buildings Directive has been in force since 2002. Proposed modifications, currently out for consultation, include the requirements that all refurbished or extended buildings and all buildings owned by public authorities,, or frequently visited by the public, that are over 250m² should be monitored and a Display Energy Certificate showing the annual energy use (or operational rating) should be prominently displayed (EU, 2010). The current average rating of UK non-domestic buildings is 'E'; if an 80% cut is to be achieved in this sector, the average rating must improve to 'C' by 2020 and 'A' by 2050 (Carbon Trust, 2009)[4]. But given the diversity and complexity of the geometry, construction, and energy services of many non-domestic buildings, and restrictive tenure and lease arrangements, together with the often short occupation periods, this is daunting task. Clearly, if local authorities are to manage carbon emissions effectively, they need specific targets and planning support tools for the non-domestic sector.

The UK Department for Transport has made sustainability central to their plans for 2014 and beyond, as outlined in the 'Towards a Sustainable Transport System' (DfT, 2007) and the 'Delivering a Sustainable Transport System' (DaSTS) publications (DfT, 2008). These are associated with the roll out of Automatic Traffic Management on motorways, electric vehicles, shifts towards greater public transport use, promoting cycling and walking, green travel plans and intelligent transport systems. The Commission for Integrated Transport has made recommendations to deliver cost-effective carbon savings from transport by 2020, aiming for a 14% reduction against 1990 levels (CfIT, 2007). The modelling of traffic flows in UK cities is relatively well developed, driven primarily by congestion and air quality concerns. These same models can be used to estimate carbon emission but the figures are crude, failing to account for the large difference in emissions between free-flowing (off-peak) and on-peak travel, and the types of vehicle on the move at different times. These weaknesses need to be overcome to create appropriate tools for designing effective low carbon transport policies.

The need to cut emissions from transport and buildings is self evident. However, in order to meet national and international obligations to produce national inventories of greenhouse gas emissions by sources and removal by sinks, as well as meeting reporting requirements under the Kyoto Protocol, UK biological carbon emissions and sequestration arising from different land uses, land use change and forestry must also be accounted for (Dyson et al, 2009). This includes estimating the carbon loss associated with the conversion of land through the process of urbanisation (e.g., from areas of agricultural production, grassland, forest). Yet, once land is considered to be urban, biological carbon density at equilibrium is assumed to be zero (Dyson et al, 2009). Contrary to this assumption, recent research conducted in North America (e.g., Nowak & Crane, 2002; Pataki et al, 2006; Pouyat et al, 2006) has suggested that urban carbon pools associated with vegetation and soils warrant closer appraisal as, although small compared to overall carbon emissions, they could provide a valuable contribution reducing net emissions. Nonetheless, findings from North America cannot simply be extrapolated to Western Europe, as the patterns of urbanisation are substantially different. In North America, the trend has been towards progressively more dispersed patterns of settlement referred to as 'sprawl', which are driven by the construction of large, low density residential developments beyond the urban periphery (Hansen et al, 2005). In contrast, within the UK and other parts of Europe, there is a tendency to densify existing urban areas, with remaining urban green space being built upon, particularly domestic gardens (a phenomenon commonly referred to as 'back-land development' or 'garden grabbing'; Burton, 2000; Goode, 2006; ODPM, 2006). The 4M project will be the first to determine the value of biological carbon pools within an urban area in Europe.

It should be evident from this overview that UK carbon emission targets and trajectories have been set and policies, which will work towards achieving them, put in place. However, the emissions reductions required at regional or city scales have not been prescribed and it is unlikely that all cities can realistically achieve the same emissions cut over the same time period and at a similar cost. So, whilst local government and city authorities are in the front line of the national struggle to cut emissions, there is no fair and transparent system for determining the reduction targets for individual urban areas, a time-frame over which these reductions must be made, and the probable costs. City authorities desperately need reliable data and models to help them establish realistic carbon emission targets, emission reduction trajectories, and acceptable and robust policies for meeting these.

The City of Leicester and Emissions Reduction

Leicester is geographically central in England. With a resident population of 280,000 in 2007, living in over 110,000 homes (ONS, 2010), and with 70,000 or so non-domestic buildings it is the UK's 15th largest city. The households in the city cover a wide range of socio-economic categories, from affluent to disadvantaged. Since 1991 the population has expanded by 3.5%, compared to the national average of 4.5%. The city, and thus the 4M study area, has a clearly defined edge with major transport arteries connected by an inner, middle and outer ring road (Figure 1)[5] and good transport links via the M1 motorway (to Nottingham, Derby and Northampton) and the M69 (to Birmingham). London is just ninety minutes away by mainline rail and an international airport is just 32 km from the city centre.

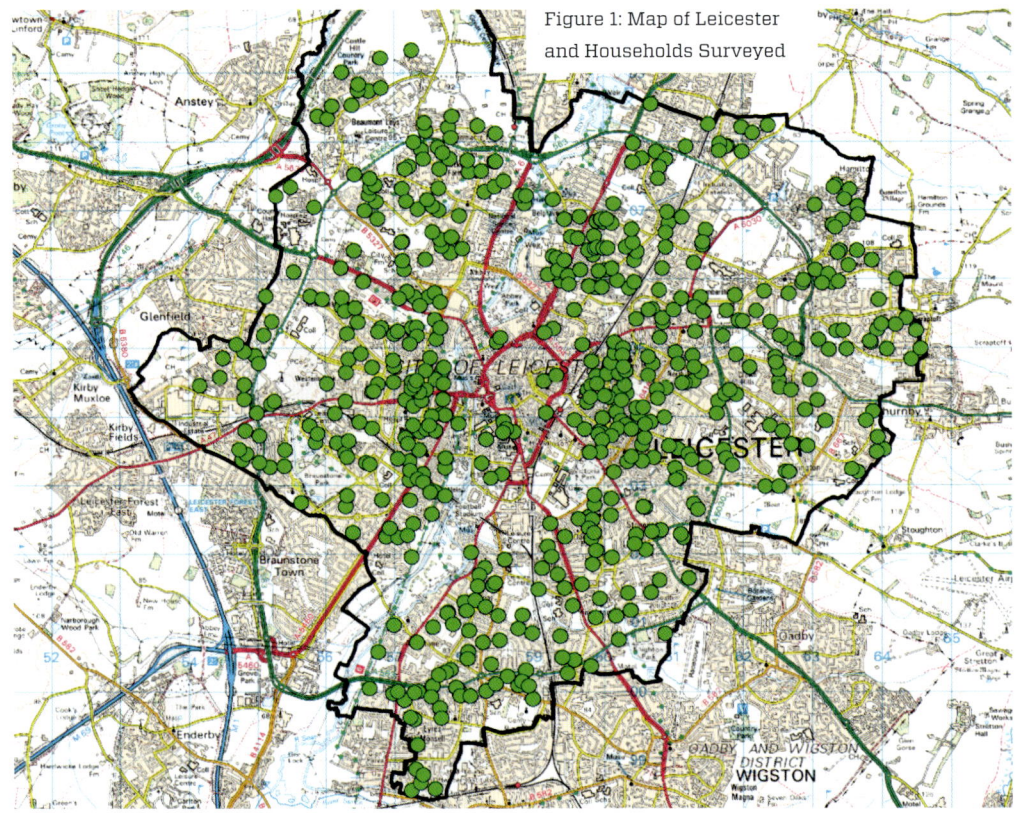

Figure 1: Map of Leicester and Households Surveyed

Green space, which accounts for 57% of land cover within the local authority boundary, includes individual street trees, road verges, public parks, allotments, riparian zones, golf courses, schools' grounds and brownfield sites. The city council is responsible for maintaining and managing approximately 23% of this 41.7 km^2 of green space. Domestic gardens constitute just over a quarter of total land cover (Loram et al, 2007), which is comparable with other UK cities.

The city council has a longstanding commitment to combating climate change. In 1990 it was voted Europe's first environment city and during the 1990s was part of the International Cities for Climate Protection network. Historically, the council's action on environmental issues has primarily focused on sustainable energy use and identifying the non-energy benefits of energy efficiency and renewable energy policies. The city council's climate change strategy (City of Leicester, 2003) declares *"a target of 50% reduction on 1990 levels of CO_2 emissions by 2025".* The council *"recognised the importance of having an accurate emissions inventory in order to identify the main users of energy, the effectiveness of measures adopted and the progress towards targets".* However it was also noted that *"since 1996 there has been much greater difficulty in obtaining good quality data at a high enough resolution to inform the modelling".*

The city council has built a strong working relationship with UK universities, and, importantly, has contributed data and information to their research endeavours. Since 1987, the instrumented City (iC) initiative has recorded traffic flows and delays, and since 1997 data from 13 indicative pollution monitors has been collected. The iC has provided a solid foundation for work at Leeds University and latterly Newcastle. Several collaborative partnerships, between universities and Leicester City, County and District Councils, has resulted in the implementation and evaluation of priority public transport corridors, bus tracking devices to provide real-time information at bus stops, and personalised messaging to travellers (Chen & Bell, 2002). Since 2001, the city council has monitoring half-hourly energy and water use in over 300 public buildings. These data are available for analysis by De Montfort University (Brown et al, 2010).

Since April 2008, the performance of local authorities throughout the UK has been measured against 198 National Indicators (NI). Local authorities agree priorities for improving the local area in conjunction with other public sector agencies, through three yearly Local Area Agreements (LAAs). These contracts with central government include no more than 35 negotiated NIs as well as 18 other statutory targets. Leicester's LAA for 2008-11 includes NI 186 - Per capita CO_2 emissions in the local authority area, with a city target *'To reduce emissions to 6.1 t CO_2 per person by 2011'* (One Leicester, 2009) as well as NI 188 - Adapting to climate change, *'To reach level 4 of 5, in developing and maintaining an action plan, by 2011, from a baseline of level 2 in 2008'* and NI 167 - Congestion – average person journey time per mile during morning peak flow, *'To only increase to 4.89 minutes per person mile, by 2011, from a baseline of 4.6 minutes in 2004/5'.* The DECC publishes statistics that chart progress against NI 186. These figures exclude emissions over which local authorities have no influence, such as motorways and some installations covered by the EU emissions trading scheme. Over the period for which figures are available, Leicester has reducing annual emissions from 7.1 t CO_2 per person in 2005, to 6.96 and 6.6 tonnes CO_2 in 2006 and 2007 respectively (DECC, 2009d). The emissions for 2007 are

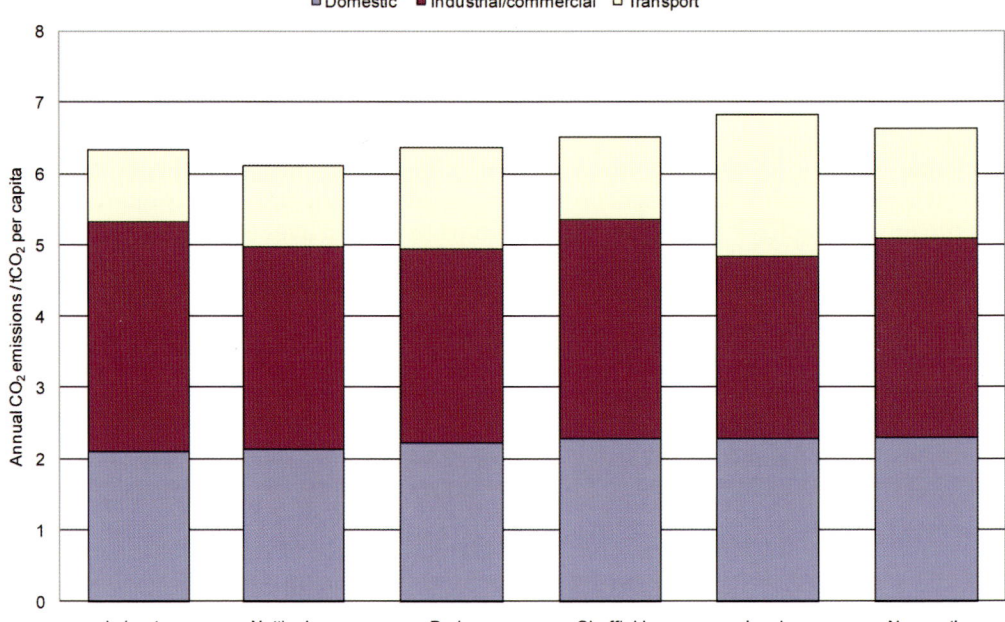

Figure 2: Comparison of per capita CO_2 emissions of Leicester and five other UK Cities derived from data published by the Department of Energy and Climate Change

comparable to those for other UK cities (Figure 2).

Whilst valuable, such aggregated data cannot answer questions that are key to urban carbon management, for instance:
- What effects will refurbishing homes have?
- Is home improvement more effective than traffic management?
- What contribution may other initiatives have (e.g., biological carbon sequestration, district heating schemes)?
- What provides greatest CO_2 reduction per £ spent?
- How would citizens react to each initiative?
- What would be the costs and benefits?
- The 4M project seeks to provide new insights that will help answer such questions.

Measuring and Modelling City Carbon Emissions

The 4M project, now in its second year, has focussed to date on measuring carbon emissions and stores across the city of Leicester, in order to enhance existing, and develop new, carbon models. The following sections describe the measurements made and the initial results from modelling.

The Living in Leicester survey

An ongoing investigation of a representative sample of Leicester households is key to understanding the relationships between household composition, socio-economic status, house type, and the energy used in homes and for travel. It also provides insights into the way people use and manage any outdoor space that maybe associated with their dwelling. The Living in Leicester survey has therefore provided a unifying focus to the measurement part of the project, and a consistent and comprehensive data set; the first such data set collected in the UK.

The face-to-face computerised questionnaire was administered at 575 homes (i.e. one in 50 Leicester homes), which were randomly selected after stratifying by percentage of detached homes and percentage with no dependent children in each of the 36 MLSOAs[1] in Leicester. The home questionnaire was devised by the 4M team and conducted on their behalf by NATCEN (the National Centre for Social Research). NATCEN's surveyors were trained with help from the 4M team and included individuals with Asian language skills (Leicester has a large Asian population)[6]. Additionally, two temperature loggers were left to record internal temperatures over a seven month period, initial gas and electricity meter readings were made at the time of interview with a final set of readings made by the 4M team after one year. More recently a detailed postal questionnaire of domestic appliance ownership and usage has been conducted, results of which have updated DECC's understanding of the patterns of appliance use. A detailed travel questionnaire is also planned.

Later in the 4M project, to probe the reasons for some of the relationships found in the survey, detailed face-to-face interviews will be conducted with approximately 50 the householders. Interviewers will present householders with their energy consumption data and the impact of travel patterns for that household. The interview will also explore knowledge of building energy conservation, willingness to invest in energy efficiency measures, implications of travel choices, and willingness to make changes to driver and travel behaviour. Results will shed light on the likely impact of the national FITs, RHI and PAYS schemes and feed into DaSTS strategy formulation.

Domestic buildings
The UK housing stock has been constructed, demolished and refitted over many centuries. Nationally, 64% of UK houses were built when no thermal standards for construction existed, including large areas of solid-wall terrace housing and post-war (1940s and 1950s) semi-detached estates. Today gas fired boilers provide central heating and hot water around 83% of homes and nearly all the rest have a combination of electric storage and fixed room heaters (BRE, 2006). In Leicester, the most frequent housing types are semi-detached dwellings (37% of the city's housing stock) and terraces (36%), which proliferate towards the city centre (Figure 3) along with flats (18%). In contrast, the detached houses are found primarily in the suburbs (10%), (ONS, 2010). Over the years many homes have been made more energy efficient by insulation and use of more modern boilers and controls.

A Community Domestic Energy Model (CDEM), (Firth et al, 2010) has been designed for predicting national carbon emissions in a previous project[7]. It is based on the steady-state energy model BREDEM-8, the Building Research Establishment Domestic Energy Model version 8 (Anderson et al, 2002) and predicts monthly space heating energy use and estimates the energy use for hot water heating, cooking, and for lights and appliances.

CDEM is designed around the assumption that English dwellings can be divided into distinct types with energy predictions made for each type rather than for each individual property: a technique that is well established in the UK for stock modelling. In CDEM, 47 archetypes, representing different geometries and ages of dwelling, are used. The number of dwellings of each geometry is derived from the last Census (ONS, 2010) and the English House Condition Survey (DCLG, 2007) enables the proportions with different heating systems,

Figure 3: Terraced housing, which is superficially easy to renovate and insulate is, in the detail, surprisingly complex, especially at the rear.

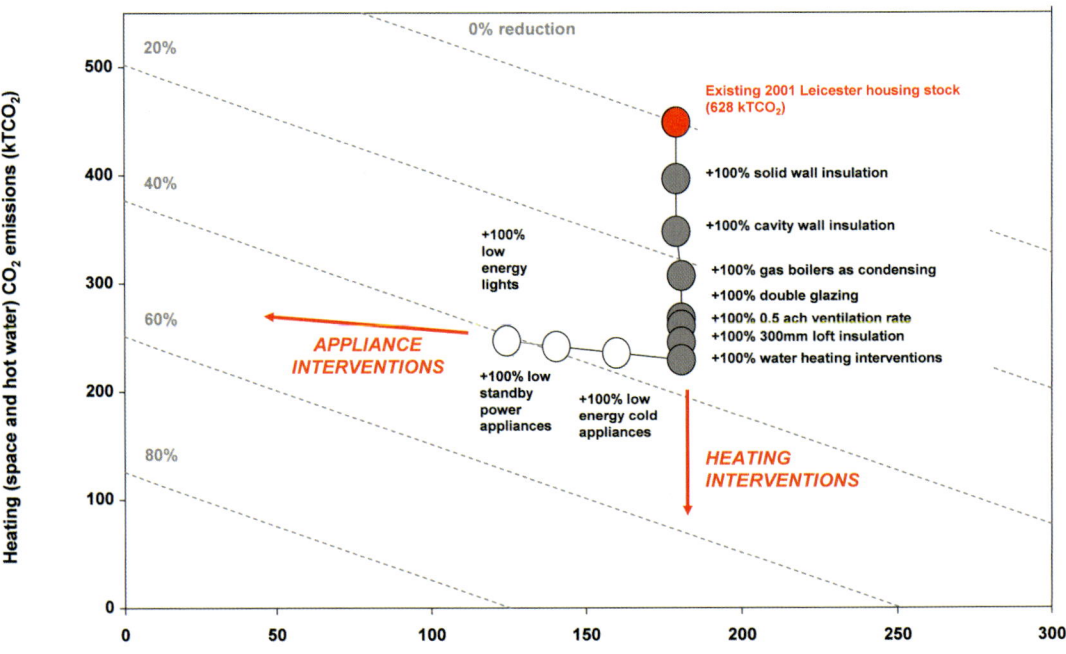

Figure 4: Predicted reductions in appliance and heating CO_2 emissions though refurbishment of the Leicester housing stock.

constructions (i.e. wall, roof and floor U-values), etc to be defined. The proportion with low energy lighting and the distribution of cooker types is provided by the Market Transformation Programme (MTP, 2007a; MTP, 2007b).

The CDEM model predicted that the 2001 Leicester housing stock of 115,752 homes had appliance CO_2 emissions of 628.0 kt CO_2 based on the 30 year average climate data, which is 5.4 t CO_2 per dwelling. This equates to 66 kg CO_2 per m^2 of dwelling floor area or 2.1 t CO_2 per person. Despite their greater exposed area, because they are newer and tend to be better insulated, detached dwelling had the lowest emission per unit floor area (62 kg CO_2 per m^2) whilst end terraces had the highest (71 kg CO_2 per m^2).

By separating out the total emissions for space heating and hot water, (primarily from burning gas), 449.0 kt CO_2, from the emissions for lighting, cooking and appliances (primarily electricity), 179.1 kt CO_2, and plotting them, respectively, on the y- and x-axis of a graph, the impact of different energy efficiency measures can readily be seen (Figure 3). On this figure, the dashed lines show contours of equal emissions and the reductions in emissions due to the complete deployment of various energy efficiency measures (i.e. insulating the 99% of Leicester homes with solid walls that are not already insulated, and filling the 69% of wall cavities that are not filled).

The measure with the most potential to reduce CO_2 emissions is to insulate solid walls; this would reduce emissions by 8% overall (Figure 4). By implementing all possible heating energy efficiency measures the overall heating CO_2 emissions are reduced to 230.8 kt CO_2 (i.e. by 35% of the total emissions). The combined effect of using low energy cold appliance, electrical items with low standby power and low energy lights, is to reduce appliance CO_2 emissions to 122.6 kt CO_2 (i.e. by 19% of the total), however the reduction in electricity consumption reduces internal heat gains and so the heating CO_2 emissions increased slightly (from 230.8 kt CO_2 to 248.6 kt CO_2). Overall therefore, it is estimated that the combined effect of the heating and appliance measures would reduce the overall 2001 Leicester housing stock CO_2 emissions by around 41%.

The overriding messages from such modelling are that it is much more effective to focus on heating energy demand reduction than appliance energy demand reduction. But, even if all possible conventional energy efficiency measures are undertaken in every possible house the emissions reduction could not possibly approach 80%. Clearly, embedded new and renewable energy systems, district heating and other initiatives must also be adopted if deep cuts in emissions are to be achieved from the housing stock. Energy efficiency measures are likely to achieve much less in practice because many home owners will not invest - despite the incentive offered through PAYS. The follow-up household interviews seek to place a figure on the number of home owners that might take up such measures and also on the number that might adopt new and renewable energy systems.

Non-domestic buildings
Non-domestic buildings are, roughly speaking, all those that are not dwellings and so the range of sizes and shapes, construction types, occupancy patterns and heating, cooling, ventilating and lighting strategies is consequently very wide. Cinemas, hospitals, department stores, office blocks, corner shops, factories, supermarkets, workshops, schools, data centres and warehouses are all examples. This diversity makes it extremely difficult to develop robust models to predict the energy demands and thus the CO_2 emissions. Nevertheless, the 4M project is attempting to do this, and to do it in a way that

will enable the many thousands of non-domestic buildings in Leicester to be analysed.

There are two main alternatives for modelling such large numbers of buildings. One option is to assign all buildings to a small set of distinct archetypes, based on their built form. These archetypes are then modelled in detail using dynamic thermal models that can predict the hourly energy demands and internal temperatures. The results are then combined in proportion to the Leicester's actual building stock composition to represent the overall behaviour at the city scale. The alternative approach is to model every building, however with this approach, dynamic thermal modelling is not feasible because the computing resource requirements would be excessive. With either option, knowledge about buildings' construction, energy systems and occupancy, is insufficient to justify the use of dynamic models.

These problems can be avoided by using simpler reduced-dataset models, which then enable each individual non-domestic buildings to be modelled. The model used in 4M is based on the European Standard BS EN ISO 13790:2008 (BSI, 2008) which is used in a range of models, including the UK's simplified building energy model (DCLG, 2008). It includes a representation of the building physics, albeit simplified, allowing the effect of changes in insulation, energy system, occupancy period etc to be explored. Although this approach reduces the quantity of data required about each building, the amount of information needed on the non-domestic stock of Leicester is still considerable, and its collection represents a major challenge.

It is well known (e.g. Mortimer et al, 2000a) that one of the fundamental determinants of energy use in non-domestic buildings is what they are used for. The business taxation database of the

Figure 5: LIDAR-derived 2.5D building block model and corresponding image of building

Valuation Office Agency (VOA) provides this information and the floor areas associated with that use. For this reason the VOA database is the most important source available. However, the VOA database deals not with *buildings* but with *premises* and the relationship between the two is complex. Buildings can contain single or multiple premises and premises can consist of parts of a building, a whole building, multiple buildings or a combination of multiple and part-buildings. What is needed is a way to relate premises and buildings that allows the modelling of buildings despite using premise-based data. This was achieved by using Leicester City Council's Local Land and Property Gazetteer (LLPG) which provides a link between premises and buildings. Analysis of the LLPG enabled the 4M team to produce an initial list of the non-domestic buildings in Leicester and the floor area given over to various activities.

The exposed wall area of each building, i.e. the area that is not touching an adjacent building, was estimated from a 2.5D model[8] of the city if Leicester (e.g. Figure 5) and from this the energy model can estimate the heat losses and gains and thus the energy necessary to heat and cool the building.

Detailed surveys of 340 premises in four cities, were undertaken between 1992 and 2002 (Mortimer et al, 2000b). These room-level surveys recorded the activity, floor area and the associated electrical equipment. Together with the period of room occupancy and the usage of the equipment and lights the energy demand profile per m^2 for each activity can be estimated. These data can then be used to generate the electrical energy demands and associated internal heat gains for lights and equipment.

Other required data pose even more formidable challenges. For example, the model requires a measure for each building's thermal mass, and sensitivity analysis shows that this has a significant impact on the results. In the absence of any direct methods of determining this parameter, which in any case is rather ill-defined, it may be necessary to combine a range of techniques such as surveys, historical mapping and written records.

The 4M non-domestic model, when completed, will allow the impact on CO_2 emissions of a range of interventions to be assessed, such as wall insulation, improved glazing and shading devices, more efficient electrical lighting, connection to a district heating system, and provision of local renewable energy generation.

Transport
Using the data from the transport section of the domestic household questionnaire, the CO_2 emissions generated by Leicester residents through travel for work, shopping, leisure and trips to take children to school can be estimated. The questionnaire focussed on journeys that began or ended at home - including multistage journeys such as home-school-work-shops-home; commuting on business to the airport, rail station etc. Raw data were collected on each household's vehicles (type, fuel use, engine size, age) and the monthly usage (frequency and occupancy) for different journey types. The journey types were split into four categories - very short (0-3 miles), short (3-8 miles), medium (8-50 miles) and long (50-100 miles). All journeys made were assumed to begin within the Leicester city boundary and through trips on the motorways were not included. The results produced an estimate for annual CO_2 emissions for such journeys of this type of around 0.6 t CO_2 per person, with trips of medium length, typically commuting to work, being responsible for 45% of these emissions.

The distribution of CO_2 emissions across the city has been estimated through the use of the Airviro Air Quality Management System (SHMI, 2009), combined with the latest emissions factors from the Department for Transport (Boulter et al, 2009). Traffic flows used in the estimation are obtained from a SATURN (Atkins, 2010) model of 3715 links within the city, combined with count data from approximately 952 sites.

The distribution of traffic, and therefore emissions, for 2005 represents the baseline against which traffic management scenarios will be tested, and is shown in Figure 6. Future work will compare the predictions from micro-simulations with detailed road-side emissions measurements to improve estimates of the local scale emissions. This improved model, combined with air dispersion models, will enable the concentration of emissions and their variation with time across the city to be estimated more accurately. The study of transport emissions management focuses on the impact of road traffic schemes and green transport plans. A self-completed web-based questionnaire targeted at 30 schools and 30 places of work within the city will provide data to enable an estimate of the carbon emissions associated with regular travel to be estimated and the likely uptake of green travel plans[9] to be explored. Various traffic management schemes will also be explored and of particular interest are: shifting from private car usage in favour of walking; cycling and public transport; reduction of vehicle speeds; changes in vehicle fleet composition including increased use of electric and hybrid vehicles; and the integration of new Park and Ride services. By combining these data with those from the detailed household survey (see above), and by using the enhanced road transport models, the impact on the spatial distribution of emissions will be better understood.

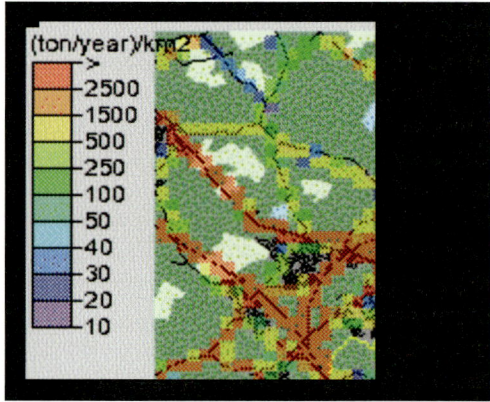

Figure 6: Distribution of annual CO2 emissions form Leicester road traffic as predicted by the Airviro programme suite
(resolution 250mx250m squares)

Biological carbon storage and sequestration

Existing empirical data on biological urban carbon pools remains scarce, with inventories of trees restricted to public lands (Zipperer et al, 1997; Whitford et al, 2001) and estimates of soil carbon extrapolated from a small number of samples (e.g., Pouyat et al, 2006). Whilst this approach has generated a wealth of useful information, it does not fully account for the possible variation associated with different types of green space that occur in urban areas. At the current time, the paucity of such comprehensive information at a pertinent scale and resolution for urban landscape planning, policy-making and management is a major hurdle to our ability to understand, value and protect these above and below ground carbon pools. In the 4M project, a detailed investigation of the carbon stores associated with vegetation and soils was undertaken in different types of green space (herbaceous

Figure 7: Soil sampling and subsequent laboratory analysis enables the carbon content of urban soils to be measured. There is a substantially higher concentration of black carbon, primarily from diesel-fuelled vehicles, close to main roads.

vegetation, shrubs, tall shrubs, trees, domestic gardens and allotments) across the city. This involved surveying over 2000 trees and taking soil cores from approximately 200 independent sites. Subsequently, these data have been used to generate and parameterise models that estimate urban carbon storage.

The significance of urban biological carbon stores is ultimately dependent on the management they receive. For example, the generation of carbon emissions arising from day-to-day management activities (e.g., through the use of lawn mowers, chainsaws, vehicles, chipping machines, fertilizer application) may even potentially negate any positive sequestration effects if they are not minimised. Information derived from Leicester City Council and the Living in Leicester household questionnaire will improve our understanding of such matters for both public and privately owned green spaces.

In the long-term, the carbon sequestered into vegetation will eventually be returned to the atmosphere when it dies or is destroyed, and replacement is therefore necessary to counterbalance the CO_2 released by decomposition (Nowak et al, 2002). Similarly, where possible, the decomposition of waste material should be limited via lasting carbon storage solutions (e.g. wood products) or the biomass used as an alternative renewable fuel source so that the release of CO_2 is accompanied by substitution for fossil fuel energy sources (Nowak et al, 2002; MacFarlane, 2009). In some instances, trees lost in urban areas will be replaced through natural regeneration, but the majority are likely to require active replanting in order to maintain current stores of carbon (Rowntree & Nowak, 1991). This is of particular importance on public land,

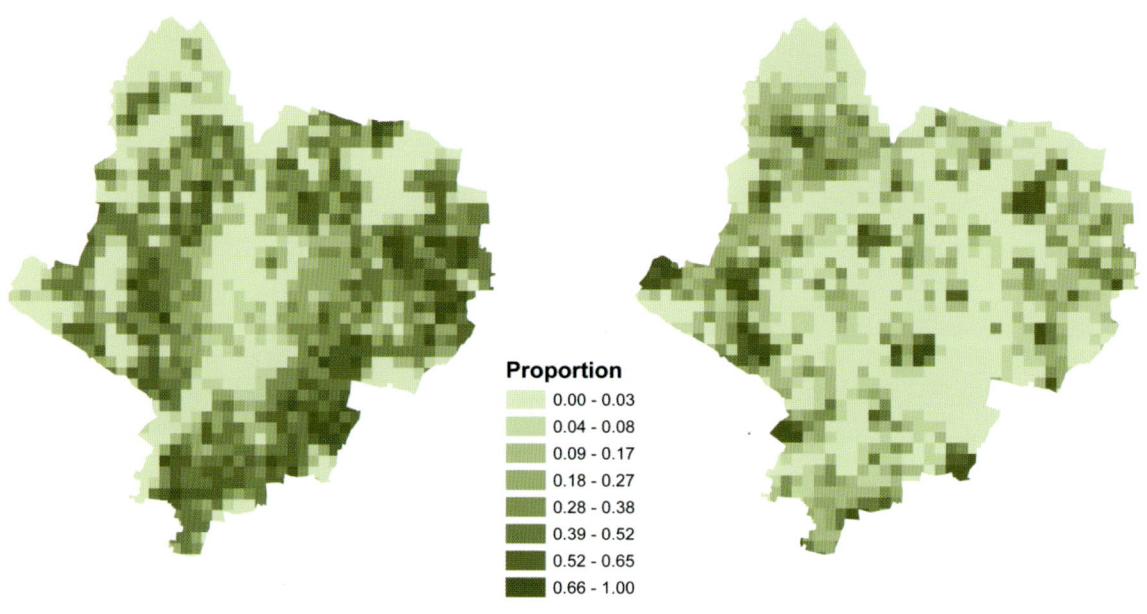

Figure 8: The distribution and proportion of (a) domestic gardens and (b) council managed land occurring across Leicester (resolution 250m x 250m squares)

where trees are frequently removed or subject to surgery in response to concerns about subsidence or human safety (London Assembly Environment Committee, 2007; Britt & Johnson, 2008). However, this issue cannot be addressed simply by top-down policies focused on land that is publicly controlled, as much of the urban landscape is privately owned. Bottom-up policy schemes encouraging householders to participate in strategies to augment urban biological carbon pools must therefore also be prioritised. In the UK this is particularly pressing due to increased infill development and the 'garden grabbing' phenomenon, as well as a growing trend to pave over front gardens to create off-road parking (RHS, 2007).

In order to facilitate the development of targeted policies that will maximise biological carbon storage through increased sequestration, above and below ground carbon pools are being mapped to assess how they vary in relation to land ownership (Figure 7). It is anticipated that policies to increase carbon storage within gardens, and other privately owned lands, will be seen as more creative and positive by the general public than many other approaches to mitigating emissions, such as energy from waste schemes and road use taxation.

The impact on below-ground carbon stores of capping formerly biological active soil with impervious surfaces is, as yet, unclear and has received little attention by researchers (Lorenz & Lal, 2009). Within urban areas, artificial surfaces (e.g., roads, pavements, hard standing, car parks, patios) make up a significant proportion of overall land cover. Indeed, in Leicester approximately 27% of land is capped in such a manner. The next phase of work has begun to address this issue and further refine soil carbon storage estimates.

Outcome and Conclusions

The 4M consortium have collected primary data and combined this with secondary data as a basis for understanding the carbon footprint of the UK city of Leicester. These data will assist the development of models describing domestic and non-domestic building energy demand, traffic emissions and biological carbon storage in vegetation and soils. Some initial observations can be made from the work undertaken so far.

Questionnaire surveys have provided *in situ* insight into household energy, travel and garden management behaviour through the involvement of individuals within their own homes. This has proved invaluable for development of an integrated dataset of information about three sectors that are typically studied separately. The next phase of analysis will seek to identify patterns across the participating households for use in follow-up interviews and inclusion in model development.

A community domestic energy model has indicated that refurbishment of the Leicester housing stock, could achieve a maximum reduction in household carbon emissions of about 41%. The model is being refined, and further data will be collected, so that the emissions cuts possible by individual households and the costs of achieving these can be calculated.

A non-domestic energy model capable of deployment at the city scale is being developed by integrating available diverse datasets. The model will be combined with digital mapping resources to realise a powerful support tool that will enable planning mechanisms to play an effective role managing carbon emissions from non-domestic buildings.

The calculation of carbon emissions associated with travel will extend current knowledge by estimating the carbon emissions associated with congestion. The enhanced models will allow the emissions reduction due to changes made by individual travellers to be established as well as the knock-on effects on other road users. Questionnaires will provide a better understanding of the trip characteristics of gross emitters and inform policy aimed at modifying travel behaviour.

The carbon stored in urban soils and vegetation is much greater than previously assumed. Indeed, on a per unit area basis, urban carbon pools are substantially larger than those associated with agricultural land. Future work will focus on determining how to enhance the capacity of urban areas to sequester carbon through further 'greening' of the environment and careful management of green spaces.

The findings from Leicester, and the data collection and modelling tools developed, will, when the project is complete, open up the possibility of measuring, modelling, mapping and managing the carbon emissions of other cities in the UK, Europe and beyond.

Acknowledgements
The authors are particularly grateful to Leicester City Council employees for their assistance, in particular, Satish Shah, Jolanta Obszynska, Jay Parmar, Duncan Bell and David Mee, Ruth Hamilton. The 4M project has been assisted by the efforts of several higher degree students: Rory Jones, Tom Kane and Jon Morris (Loughborough University), Jill Fisher and Rob Liddiard (De Montfort University), Justin Cairns (Newcastle University) and Sarah McCormack (University of Sheffield). The team are assisted by an international advisory panel that represents a range of stakeholders. Infoterra kindly provided access to LandBase, and with permission from the City Council also provided aerial LiDAR and building height information. Ordnance Survey MasterMap data were provided through EDINA/DigiMap or directly from the Ordnance Survey. The 4M consortium is funded for four years by the Engineering and Physical Sciences Research Council (EPSRC) under their Sustainable Urban Environment programme (grant EP/F007604/1).

—

Endnotes

1. The benefits that humans receive from ecosystems, such as the atmospheric, water & nutrient cycles and recreational opportunities.

2. DECC publishes regional and local authority fuel consumption figures for: electricity, gas, road transport, remaining fuels (coal, manufactured solid fuels, non-road transport petroleum and renewables) and total energy consumption (DECC, 2009a). Electricity and gas consumption data (domestic and non-domestic) are also available at middle layer super output area level (MLSOA, minimum population 5,000, approximately 2,000 households) and lower layer super output area level (LLSOA, minimum population 1,000, approximately 400 households) in England and Wales; as well as at intermediate geography zone level (IGZ, minimum population 4,000, approximately 2,000 households) in Scotland (DECC, 2010b). The gas and electricity consumption figures are based on sales figures estimated from metered consumption whereas road transport and other fuels are modelled by AEA Energy and Environment on behalf of DECC, using a number of data sources. Total fuel use is simply the aggregate of the others. At MLSOA and LLSOA there are some problems with misallocation (incorrect sector or incorrect geographical area) and issues of disclosure prevent proper allocation in commercially sensitive areas with significant consumers.

3. Electricity meters that record half-hourly energy use and relay the data to a central database. Feed-back to householders is possible, which can aid their understanding of the link between their activities and the resulting energy demand.

4. The Carbon trust has indicated that the carbon footprint of the UK's non-domestic buildings can be reduced by over a third by 2020 given appropriate strategies, including all feasible energy efficiency measures, improved lighting, and heating and lighting controls (Carbon Trust, 2009).

5. The data points bear no direct relationship to the households surveyed but preserve a sense of the number and rough location of those interviewed.

6. All the interviews were undertaken between 17/3/09 and 18/7/09 and each interview lasted about 45 minutes and had at least 247 questions supported by 51 show cards. There are 1411 anonymous and 157 confidential variables in the complete data set.

7. The 'Carbon Reduction in Buildings: a Socio-technical, Longitudinal Study of Carbon Use in Buildings' (CaRB) consortium of 5 universities sought to: improve the understanding of how people actually use energy in buildings; formalise this understanding in models that describe the current domestic and non-domestic building stock and the patterns of

energy use; and produce tools to assist policy makers, consultants and others in their efforts to reduce national CO2 emissions (see Lomas 2010 and at http://www.carb.org.uk/).

8. The 2.5D model was created using LIDAR technology, in which a plane overflies the city so that a laser can rapidly scan the surface below. By analying the reflected light the relative heights of objects, such as trees and buildings, can be estimated. Combining this data with Ordnance Survey MasterMap data, enables the heights and exact perimeter position of buildings to be deduced and a 2.5D building block model produced.

9. Schemes such as ride sharing, using buses, minibus services, walking, providing safe routes to schools, provision of shower facilities, recycling of bicycles in schools, and providing loans for purchasing bicycles.

References

Anderson, B., Chapman, P., Cutland, N., Dickson, C., Doran, S., Henderson, G., Henderson, J., Iles, P., Kosmina, L, & Shorrock, L. (2002) BREDEM-8: Model Description 2001 Update. Building Research Establishment, Watford, UK.

Atkins. (2010) SATURN (Simulation and Assignment of Traffic to Urban Road Networks). WS Atkins and The Institute for Transport Studies, University of Leeds. [Online] Available from: https://saturnsoftware.co.uk/index.html [Accessed 30th June 2010].

Boulter, P.G, Barlow T. J., McCrae, I.S. and Latham, S. (2009) Emissions factors 2009 Final summary report. Report prepared by the Transport Research Laboratory (TRL) on behalf of the UK Department for Transport. [Online] Available from: http://www.dft.gov.uk/pgr/roads/environment/emissions/summaryreport.pdf [Accessed 28th June 2010].

BRE. (2006) Energy use in homes: space and water heating. Building Research Establishment. [Online] Available from: http://projects.bre.co.uk/energyuse/pdf/2003/Space_and_Water_Heating_2003.pdf [Accessed 8th July 2010].

Britt, C. & Johnson, M. (2008) Trees in Towns II: A New Survey of Urban Trees in England and their Condition and Management. Department for Communities and Local Government, London.

Brown, N., Wright, J.A., Shukla, A. & Stuart, G. (2010) Longitudinal analysis of energy metering data from non-domestic buildings. Building Research & Information, 38(1), 80-91.

BSI. (2008) BS EN ISO 13790:2008. Energy performance of buildings- Calculation of energy use for space heating and cooling. London, British Standards Institution.

Burton, E. (2000) The compact city: just or just compact? A preliminary analysis. Urban Studies, 37, 1969-2001.

Carbon Trust. (2009) Building the future today: transforming the economic and carbon performance of the buildings we work in. Carbon Trust. Report CTC765. [Online] Available from: http://www.carbontrust.co.uk/Publications/pages/publicationdetail.aspx?id=CTC765 [Accessed 8th July 2010].

CCC. (2008) Building a low-carbon economy – the UK's contribution to tackling climate change. Committee on Climate Change. [Online] Available from: http://www.theccc.org.uk/pdf/TSO-ClimateChange.pdf [Accessed 8th July 2010].

CCC. (2009) Meeting Carbon Budgets – the Need for a Step Change. Committee on Climate Change. [Online] Available from: http://downloads.theccc.org.uk/21667%20CCC%20Report%20AW%20WEB.pdf [Accessed 8th July 2010].

CfIT. (2007) Transport and Climate Change: Recommendations to deliver greater cost-effective carbon savings from transport by 2020. Commission for Integrated Transport. [Online] Available from: http://cfit.independent.gov.uk/pubs/2007/climatechange/pdf/2007climatechange.pdf [Accessed 8th July 2010].

Chen, H and Bell, M.C. (2002) Instrumented city database analysts using multi-agents. Transportation Research Part C: Emerging Technologies, 10(5-6), 419-432.

City of Leicester. (2003) City of Leicester Climate Change Strategy, October 2003. Leicester Partnership and Leicester Environment partnership. [Online] Available from: http://www.leicester.gov.uk/your-council-services/ep/the-environment/climate-change/climate-change/strategies-plans-and-guides/climate-change-document-folder/ [Accessed 8th July 2010]

CLG. (2006) Building a greener future: towards zero carbon development. Communities and Local Government. [Online] Available from: http://www.communities.gov.uk/documents/planningandbuilding/pdf/153125.pdf [Accessed 8th July 2010].

DCLG. (2007) The English House Condition Survey. Department of Communities and Local Government. [Online] Available from: www.communities.gov.uk/ehcs [accessed 17th July 2007].

DCLG. (2008) SBEM Technical Manual. Department for Communities and Local Government. [Online] Available from: http://www.ncm.bre.co.uk/files/SBEM_Technical _Manual_v3.0.b_24Oct08.pdf [Accessed 9th July 2010].

DECC. (2009a) Guidance note for regional energy data. Department of Energy and Climate Change. Publication URN 09D/857. [Online] Available from: http://www.decc.gov.uk/en/content/cms/statistics/regional/regional.aspx [Accessed 15th June 2010].

DECC. (2009b) Be part of the Great British Refurb – to cut emissions and cut energy costs. Department of Energy and Climate Change. Press release. [Online] Available from http://hes.decc.gov.uk/news/press-notice-from-ed-miliband/index.html [Acessed 8th July 2010].

DECC. (2009c) Towards a smarter future: Government response to the consultation on electricity and gas smart metering. Department of Energy and Climate Change. [Online] Available from: http://www.decc.gov.uk/assets/decc/Consultations/Smart%20Metering%20for%20Electricity%20and%20Gas/1_20091202094543_e_@@_ResponseElectricityGasConsultation.pdf [Accessed 8th July 2010].

DECC. (2009d) Local and Regional CO2 Emissions Estimates for 2005-2007. Department of Energy and Climate Change spreadsheet. [Online] Available from: http://www.decc.gov.uk/en/content/cms/statistics/indicators/ni186/ni186.aspx [Accessed 15th June 2010].

DECC. (2010a) UK Climate change sustainable development indicator: 2009 Greenhouse gas emissions, provisional figures and 2008 greenhouse gas emissions, final figures by fuel type and and-user. Department of Energy and Climate Change. [Online] Available from: http://www.decc.gov.uk/assets/decc/statistics/climate_change/1_20100325084241_e_@@_ghgnationalstatsrelease.pdf [Accessed 9th July 2010].

DECC. (2010b) Guidance note for the DECC MLSOA/IGZ and LLSOA electricity and gas consumption data. Department of Energy and Climate Change. Publication URN 10D/668. [Online] Available from: http://www.decc.gov.uk/en/content/cms/statistics/regional/mlsoa_llsoa/mlsoa_llsoa.aspx [Accessed 15th June 2010].

DECC. (2010c) Feed-in tariffs: Governments response to the summer 2009 consultation. Department of Energy and Climate Change. [Online] Available from: http://www.decc.gov.uk/assets/decc/Consultations/Renewable%20Electricity%20Financial%20Incentives/1_20100204120204_e_@@_FITsconsultationresponseandGovdecisions.pdf [Accessed 8th July 2010].

DECC. (2010d) Renewable heat incentive: consultation on the proposed RHI financial support scheme. Department of Energy and Climate Change. [Online] Available from: http://www.decc.gov.uk/assets/decc/Consultations/RHI/1_20100204094844_e_@@_ConsultationonRenewableHeatIncentive.pdf [Accessed 8th July 2010].

DfT. (2007) Towards a sustainable transport system: supporting economic growth in a low carbon world. Department for Transport. [Online] Available from: http://www.official-documents.gov.uk/document/cm72/7226/7226.pdf [Accessed 8th July 2010]

DfT. (2008) Delivering a sustainable transport system: main Report. Department for Transport. [Online] Available from: http://webarchive.nationalarchives.gov.uk/+/http://www.dft.gov.uk/about/strategy/transportstrategy/dasts/dastsreport.pdf [Accessed 8th July 2010].

Dyson, K.E., Mobbs, D.C. & Milne, R. (2009) Annual inventory estimates for the UK (WP 1.1). In: Dyson, K.E. (ed.) Inventory and projections of UK emissions by sources and removals by sinks due to land use, land use change and forestry. Annual report, July 2009, Contract GA01088. Department for the Environment, Food and Rural Affairs, London. pp. 13-49.

EU. (2010) Directive 2010/31/EU of the European parliament and of the council, of 19 May 2010, on the energy performance of buildings (recast). European Union. [Online] Available from: http://eur-lex.europa.eu/LexUriServ/LexUriServ.do?uri=OJ:L:2010:153:0013:0035:EN:PDF [Accesses 9th July 2010].

Firth, S.K., Lomas, K.J. & Wright, A.J. (2010) Targeting household energy-efficiency measures using sensitivity analysis. Building Research & Information, 38(1), 25-41.

Goode, D. (2006) Green Infrastructure. Report to the Royal Commission on Environmental Pollution, London.

Great Britain. (2008) Climate Change Act 2008: Elizabeth II. Chapter 27. London, The Stationery Office.

Hansen, A.J., Knight, R.L., Marzluff ,J.M., Powell, S., Brown, K., Gude, P.H. & Jones, A. (2005) Effects of exurban development on biodiversity: patterns, mechanisms and research needs. Ecological Applications, 15, 1893-1905.

HM Government. (2010) Warm homes, greener homes: a strategy for household energy management. Department of Energy and Climate Change. [Online] Available from: http://www.decc.gov.uk/assets/decc/What%20we%20do/Supporting%20consumers/Household%20Energy%20Management/1_20100331101157_e_@@_warmhomesgreenerhomeshemstrategy.pdf [Accessed 8th July 2010].

HM Treasury. (2008) Budget 2008. HM Treasury. Report HC388. [Online] Available from: http://webarchive.nationalarchives.gov.uk/+/http://www.hm-treasury.gov.uk/media/9/9/bud08_completereport.pdf [Accessed 8th July 2010].

IEA. (2009) Key World Energy Statistics 2009. OECD/International Energy Agency.

IPCC. (2007) Climate Change 2007: Synthesis Report, Summary for Policymakers. Intergovernmental Panel on Climate Change. [Online] Available from: http://www.ipcc.ch/publications_and_data/ar4/syr/en/spm.html [Accessed 9th July 2010].

Lomas, K. J. (2010) Carbon reduction in existing buildings: a transdisciplinary approach. Building Research and Information (Special Issue CaRB Project), 38(1), 1-11.

London Assembly Environment Committee. (2007). Chainsaw massacre: a review of London's street trees. Greater London Authority, London.

Loram, A., Tratalos, J., Warren, P.H. & Gaston, K.J. (2007) Urban domestic gardens (X): the extent and structure of the resource in five major cities. Landscape Ecology, 22, 601-615.

Lorenz, K. & Lal, R. (2009) Biogeochemical C and N cycles in urban soils. Environment International, 35, 1-8.

MacFarlane, D.W. (2009) Potential availability of urban wood biomass in Michigan: implications for energy production, carbon sequestration and sustainable forest management in the USA. Biomass and Bioenergy, 33, 628-634.

Mortimer, N.D., Elsayad, M.A., Grant, J.F. (2000a) Patterns of energy use in nondomestic buildings. Environment and Planning B: Planning and Design, 27, 709-720.

Mortimer, N.D., Ashley, A. and Rix, J.H.R. (2000b) Detailed energy surveys of nondomestic buildings. Environment and Planning B: Planning and Design, 27, 25-32.

MTP. (2007a) Assumptions for Energy Scenarios in the Domestic Lighting Sector. Market Transformation Programme. Briefing Note No. BNDL01. [Online] Available from: http://www.mtprog.com [Accessed 17th August 2007].

MTP. (2007b) Assumptions Underlying the Energy Projections of Cooking Appliances. Market Transformation Programme. Briefing Note No. BNCK01. [Online] Available from: http://www.mtprog.com [Accessed 17th August 2007].

Nowak, D.J. & Crane, D.E. (2002) Carbon storage and sequestration by urban trees in the USA. Environmental Pollution, 116, 381-389.

ODPM. (2006) Land Use Change in England: Residential Development to 2004 – January update. Office of the Deputy Prime Minister. [Online] Available from: http://www.communities.gov.uk/documents/planningandbuilding/pdf/143738.pdf [Accessed 9th July 2010].

One Leicester. (2009) Leicester's Local Area Agreement (revised March 2009). One Leicester. [Online] Available from: http://www.oneleicester.com/leicester-partnership/leicesters-local-area-agreement/. [Accessed 8th July 2010].

ONS. (2009) National population projections, 2008-based. Office for National Statistics. [Online] Available from: http://www.statistics.gov.uk/pdfdir/pproj1009.pdf [Accessed 9th June 2010].

ONS. (2010) Results of the 2001 Census. Office for National Statistics. [Online] Available from: www.neighbourhood.statistics.gov.uk [accessed 17th June 2010].

Pataki, D.E., Alig, R.J., Fung, A.S., Golubiewski, N.E., Kennedy, C.A., McPherson, E.G., Nowak, D.J., Pouyat, R.V. & Romero, Lankao P. (2006) Urban ecosystems and the North American carbon cycle. Global Change Biology, 12, 2092-2102.

Pouyat, R.V., Yesilonis, I.D. & Nowak, D.J. (2006) Carbon storage by urban soils in the United States. Journal of Environmental Quality, 35, 1566-1575.

PRB. (2009) 2009 World Population Data Sheet. Population Reference Bureau. [Online] Available from: http://www.prb.org/pdf09/09wpds_eng.pdf [Accessed 7th June 2010].

RHS. (2007). Gardening Matters. Royal Horticultural Society, London.

Rowntree, R.A. & Nowak, D.J. (1991) Quantifying the role of urban forests in removing atmospheric carbon dioxide. Journal of Arboriculture, 17, 269-275.

Schoon, N. (2001) The chosen city. London, Spon Press. ISBN 0-415-25802-2.

SDC. (2010) Sustainable Development Commission: Transport. Sustainable Development Commission. [Online] Available from: http://www.sd-commission.org.uk/pages/transport.html [Accessed 22nd July 2010].

SMHI. (2009) SMHI Airviro. The Swedish Meteorological and Hydrological Institute. [Online] Available from: http://www.smhi.se/airviro [Accessed 28th June 2010].

UN. (2010) Millennium Development Goals indicators, Carbon dioxide emissions (CO_2), thousand metric tons of CO_2. Produced by the Carbon Dioxide Information Analysis Center (CDIAC) for the United Nations Statistics Division. [Online] Available from: http://mdgs.un.org/unsd/mdg/SeriesDetail.aspx?srid=749&crid= [Accessed 9th July 2010].

UNFPA. (2007) 2007 State of World Population. The United Nations Population Fund. [Online] Available from: http://www.unfpa.org/pds/urbanization.htm [Accessed 7th June 2010].

Whitford, V., Ennos, A.R. & Handley, J.F. (2001) "City form and natural processs"– indicators for the ecological performance of urban areas and their application to Merseyside, UK. Landscape and Urban Planning, 57, 91–103.

Wiedmann, T. & Minx, J. (2008) Chapter 1: A Definition of 'Carbon Footprint'. In: Pertsova, C. C. (ed.) Ecological Economics Research Trends. Hauppauge, Nova Science Publishers. pp. 1-11.

Zipperer, W.C., Sisinni, S.M. & Pouyat, R.V. (1997) Urban tree cover: an ecological perspective. Urban Ecosystems, 1, 229-246.

Rebuilding after a Natural Disaster: Using the Opportunity to be "better than ever"

Long Beach, Mississippi, USA

Dhiru A. Thadani

Hurricane Katrina focused the world's attention on the devastation of the city of New Orleans in August 2005. Less media attention was paid to the eleven gulf coast cities in Mississippi, where over 200,000 residents were left homeless. Governor Haley Barbour organized the Governor's Commission on Recovery, Rebuilding and Renewal, which engaged in an unprecedented partnership with the Congress for the New Urbanism (CNU).

In a matter of six weeks the CNU marshaled one hundred of its experienced designers, planners, and other member professionals from across the nation, to join forces with a like number of Mississippi based architects and planners. These volunteers conducted the

Top:
Photograph of the City of Long Beach taken shortly after Hurricane Katrina struck the coast. The main street, Jeff Davis is marked with a yellow dash line. The east-west railroad tracks that run parallel to the coastline served as a levee, a barrier for the flood waters.

Bottom:
The Mississippi Rebuilding Forum was held on October 11 - 18, 2005 at the Isle of Capri Casino/Hotel Ballroom in Biloxi. Within the ballroom designated work areas were assigned to each of the eleven coastal towns. Approximately 200 volunteers participated in the forum.

Washington DC based architect Katie Poindexter reviewing satellite imagery of Long Beach at the Mississippi Rebuilding Forum.

Long Beach Alderman and architect Mark Lishen and local architect Lisa Herron collaborate on the master plan drawing.

Team Leader, Dhiru Thadani discusses the plan with Long Beach officials and stakeholders.

six-day Mississippi Rebuilding Forum, a participatory public workshop held in a partially habitable casino hotel in Biloxi. This round-the-clock collaborative meeting pooled designers with local officials, citizens, and stakeholders who together discussed ideas and brainstormed solutions for rebuilding the eleven devastated coastal cities. The goal was to rebuild in a better way with a consensus vision and practical plans based on the spirit of place, while incorporating the natural conditions of local climate, topography, soil, and cultural context.

At the end of the forum, each coastal community was provided with a rebuilding master plan that was based on the principles embodied in the Charter of the Congress for the New Urbanism. The ease with which the design team arrived at eleven consensus-based plans can be attributed to close adherence to the principles of the CNU Charter, which are organized into three scales: 1) the region: metropolis, city, and town; 2) the neighborhood, district, and corridor; and 3) the block, street, and building.

The plans organized metropolitan regions composed of well-structured cities, towns, and neighborhoods with identifiable centers and edges. New development was to be compact and designated in urban areas, whereas farmland and environmentally sensitive areas were to be preserved in rural areas. This was a direct response to the failures of pre-Katrina planning paradigms that had resulted in a weakening sense of community and public life, a non-existent public realm, and a lack of identifiable places.

The Commission understood the benefits proposed, which emphasized civic life, public space, and schools located within walking distance of students. They were anxious for local jurisdictions to adopt these principles, seize the opportunity presented by Hurricane Katrina, and make the coast "better than ever." Furthermore there was overwhelming sentiment to rebuild sustainable and

Banner sign that was hung soon after the hurricane.

Damage Assessment Diagram which graphically illustrates the preliminary assessment of damage caused by Hurricane Katrina. The information shown is a combination of the City of Long Beach's Parcel Damage Assessment Map, post-Katrina aerial photographs, and citizen reports.

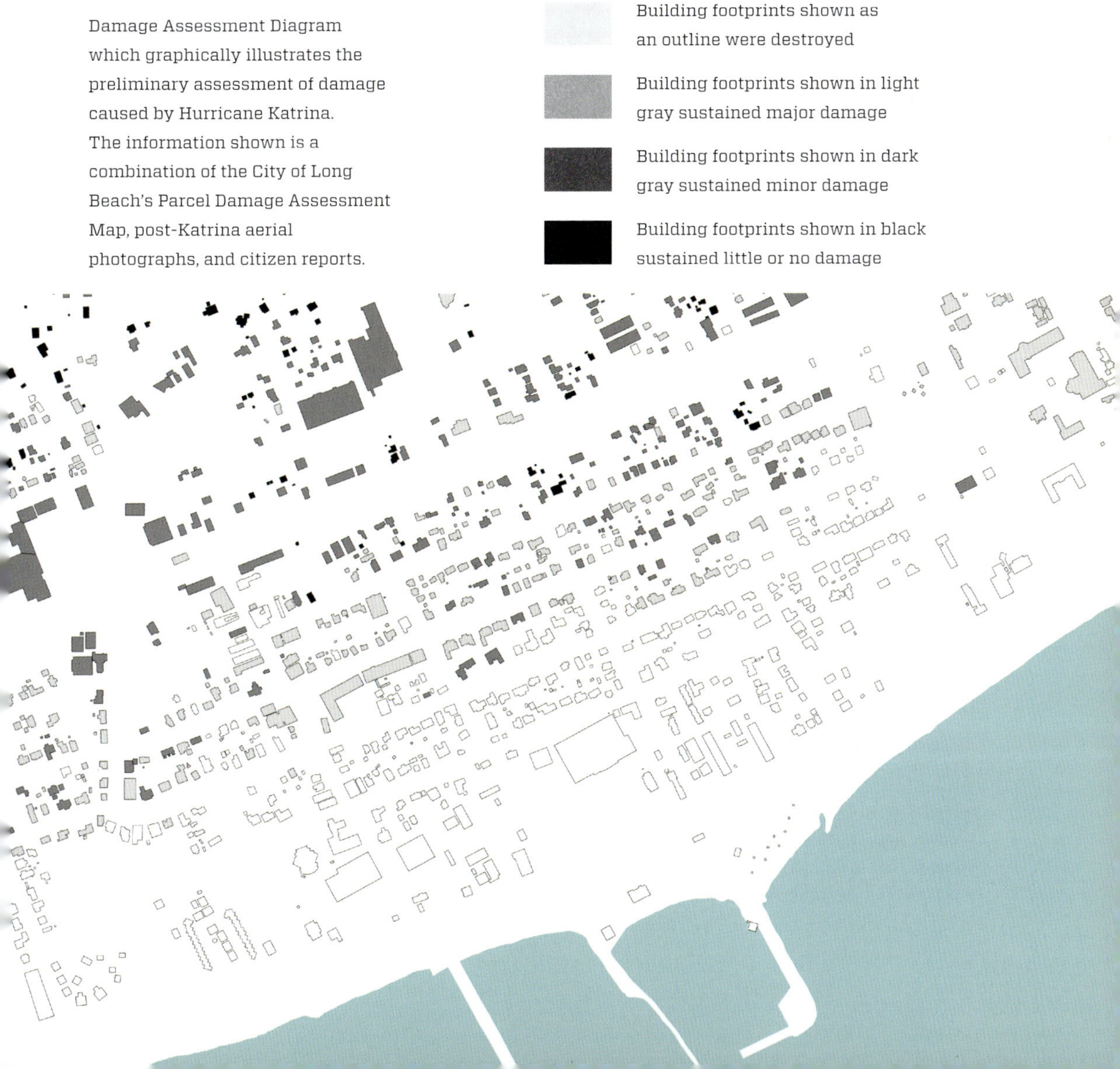

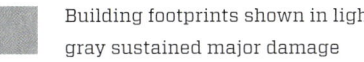 Building footprints shown as an outline were destroyed

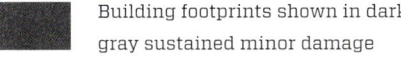 Building footprints shown in light gray sustained major damage

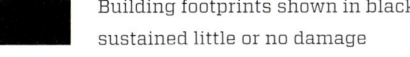 Building footprints shown in dark gray sustained minor damage

Building footprints shown in black sustained little or no damage

visually pleasing communities, while excluding patterns of sprawling development that plagued the coastal towns.

The forum established precedence for a participatory planning process that focused on socio-economic issues as well as preservation of environmentally sensitive lands. Additionally, plans suggested mitigating sprawl by increasing density in urban areas, overturning obstacles to infill development, and providing incentives for mixed-use projects.

Furthermore, compact and well-connected developments will be more economically efficient to build than typical suburban development.

Given the urgency to produce rebuilding plans in a short time frame, under less than ideal conditions, and with limited factual data, the Mississippi Rebuilding Forum was remarkably successful. Most of the rebuilding plans received additional funding from the Mississippi Development Authority, to

Figure Ground (Pre-Katrina and Proposed)
Cities are not measured by how many great buildings exist within their boundaries, but how these buildings coexist to form memorable spaces. The critical role of buildings within a city is to define the public realm, the space that a resident or visitor will experience. The opportunity to rebuild neighborhoods is also a chance to improve existing patterns. It is within this spirit that the master plan proposals have been made.

Buildings along the main street, Jeff Davis are closely grouped together to help define the thoroughfare corridor. Spacing between buildings is tighter to create a seamless pedestrian experience.

Buildings along Beach Boulevard (Highway 90) facing the Gulf are also grouped to form a shallow curve that relates to Oak Park and the marina. Similarly buildings around the civic squares also work together to define outdoor public rooms. The walls of these public rooms are the facades of buildings that enfront the space, and help create a well defined public realm.

Southern Mississippi University
The figure ground drawing above and illustrative master plan on the following page shows the reconfiguration of the university located in the south east corner of the city. The plan proposes remodeling, renovation and expansion of the university, along with the rebuilding of a church that was destroyed by the hurricane.

The historic Bear Run Creek which had been buried in a culvert is proposed to be daylighted and rebuilt not only for aesthetic reasons but to function more effectively within the storm water management system. A walkway along the creek connects the university to the marina.

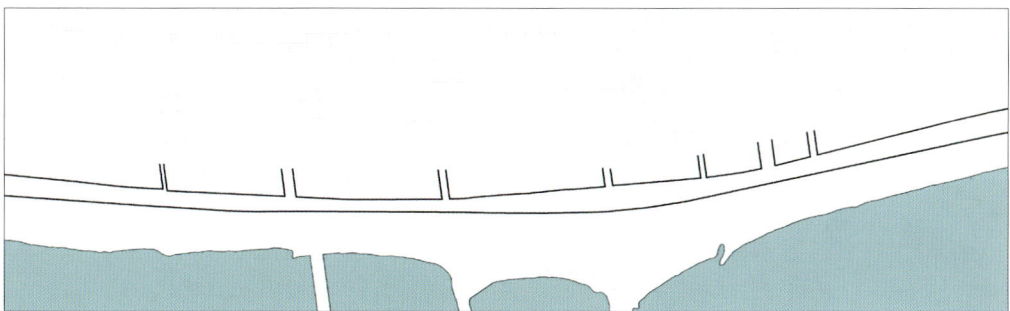

The existing alignment of Highway 90, which currently passes along the southern edge of City of Long Beach.

The properties affected by the creation of Oak Park and new thoroughfare alignment that includes the Federal Emergency Management Agency (FEMA) flood zone areas.

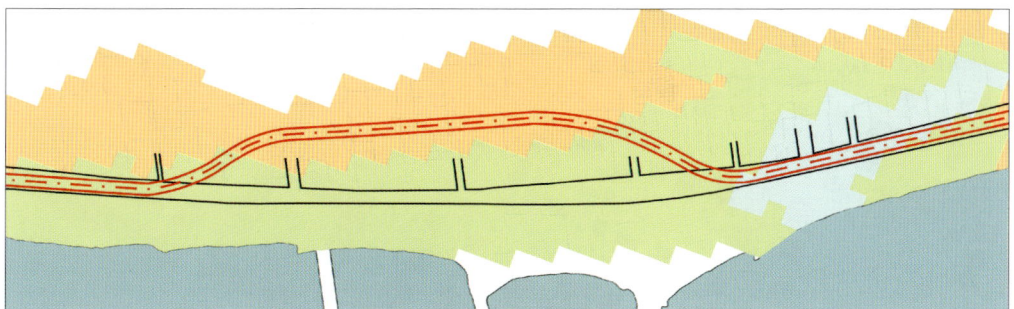

The new thoroughfare alignment is overlaid on the FEMA high-risk flood zones that identify coastal areas with an annual 1% or greater chance of flooding and an additional hazard associated with storm wave action.

The proposed plan illustrating Oak Park and the daylighted Bear Run Creek (to the East). The transformed thoroughfare Highway 90 is renamed Beach Boulevard and permits frequent access to the park and coastline.

Long Beach, Mississippi
Master Plan 2006

continue to refine the plans that were started at the forum. New urbanist firms have continued to work in the region, successfully replacing antiquated Euclidean codes with form-based codes.

Long Beach
At the Mississippi Rebuilding Forum the author led a team that worked on the City of Long Beach, a quaint community consisting of 17,300 residents. The city form is bifurcated by railroad tracks that sit on an elevated levee that runs east-west and parallel to the coast line. The area south of the tracks and closest to the water's edge was devastated by flooding and wave action that reached levels 22 feet (6.7 meters) above sea level. The area to the north of the tracks was mainly damaged by high-speed winds, which reached a maximum of 175 mph (280 km/h).

Similar to other coastal cities in Mississippi, pre-Katrina Long Beach was

Block Structure (Pre-Katrina and Proposed)
The two plan diagram above represents the existing network of streets that create elongated blocks running parallel to the coast. A typical block is currently between 800 and 900 feet long. This dimension discourages walking and limits access to the waterfront. The proposed master plan strives to provide a maximum block dimension of 250 feet deep by 600 feet long. Precedent studies suggest that this smaller block dimension is conducive to the creation of a pedestrian-friendly community.

To create connectivity and encourage a pedestrian friendly environment, the following changes are recommended:

1. Transformation of the existing thoroughfare section of Highway 90 to create a scenic Beach Boulevard thoroughfare.
2. Extend the main street, Jeff Davis to the north past the railroad tracks to terminate at a proposed civic square.
3. Remove the railroad tracks and transform the two streets on either side of the railroad right-of-way into a parkway with a landscaped median, connecting Long Beach to other coastal towns.
4. Insert several north-south residential streets to subdivide the elongated blocks and increase connectivity to the gulf coastline.
5. Incorporate a system of alleys to provide a right-of-way for utilities as well as access for service vehicles and garages.
6. Incorporate several on-grade street crossings across the existing railroad tracks to increase connectivity from the north side of the tracks to the Gulf coastline.

Long Beach Marina

The Long Beach Marina is proposed to be repaired and expanded to the west. The marina will serve as a focal point for the town's new open space, Oak Park.

The marina is one of the few marinas along the Gulf Coast that provides visitor boat slips, and will help anchor the town's tourism industry. Developing this unique asset has the potential to set Long Beach apart as a jewel along the coast. Residential condominium development above retail along Beach Boulevard creates a backdrop for the Marina.
Aerial photograph on right was taken a few weeks after Hurricane Katrina made landfall.

Long Beach Mississippi
Aerial View of Marina
and Oak Park

Opposite top:
Aerial view looking south down Jeff Davis, from the existing railroad tracks. The retail street will be terminated by a new lighthouse that will mark the Long Beach Marina.

Opposite bottom:
Plan view of Jeff Davis, the main street of Long Beach.

Top:
Street level view looking south down Jeff Davis showing the preservation of an existing building (barber shop at far right) with new infill development.

RAILROAD STREET

Railroad Street runs as a pair of streets on either side of the railroad track right-of-way. The master plan proposes reusing the existing freight railroad tracks for commuter rail or transforming the right-of-way to a dedicated rapid bus thoroughfare which would connect Long Beach to the other coastal communities.

Above:
The rendering illustrates main street (Jeff Davis) as it crosses the tracks and continues northward to the new civic square.

Left:
Existing condition of Jeff Davis and Railroad Street showing haphazard building placement and under utilized land parcels. These sites adjacent to the rail corridor are prime sites for transit oriented development.

Figure ground showing existing building footprints pre-Hurricane Katrina, alongside the railroad tracks.

Proposed master plan with the railroad remaining and the North and South Railroad Street transformed to a tree lined parkway.

Proposed master plan showing commuter parking buffered by tree-lined thoroughfares to the north and south. Due to a lack commuter rail service in the US, an option that removes the railroad tracks and transforms the easement to a dedicated rapid bus corridor is proposed. Given the scale of Long Beach, residents living on the edges would most likely drive from their home to the transit corridor requiring commuter parking as shown in the plan diagram above.

a sprawling low-density accumulation of buildings that lacked a center or identifiable core. Auto-dependent and hostile to pedestrian activity the city was far from autonomous, with most residents working and shopping in adjacent communities. Although the city had a reputation for its stellar school system, the reality was an inadequate tax base, failing infrastructure, a backlog of maintenance, and diminishing population. Ineffective city management had failed to leverage the city's two unique assets, the marina and the college.

Post-Katrina Long Beach has the possibility of capitalizing on these city assets and becoming a model for sustainable development. The strategies for redevelopment were based on time-tested urban design principles overlaid onto the existing city framework. They included:

1. Move development away from the coastline, north of the newly prescribed FEMA high-risk flood velocity zone.
2. Convert the existing coastal highway to a tree-lined beach boulevard. This slower thoroughfare would be pedestrian-friendly and provide walkable links to the park and coastline.
3. Create a public park between the newly prescribed building edge and the water's edge. The park could appropriately be named Oak Park for the surviving resilient species of coastal oak trees that lived through the hurricane.
4. Concentrate compact mixed-use development adjacent to Oak Park.
5. Reconfigure the existing main street in the city with higher density buildings and a streetscape conducive to pedestrian activity.
6. Designate a hierarchy of thoroughfares throughout the city.
7. Discourage development on the periphery as well as thoroughfare corridors, to encourage densification and building activity in the core of the community.
8. Encourage rebuilding and expansion of the harbor and the college to serve as economic engines to power the city's future.
9. Sub-divide existing blocks with new streets to create a porous network and increase connectivity to the beach frontage. Engineer existing and new north-south streets to drain storm water.

Conclusion
Natural disasters and man-made catastrophes are extremely unfortunate events. It is hard to imagine the disruption, turmoil, and angst caused within a household. The general reaction immediately following the calamity is for the victims to yearn for a return to normalcy, which usually translates to rebuilding exactly what was there before.

Insurance companies require strict adherence to cataloguing what was lost and applying archaic devaluation formulas that result in replacement values that usually steer victims to rebuild and replace exactly what they once had. Unfortunately, the replacement of goods and structures are usually of lower quality, given the formulaic economics of replacement value.

It is important for designers to empathize with the victims, yet carefully suggest alternatives to the rebuilding efforts. Across the country, the practices of the last fifty years were far from sustainable, as most of America was built to be predominantly auto-dependant and wasteful in their energy consumption. With the burgeoning crisis of the peak-oil era, no country, no matter how wealthy, can afford to waste energy in the same way again.

It is essential that all new construction and rebuilding efforts after a disaster must consider the life-cycle cost and carbon footprint of the new structure and mandatory appliances, as well as the transportation cost getting to and from the buildings. Studies clearly indicate that energy consumed traveling between

Katrina Cottage

A highly successful by-product of the Mississippi Rebuilding Forum was the development of the Katrina Cottage. The 330 square foot (33 square meters) affordable cottage can factory built and trucked to the site as an alternative to the metal Federal Emergency Management Agency (FEMA) trailers. The cost for the cottage is equivalent to the visually challenged mobile trailer unit that have commonly been deployed in similar relief efforts.

Designed for disaster relief conditions the cottage can be located on the property to serve as temporary housing, while the residents rebuild their damaged home. The cottage may stay on permanently on the property as an auxiliary unit.

In the past five years many versions and size variations of the cottage have emerged. The Katrina Cottage has engendered support outside of the Gulf Coast as an economically efficient housing alternatives for communities located in costly housing markets.

Aerial view looking west along the new Beach Boulevard (formerly Highway 90), showing the northern edge of Oak Park lined with condominiums and retail frontage.

The Congress for the New Urbanism (CNU) is an advocacy organization promoting walkable, mixed-use neighborhood development, sustainable communities and healthier living conditions.

Since 1983 CNU members have used the principles in CNU's Charter to promote the hallmarks of New Urbanism, including:

Livable streets arranged in compact, walkable blocks.
1. A range of housing choices to serve people of diverse ages and income levels.
2. Schools, stores and other nearby destinations reachable by walking, bicycling or transit service.
3. An affirming, human-scaled public realm where appropriately designed buildings define and enliven streets and other public spaces.

buildings is equal if not more significant than energy consumed by the building itself. This fact must be addressed in all rebuilding efforts.

New human habitats must be compact and well connected, with the public realm complete to accommodate private and public vehicles as well as all facets of pedestrian life: the healthy, infirmed, young, and old.

Postscript

Five years after Hurricane Katrina, the coastal communities are rebuilding slower than anyone would have anticipated, and the road to recovery is long and fraught with tragedy. The recent oil spill in the Gulf Coast is yet another major setback for the coastal States in the US.

The good intentions of the Governor's Commission and the New Urbanist volunteers have had limited success in implementation. Change is slow and even slower in States such as Mississippi where local politicians and planning boards have had very little or no experience with long-term planning.

The divide between building it better and business as usual is seen quite differently by the designers and the local community. One sees reducing car trips and walking as a priority while the other desires more convenient parking spaces and cheaper gas prices.

The rate of obesity in Mississippi is among the highest in comparison to other States and the national trend toward a healthier lifestyle and a reduction in auto-dependency has yet to be embraced by the citizenry.

No plan, no matter how brilliant, can be realized without top-down political support and bottom-up citizenry enthusiastic persistence. Similar to the saying that citizens get the government they deserve, it may also be true that in the end citizens only demand the reality that they can imagine.

-

The Loss of Green Spaces in and around City Areas: Learning from Syria

The Use of Medium Resolution Satellite Images in Examining the Impact of City Expansion on Urban and Peri-urban Green Areas in Syria

Peter Ross

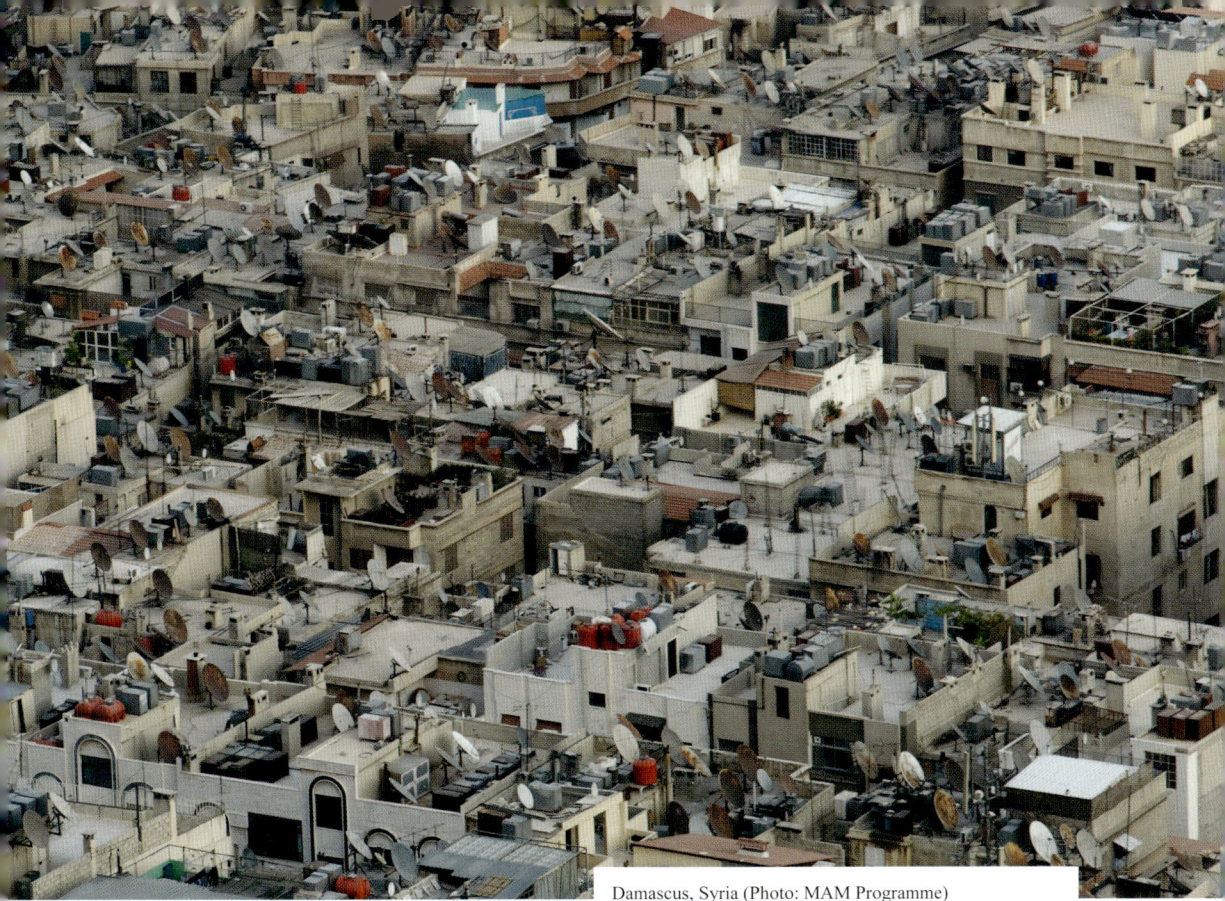
Damascus, Syria (Photo: MAM Programme)

The paper relies heavily on work undertaken by Eng. Huda Basal and colleagues at the Ministry of Local Administration, Syrian Arab Republic

—

Introduction

Urban greening becomes ever more important at both a macro and a micro level, as issues of climate change and urban livability become pressing in the world's cities. In Syria there is an increasing concentration on the issue.

It is thus very useful when a donor agency is prepared to fund in-depth work on crucial practical urban issues in specific locations, and to encourage a rigorous approach to the issues. One such project has been the EU/Syrian Government funded Municipal Administration Modernisation Programme (MAM), one of the largest such programmes in Syria (www.mam-sy.org). The Programme aimed to improve the quality and effectiveness of local government, especially in managing urban growth. Over more than four years the Programme has delivered a series of interlocking action plans covering legislative, financial and administration reform. Important work strands of MAM have covered urban planning and related topics: GIS, PPP, property management, Agenda 21, solid waste disposal, old cities and heritage sites of world importance, traffic and transportation, regional planning and institutional structure and processes redesign. One major achievement was the establishing of the Damascus Regional Centre for Sustainable Local Development (RCSLD)

Many of the strands of MAM are relevant to the overall question of environmental sustainability in Syria. This paper concentrates on one particular aspect, in which input from Syrian partners, notably the Ministry of Local Administration, has been critical in developing new ways of analysis, and in pushing forward realistic policies for the retention and expansion of green spaces in and around city areas.

Urban Development in Syria

As in many countries Syria has experienced significant urban development over recent decades with annual growth rates in some years as high as 5%. Over 50% of the total population now lives in urban areas, and this proportion is expected to rise to 75% by 2050 (see end note 3). As would be expected there are familiar factors underlying this process of rapid urban development:
- Rural-urban migration, as people seek better lives for themselves and their children. In Syria this trend is exacerbated by increasing dryness in some rural areas.
- The flight to the suburbs, as families with increased wealth seek more space and a higher perception of security.
- Rising land, and consequently house, prices in central city areas.
- Increasing vehicle ownership leading to more pressure to extend the road system, and parking pressures on the public domain, leading to higher space demands and conflicts with existing uses, for example street markets. Increased pollution from urban traffic is also a problem.
- Commercial development: increased wealth brings an increased need for shops and related facilities. An increase in square metres for each person is coupled with an increase in size of the grain pattern of the urban fabric – not only are more shops being sought, but also larger ones – often in the form of shopping malls. The existing urban fabric – for a variety of reasons – presents few opportunities for renewal to include such facilities.
- Similar problems are faced in the provision of facilities for financial and technical services, coupled in this case with the dominance of the need for high quality electronic service networks.
- Especially in the most valued historical parts of cities, and in rural and peri-urban areas, tourism is growing, seeking its own share of the public space and systems.
- Quality of life improvements: existing city residents have normal expectations of improvements in social, health, educational and other services. Incomers also – perhaps with greater need and intensity – have these expectations.
- Of historical, current and future importance is Syria's role as an entrepôt; its position in trans-continental trade and traffic. This leads to a strong need for port facilities, and for high standard roads and railways. It places demands on local urban systems, but provides only limited advantage to the cities in which the extensive facilities are located.

However there are other, particular, forces at work in Syria which are directly relevant to the rate of urban development, including, above all, the generous Syrian hospitality to a large number of regional refugees: at an earlier date from Palestine and Lebanon, and more recently from Iraq. Syria has reportedly received between 1.5 and 2 million Iraqi refugees in recent years.

Above all perhaps, is the speed at which these forces are changing the shape and nature of Syrian cities.

Pressure for urban development has

An informal settlement in Damascus
(Photo: MAM Programme)

increasingly been resolved by city expansion, external and internal, formal and informal, at the expense of green areas.

The Impact of Informal Settlement Areas

In this context it is worth considering informal housing development in a little detail. In Syria we are not typically talking about the usually envisaged form of informal housing. Yes, there are deprived communities, some seriously so, and some such communities are informal, but in Syria as a rule informal does not equate to the normal image of insanitary totally unserviced slums, commonly experienced in South America, Africa and South East Asia. Indeed there are many informal settlements occupied by middle-class groups living in expansive, and expensive, villas.

The MAM Programme was fortunate to be able to look at four Syrian informal settlements in detail, and a rich variety of urban form and social composition was found. The general conclusions of this work can be explored in detail elsewhere (www.mam-sy.org/index.php?p_id=29). However, there are two aspects of this situation that are particularly relevant to the current discussion.

Firstly, almost all informal settlements lack adequate public open space; thus increasingly large areas of Syrian cities are without such provision.

However, one has to move outside the settlements themselves to observe the biggest non-personal impact of informal settlements in Syria, which can be ascribed entirely to their informal nature: the significant loss of the benefits of urban structure planning. If it is now accepted that informal development accounts for 50% of urban growth on the outskirts of conurbations in Syria, then it is clear that there has been a noticeable lessening of control over the shape and organisation of cities. The implications of this point are significant in terms of the use of so far undeveloped land. If there is little control over city expansion, there is equally little control over the nature of the land that is lost to development.

This, of course, has implications for the future of urban Syria, and for urban planning processes. As elsewhere development pressures reveal the strengths and weaknesses of urban planning systems. If half the urban population only has access to land and housing through informal processes, or chooses to, and is able to, ignore for whatever reason the formal system, then there are questions that need to be asked concerning the overall system in place to respond to such basic needs.

Urban Planning in Syria

Syria has a well developed urban planning system, which drew on the best that planners in Europe and elsewhere provided as examples, and which was set in place in a comprehensive manner. However the growth of informal settlements, and other evidence, provides a clear demonstration that the current formal system cannot keep up with recent pressures. As a Government spokesperson has said:

"It is known that people's needs grow faster than the government's plans, and sometimes unforeseen issues may arise and cannot wait for the plan's implementation" (Syrian Times, 9th August 2005).

From the legal point of view, including general urban planning legislation, whilst the concept of preserving urban green area is evident in different elements of laws and decrees, until recently there has been no specific legal framework to address the issue. The only available Act specifically concerning urban green areas has been Law no.49 of 2004 concerning the "Cleanliness and Tidiness of Administrative Units". In Article no. 35, this law bans the removal of trees within cities, in both public and private areas. However by definition this legislation has not served to control loss due to city expansion, formal or informal.

More recently, however, various instructions from the Minister of Local Administration, supported by a Prime Ministerial Decision (Decision no. 7334/15 of 2009) has assessed the problem from a broader perspective. Through this Decision local authorities are now obliged to seek approval for expansion on green or agricultural lands from the Ministry of Agriculture. In conjunction with this Decision the Ministry of Agriculture is currently developing a database of agricultural land quality.

The latest, and probably the most relevant initiative has been the introduction of the first Syrian Regional Planning Legislation – Law no. 26 of 2010 – brought about with the substantial assistance of the MAM Programme. In the press conference following the enactment of the legislation the Minister of Local Administration made it clear that one of the main aims of the legislation was to protect green areas through the better regulation of urban growth, especially informal areas. He went on to say that the Law will also seek to preserve the country's natural heritage.

To devise and refine the response to issues of city expansion a good understanding of the impacts is necessary. One reason that the current system cannot move quickly is that the existing information collection and analysis process is a lengthy one, often taking over three years for a straightforward local plan. Analysis must be much speedier if it is to be useful, even at the expense of complete accuracy. It is also useful to connect information collection and analysis directly to strategic decision making, with full public engagement, rather than entering directly into detailed plan making, as tends to happen currently in Syria.

Here the work of Engineer Huda Basal and colleagues from the Ministry of Local Administration is particularly important.

The Technique Used for this Analysis

Modern high resolution satellite images are well known as important tools for urban planning policy making, but in developing countries such images are frequently not sufficiently available, or are at too high a price, to be truly useful. Medium resolution images are however often more available, and are often free. Older images of the same area are equally often available, allowing period analysis to be undertaken.

Using images of this sort taken by the Landsat satellite it was possible to examine the interiors and edges of six Syrian cities for two dates, and to quantify the changes. It is not suggested that the results have 100% accuracy. However, there is enough confidence in the results to be able to draw policy conclusions.

The six cities chosen varied in size and locational aspects. Damascus and Aleppo are the two largest and most important cities in Syria, Damascus in the south, and Aleppo in the north. Government functions are concentrated in Damascus, but Aleppo has a long tradition of commercial enterprise. The official population of each is about 2.5 million, if the whole urban area is taken into account, but realistic estimates would place the figures approximately a million higher in each case. Tartous and Latakia are both port cities, lying on the Mediterranean, and in the fertile coastal plain. Their official population levels are respectively 150,000 and 400,000, but again these figures are likely to be underestimates. Homs lies in the centre of the country, north of Damascus, in the corridor between Damascus and Aleppo, with an official population of almost three quarters of a million. Der Ezzor lies in the far north-east of the country, close to the borders of both Turkey and Iraq; its official population figure is approximately 215,000. The population of Syria as a whole is a little over 20 million.

The basic information used in the analysis was as follows:

City name	Satellite	Sensor	Bands (FCC)	Date of acquisition
Damascus	Landsat	L4TM L5TM	NIR,R,G (4,3,2)	20-5-1988 1-5-2007
Aleppo	Landsat	L4TM L5TM	NIR,R,G (4,3,2)	20-5-1988 1-5-2007
Homs	Landsat	L4TM L5TM	NIR,R,G (4,3,2)	20-5-1988 1-5-2007
Tartous	Landsat	L4TM L5TM	NIR,R,G (4,3,2)	20-5-1988 1-5-2007
Deir ez zor	Landsat	L5TM L5TM	NIR,R,G (4,3,2)	16-4-1986 28-5-2007
Latakia	Landsat	L4TM L5TM	NIR,R,G (4,3,2)	20-5-1988 1-5-2007

For each city two images, each of 30m resolution, dated 1988 (1986 in one case) and 2007, were used, and through software (Erdas Image 8.4) were classified into land uses as follows:

A. Green areas
B. Dense green areas
C. Built up areas
D. Bare soil areas
E. Water areas

Green and dense green areas were separately calculated and are differentiated by the level of cover. Dense green areas have full green cover and often include many mature trees. Green areas are less entirely covered, and tend to have fewer mature trees, but nonetheless are sufficiently covered to count as green areas. Bare soil areas and built up areas, as defined in this analysis, have very little or no greenery.

For each of these areas square metres were calculated using the 30m pixels for each date, and a comparison made. The comparison was relatively easy because the administrative boundaries for the cities had not changed between the two dates; even if this had been the case a simple calculation would have resolved the difficulty.

The images chosen were taken during the same season, in most cases in the same month, to ensure that seasonal variations in green cover did not complicate analysis. Other factors causing difficulties in the image interpretation are the seasonal changes in sun-angles and differences in atmospheric characteristics.

The Results of the Analysis
The results are stark, and can be seen in the comparison images given below.

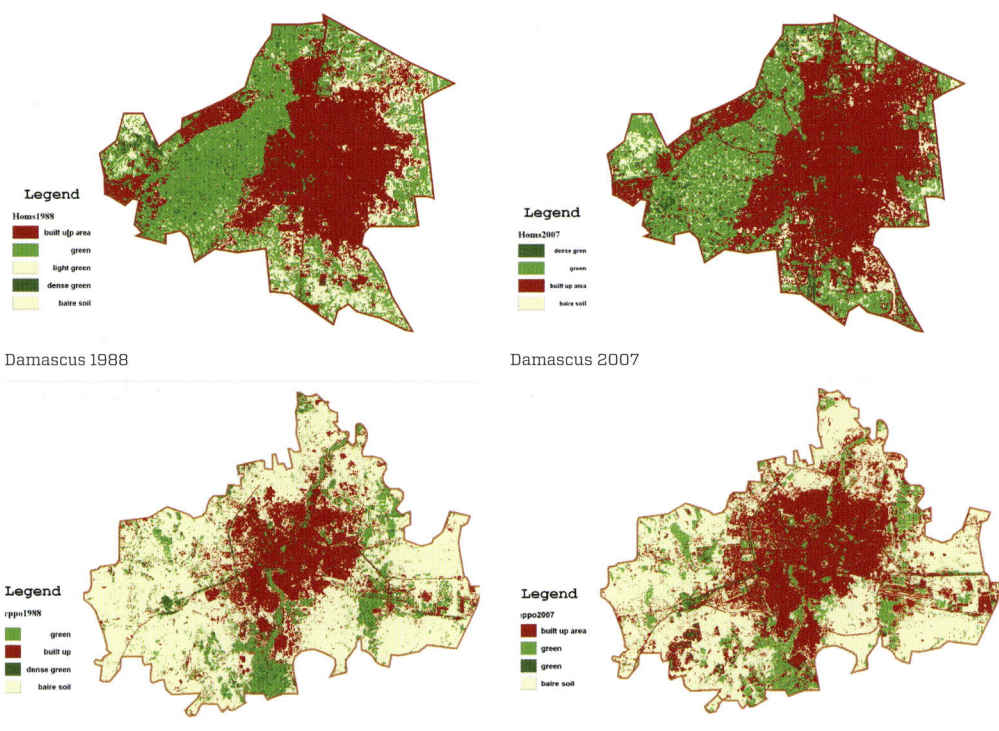

Damascus 1988

Damascus 2007

Aleppo 1988

Aleppo 2007

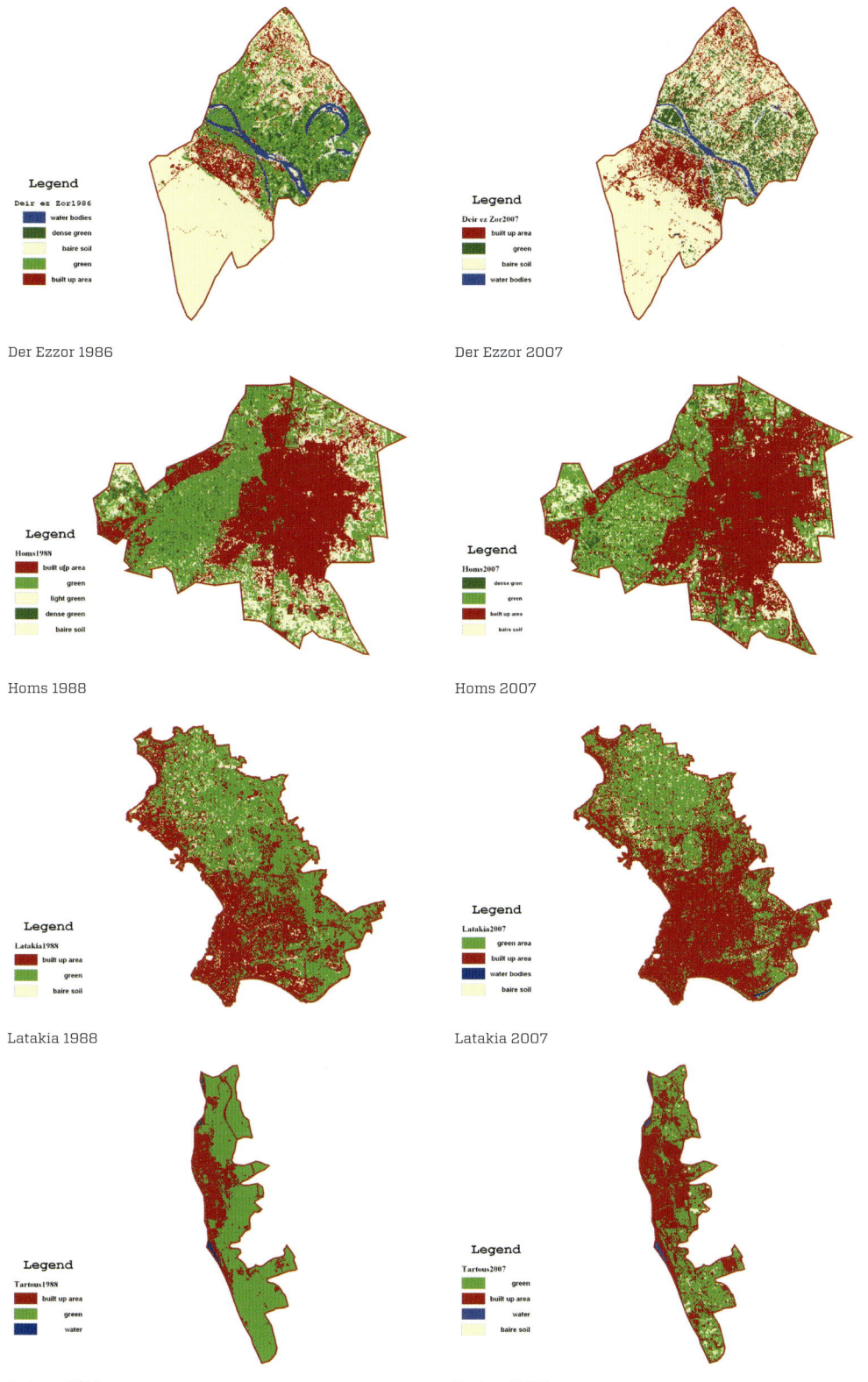

Der Ezzor 1986   Der Ezzor 2007

Homs 1988   Homs 2007

Latakia 1988   Latakia 2007

Tartous 1988   Tartous 2007

The statistical analysis that followed the graphic manipulation reveals the following information:

City	Area km2	Number of pixels	Land use
Damascus 1988	37.5408	41712	built up area
	25.4637	28293	green area
	55.0467	61183	bare soil area
Damascus 2007	53.6445	59605	built up area
	15.8652	17628	green area
	48.5595	53955	bare soil area
Aleppo 1988	69.1722	76858	built up area
	11.3535	12615	dense green
	40.9977	45553	green area
	196.1199	217911	bare soil area
Aleppo 2007	107.2809	119201	built up area
	4.0005	4450	dense green
	42.1884	46876	green area
	164.169	182410	bare soil area
Homs 1988	27.945	31050	built up area
	29.2419	32491	green area
	12.6414	14046	bare soil area
Homs 2007	35.4726	39414	built up area
	26.4708	29412	green area
	7.8849	8761	bare soil area
Latakia 1988	19.6614	21846	built up area
	27.3366	30374	green area
	3.3372	3708	bare soil area
Latakia 2007	26.5725	29525	built up area
	20.8206	23134	green area
	2.9421	3269	bare soil area
Tartous 1988	8.7795	9755	built up area
	24.0048	26672	green area
		Not measurable	bare soil area
Tartous 2007	15.2703	16967	built up area
	16.4115	18235	green area
	1.1025	1225	bare soil area
Deir Ezzor 1986	9.4518	10502	built up area
	28.8846	32094	green area
	44.7489	49721	bare soil area
	4.1508	4612	water bodies
Deir Ezzor 2007	13.2462	14718	built up area
	15.0975	16775	green area
	56.7351	63039	bare soil area
	2.1573	2397	water bodies

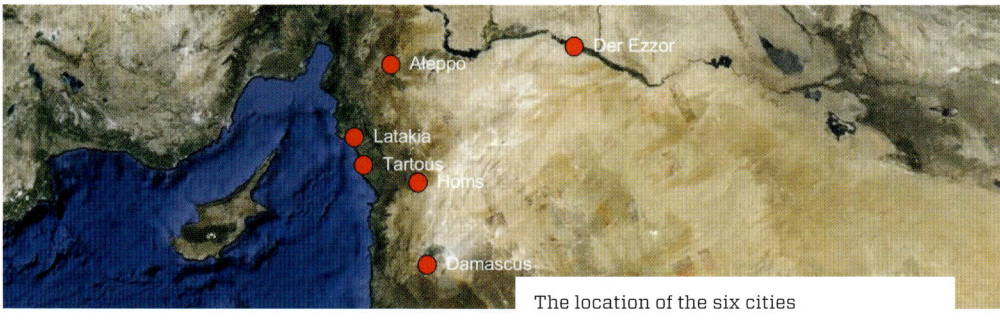

The location of the six cities

It is clear that throughout Syria there has been a significant drop in the amount of land in green areas between 1988 and 2007. City by city the loss is as follows:

City	Loss of green and dense green areas to urban development between 1988 (1986 in one case) and 2007
Damascus	38%
Aleppo	12%
Homs	10%
Latakia	24%
Tartous	32%
Der Ezzor	48%

Taken together, the analysis shows that there has been a net loss of approximately 25% of the green areas in and around six of the most important cities in Syria. This has substantially been due to urban expansion.

This in itself is a valuable, if dispiriting, conclusion. If individual areas are looked at in detail, whilst the pixels become obvious, the picture becomes even more revealing, with three main points to be made:
- The loss of green areas to urban development has been piecemeal and scattered.
- The loss has been within cities, as well as on the outskirts.
- Small extensions of urban areas can lead to major intrusions.

1. The loss of green area to urban development has been piecemeal and scattered

All the cities show this tendency, but it can perhaps be seen most clearly in Damascus.

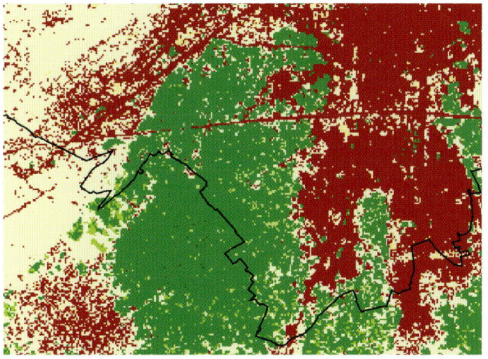

Damascus 1988: detail 1

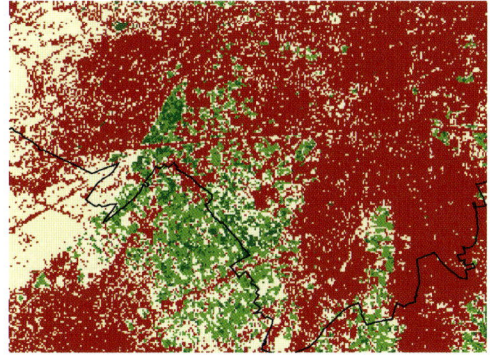

Damascus 2007: detail 1

In Damascus there is a serious fragmentation of the green around the city, leading to increased dangers of crop theft, pollution, and vandalism. In such circumstances the risks of further loss in an uncontrolled way become very great. This is particularly distressing as Damascus has been traditionally seen as a city set within an oasis. As recently as the middle of the last century this remained true, with a clear demarcation line between the city and the oasis.

Edge of Damascus 1925
(Photo: Institut Français du Proche-Orient)

Peri-urban land under threat (Photo: MAM Programme)

2. The loss has been within cities, as well as on the outskirts

Again the clearest examples come from Damascus.

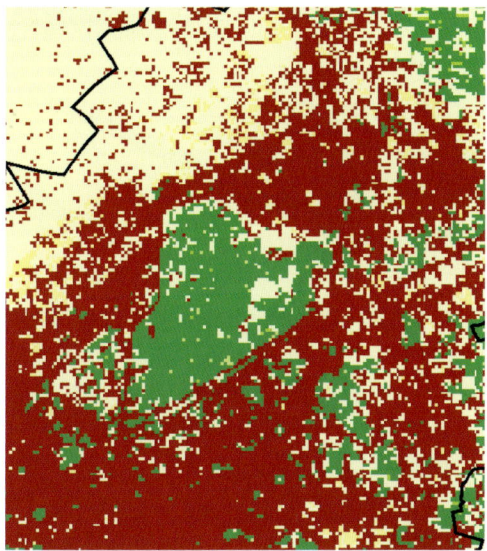

Damascus 1988: detail 2

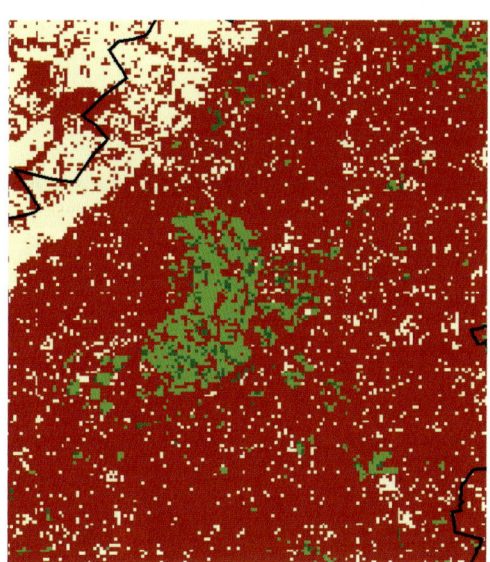

Damascus 2007: detail 2

A well maintained urban green area in Damascus
(Photo: MAM Programme)

It is not surprising that as the city facing perhaps the greatest pressures, Damascus again serves as an illustration of the consequences of relatively uncontrolled urban development. This is unfortunate as the Damascus Governorate and several foreign donors and local NGOs have been active in improving the remaining green areas in the city.

3. Small extensions of urban areas can lead to major intrusions

The dangers of ribbon development, or poorly planned and executed 'growth corridors', are well known. An example from Homs shows the potential danger clearly.

Thus not only can such images reveal a broad picture, but they can point to particular issues of urban development that require specific responses.

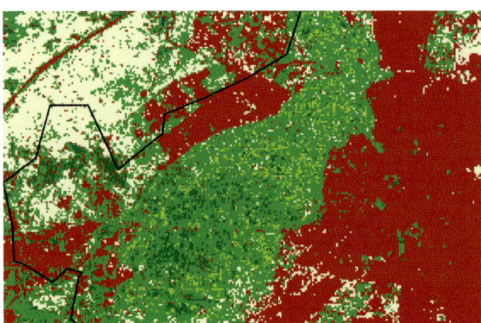

Homs 1988: detail

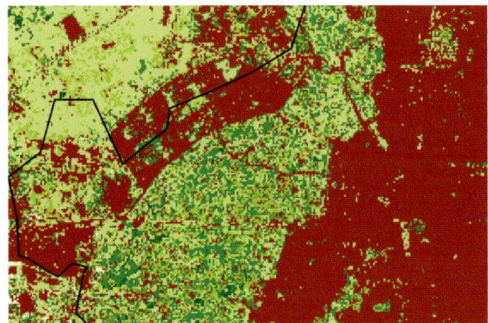

Homs 1988: detail

Beyond this Analysis

Further issues of policy importance can also be detected. For example in Der Ezzor there has been an increase in bare land of some 25% between 1986 and 2007. This is to be expected in the light of the continuing diminishing availability of water in the eastern part of the country, but the image provides not only graphic impact, but also local specificity. Drought is itself a topic for serious consideration, but will not be developed further here.

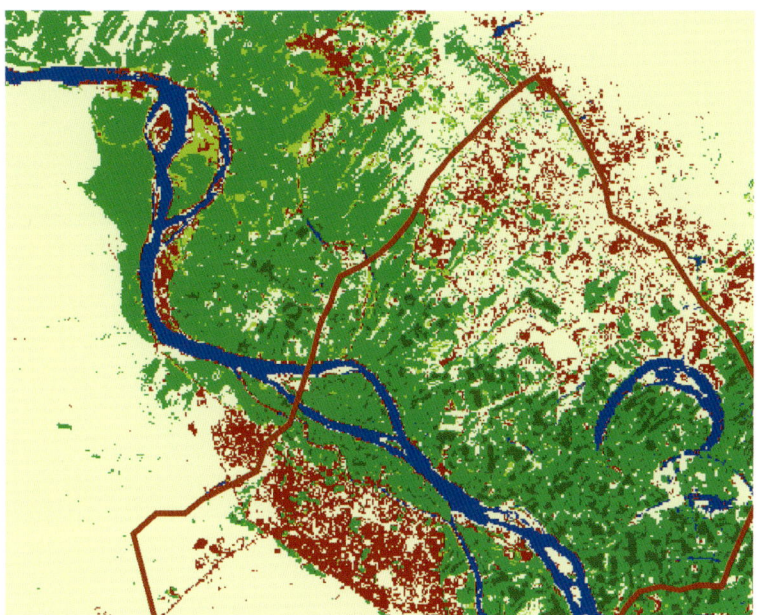

Der Ezzor: 1986 detail

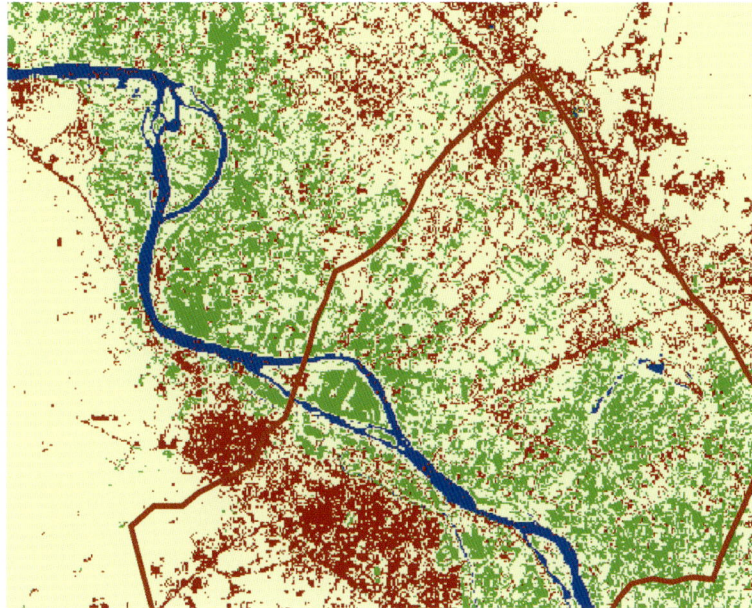

Der Ezzor: 2007 detail

Bare earth in Der Ezzor (Photo: MAM Programme)

Conclusions

As indicated the matters discussed in the paper, and other related matters, are of considerable importance to Syrian urban policy making. Two recent seminars organised by the MAM programme and the RCSLD were particularly important in moving the debate forward. The first, held in July 2009, was jointly organised with ISOCARP and allowed for a full professional exchange of views on energy-lean urban planning and urban design and management for environmentally sound cities, from a Syrian and international perspective. The second, held in April 2010, directly covered urban green issues, and was hosted jointly with the British Syrian Society. This seminar took as its main themes the introduction of green wedges from the rural edges into the hearts of Syrian cities, with proper and well identified city entrances, the provision of inter-connected, urban green networks in Syrian cities, and the legal protection of the Syrian natural environment and its biodiversity. The extensive historical photograph library of the Institut Français du Proche-Orient was of considerable importance in presenting information at this seminar.

These seminars covered not only the topics presented here, but also made important contributions to other related matters, including an understanding of the value of traditional architecture and urban design. Full details of these seminars can be found at www.mam-sy.org/isocarp-regionalcentre and www.british-syriansociety.org/green

Endnotes

1. The author of this article has been the EU Urban Development Team Leader of the MAM Programme mentioned, working as an Associate of WYG International.

2. The article draws on experienced gained in this role and on other work undertaken as part of the MAM Programme. The information, comment and opinion given in this paper however are personal to the author and cannot in any way be taken as reflecting the position of the EU, WYG International, or the Government of the Syrian Arab Republic.

3. Figures concerning demographic, urban and informal settlement growth are taken from: Lavinal, Olivier (2008) "The challenges of urban expansion in Syria: the issue of informal housing", in Villes en développement, No 79

4. The author can provide contact with Huda Basal and others at the Ministry of Local Administration for those wishing to learn more detail of the technique used.

Cultivating the Capital

How the Planning System is Vital to London's Ability to Grow its Own Food

Jenny Jones

with contribution from
Rosie Boycott

Cultivating the Capital

Jenny Jones

Introduction

As Britain's capital city, London is known as a sprawling urban metropolis. However, one of Greater London's best-kept secrets is its 500 farms, producing a rather surprising harvest: 8,000 tonnes of fruit and vegetables, including grapes, aubergines, potatoes, cauliflowers and cabbages as well as around 27 tonnes of honey, meat, milk and eggs.

But experts say this is not enough and warn that, if London does not become more self-sufficient, it faces an increasingly insecure food supply that is dependent on massive food miles, unsustainable sources and lengthy supply chains that are vulnerable to disruption.

So what's stopping London from growing more food? Ultimately it is a lack of vision as to how the city should develop. We at the London Assembly, the elected body that investigates matters of importance to the capital and scrutinises the work of the elected Mayor of London, recently looked into the issue.

The Mayor is currently delivering a programme called 'Capital Growth' [see final section] which aims to help Londoners create 2,012 new food growing spaces by the end of 2012.

We commend the aspirations of Capital Growth and its value. Our own recent investigation looked at food growing in London on a larger scale. We concluded that to really exploit London's potential to become more self-sufficient, changes are required to the planning system at a regional and local level. To set this process in play, we called for amendments to the Mayor's London Plan, the strategic master plan that sets and informs planning policy in the capital. He has since indicated that he will accept our advice and those changes.

Growing Communities grower on Allens Gardens' site in London Borough of Hackney

Volunteer at work in Forty Hall Community Vineyard in the London Borough of Enfield

Our investigation

The London Plan is perhaps the most important policy document the Mayor is required to produce as it sets out a framework for the development of London over the next 20-25 years. Crucially, it also provides the strategic, London-wide context within which boroughs must set their planning policies.

The Mayor is currently reviewing the London Plan, and has made a commitment to increasing protection for green space and growing space. The Committee set out to establish recommendations for inclusion in the London Plan that would have the most impact on increasing food production in and around the capital.

Our investigation assessed how effectively the planning system supports and encourages agriculture and commercial food growing in London and what more could be done to improve the situation. It highlights the need for amendments to the London Plan and local authority planning policies to encourage food growing in London.

London is currently very dependent on food imports. Some experts believe London may have only three or four days' stocks of food if supplies were disrupted. Tim Lang, Professor of Food Policy at City University London told Assembly Members: "We are sleepwalking into a major problem when it comes to food".

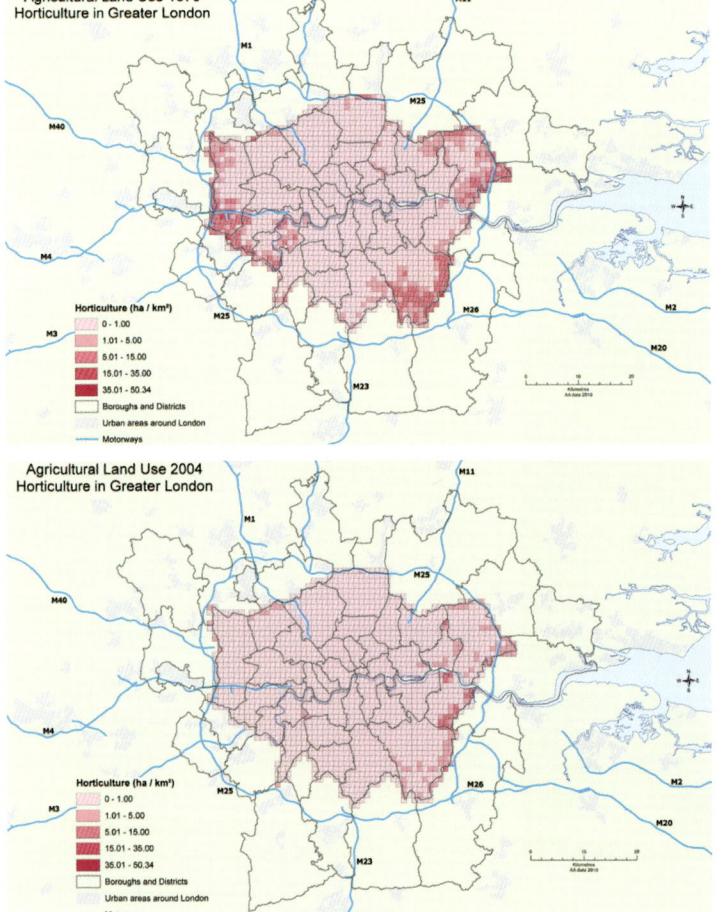

Changes in horticultural land use, Greater London 1970-2004
Source: ADAS Environment Group for Planning and Housing Committee 2010

We looked at both the challenges and the opportunities presented by current planning legislation with regards to food production. We considered whether existing commercial and social enterprise growers are adequately protected by current planning laws, and the scope for planning mechanisms to provide for growing spaces in existing urban spaces, as well as in new developments.

During the inquiry we heard from expert witnesses and consulted with a wide range of organisations and individuals. Our investigation culminated in a report, 'Cultivating the Capital: *Food growing and the planning system in London*, which was published in January this year.

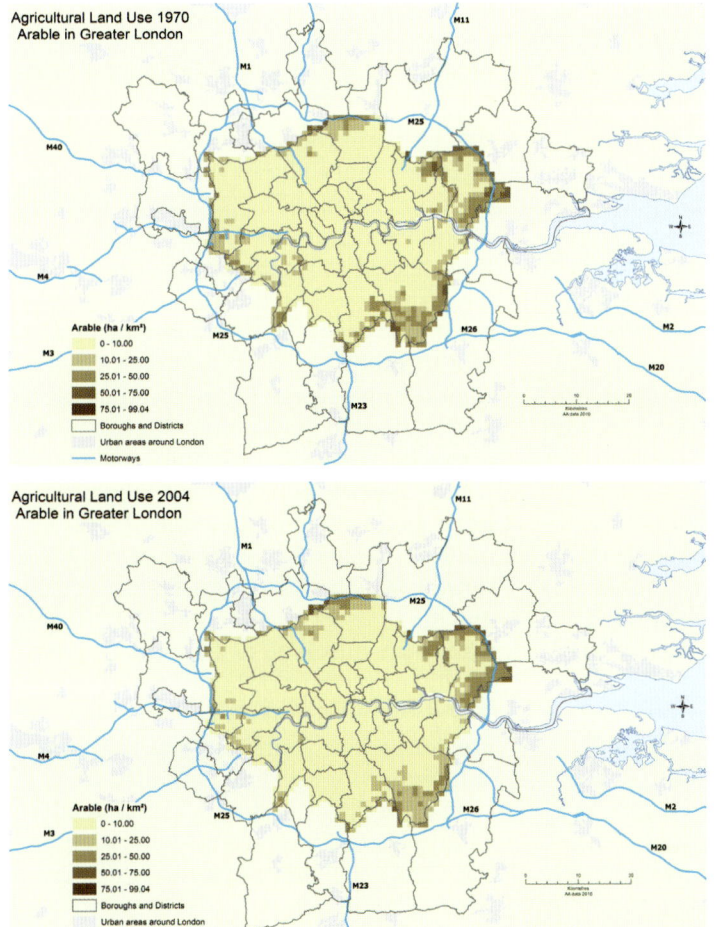

Changes in agricultural land use, Greater London 1970-2004
Source: ADAS Environment Group for Planning and Housing Committee 2010

The Way Forward

We believe the capital could produce so much more food if we make better use of the space we have available. This means all space – from rooftops and back gardens, purpose-designed growing spaces in new developments, to community allotments [2] and temporary plots, along with the swathes of land in the Green Belt that borders London. Much of this land, which makes up around 15 per cent of the capital's total area, while officially classed as "agricultural", is not actively farmed.

More locally grown and sourced food is the solution to potential supply problems in the longer-term, and meeting demand in the short-term. Increasing allotment waiting lists and the establishment of more farmers' markets in London in the last ten years demonstrate that people are keen to reap the health, economic, social and environmental benefits of locally grown food. Yet despite greater demand for locally sourced food, one estimate puts the proportion of imported food in Londoners' diets at as high as 80 per cent [3].

Our goal should be wide-scale and sustainable urban agriculture, using the city's own residents and resources in both conventional and unconventional growing spaces, using the city's organic waste as compost and bio-fertiliser and waste water for irrigation. London alone sends 370,000 tonnes of food waste to landfill each year when it could be reusing it as a resource for all Londoners.

Instead of continuing with the old development model of maximising high density living, an over-reliance on the finance and business sector, and the notion that all but a fraction of our food requirement will come from rural areas, we need a radical re-imagining of how London and other cities can thrive in a more sustainable way. Instead of maximising density, we should be optimising it while still incorporating planned growth within London's existing boundaries. It will, however, require a careful balancing act, one that must take into account the capacity of each area to accommodate growth without compromising open space and gardens, and making sure adequate transport and social infrastructure is in place.

Agriculture and the Planning System

London has a long term vision set by its Mayor - the London Plan - but the current draft mimics a vision of the past. Yet there are some practical steps that the Mayor could take to nudge London towards a new pattern of development: one which reinvigorates London's fringe, one which would support commercial growers and so boost jobs and develop new skills.

In practical terms this means tackling obstructive and old-fashioned planning rules. In seeking to protect the Green Belt, these rules have in some cases tied farmers' hands, restricting modernisation and limiting viability.

Our evidence shows that existing planning regulations, as well as regional and local planning policies, often either restrict or ignore urban agriculture as a land use. Many commercial growers in and around London have found that the changes they want to make on their farms in order to maintain a viable agriculture business often conflict with Green Belt and other planning policies.

This is especially the case when the need for a new or replacement farm building arises. For example, if you are a farmer who grows apples, planning rules can make it very difficult for you to open a shop on your land to sell apple sauce, as this would be a different "use".

With farmers already facing huge pressures from housing developments, competition from cheap imports, low farm gate prices and high crime levels, selling excess produce on-site can mean the difference between a thriving business and going bust.

These pressures were perhaps not as

Upper Hockenden Farm, Kent run by A V Produce

significant when Green Belt policy was pioneered in the UK in the 1930s. Then, the fundamental aim was to prevent urban sprawl by keeping land permanently open. And in keeping this land open a key objective was to retain land in agricultural use. It seems this objective has generally been forgotten and we believe there is an urgent need to remind policy makers and decision takers of the importance of using Green Belt land for food production.

The challenge for the statutory planning framework is to recognise and integrate food production into sustainable development strategies. We believe agriculture as a land use in the Green Belt should be given equal weight to some of the other objectives set out in national policy like those on traffic generation and loss of residential amenity.

We recommend that on a regional level, the Mayor of London should include a requirement in the London Plan for local authorities to give added weight to food growing as a one of the most productive activities in the Green Belt.

And on a local level, we also urge boroughs – through draft policy 7.22 - to incorporate urban agriculture in their Local Development Frameworks (LDF) as a desirable urban activity that can help improve the quality of urban life, food security, neighbourhood safety and environmental stewardship that utilises vacant land.

Other Measures to Promote Economic Viability

One key issue growers raised with us during our investigation is the challenge of distributing and selling produce.

Many growers are trying to tap into the expanding demand for local food by growing a variety of produce in, or close to, London. But you have to get the food to market and we found that economic circumstances and complex food supply chains often favour larger farms over smaller local suppliers.

With the largest four supermarkets controlling around 75 per cent of the grocery market, use of London wholesale markets – formerly the main hub between farmers and retailers – had in the last few decades gone into decline. Luckily, they are now showing signs of a revival, so they could once again become part of a significant distribution system for local and regional produce for schools, hospitals, restaurants, shops and street markets.

This dependence on a few major supermarkets with their long supply chains and "just in time" delivery systems cannot be sustained. We concluded that we need planning policies that improve distribution for regional producers into the capital and suitable retail outlets such as farm shops, street markets and farmers' markets.

Our report welcomes draft London Plan policy 4.8, which supports the range of street and farmers' markets and their contribution to the vitality of town centres. However, we would also like to see the London Plan specifically support the potential for farmers' markets in the public realm and in particular public squares and large open public spaces.

Farmers need to access new markets if they are to maintain their commercial viability. In order to do this, they need assistance with distribution and encouraging local markets. As well as selling their wares to Londoners, food producers from the capital and its fringes need

Fruit stall at a London Farmers' Market in Swiss Cottage

new innovative supply chains to sell their produce directly to schools, hospitals and restaurants.

Sites need to be found for organisations that will distribute locally grown food, and new or extended farmers' markets need to be accommodated by the planning system and through local authority food policies. These can provide a market for locally grown food and provide an alternative to wholesale markets for local businesses and residents.

We saw one of these services as part of our investigation. Growing Communities is a social enterprise run by local people in East London. It is working to create a more sustainable food system, supporting small organic farmers through the sale of boxes of salads and vegetables to customers from five pick-up points. It currently employs 18 part-time members of staff and is supported by up to 80 volunteers working throughout the year. [see full case study below]

This is the kind of operation we need to see more of. To this end, we want to see the proposed London Plan Town Centre Supplementary Planning Guidance (SPG) specifically include detailed guidance regarding farmers' markets and distribution networks for locally grown food.

New Growing Sites
Although our report focused on support for larger commercial growers, we also looked at the potential of smaller sites to supply London with more food.

Land along highways, railway lines and waterways not suitable for housing or other built development, along with rooftops, could provide "unconventional" spaces for food growing. The co-operation of landowners is required and lease agreements have to be negotiated. If the land is needed in the future, temporary use is viable.

We say the Mayor of London should through the London Plan encourage the temporary use of vacant public and private land for urban agriculture and encourage boroughs to include relevant policies in their Local Development Frameworks.

Longer-term, new developments should include suitable food-growing plots. These could be integrated in the overall soft landscaping strategy of the site or be allocated as flexible space depending on local demand.

In housing developments, allotments and community gardens have the most potential. In a mixed-use or commercial scheme a commercial growing operation could be accommodated, creating the opportunity for local businesses and restaurants to grow their own produce, with the excess sold to local residents.

Jenny Jones meets allotment holders at London Borough of Southwark allotment

Through Section 106 agreements, local authorities already require a range of planning contributions from applicants as part of permitting new developments, like play spaces or cycle paths. Why not require space for food growing too?

The first step is assessing the number and quality of the spaces available. Our evidence suggests that growers who are looking for additional sites to expand their business or to start a farm or food growing project are experiencing difficulties in finding suitable sites or accessing the relevant information and contacts.

Our report urges public authorities to conduct surveys or audits of potential sites that could be used for food growing. Currently, borough or city-wide strategic land assessments of vacant or underused land often concentrate on housing or business uses only.

International examples show that a borough or city-wide assessment of potential sites can pave the way for effective development strategies for vacant or temporary spaces including food growing as a land use.

Portland City Council in the USA passed a resolution in 2004 directing various city departments to conduct an inventory of their properties, with the goal of determining which might be suitable for either expanding the Community Gardens Program or for future development into other kinds of agricultural uses. The subsequent "Diggable City" study by Portland State University identified a diverse array of potential agricultural uses on city-owned lands.

Back in London, in November 2009, the Mayor announced proposals to free up under-used land owned by the Greater London Authority (GLA). He has commissioned an audit of land owned across the GLA to identify potential sites for housing development – an initiative we welcome.

However, we would like to see the audit extended to also assess the GLA's land holdings for potential for commercial or community growing. Sites that are unsuitable for housing due to their location or size may still be acceptable for food growing, such as sites under power lines or near railway tracks. By using raised beds or similar solutions for growing, contaminated sites that cannot immediately accommodate housing development, can also be utilised for food growing, even if only on a temporary basis.

Our report calls on the Mayor to commission an assessment of sites owned by the GLA group regarding their potential for short or long-term urban agriculture, including both commercial and community growing opportunities in the next two years. We urge local authorities to do the same for council-owned land, as well as existing brownfield sites through the LDF process.

Integrating Food Growing with the Mayor's Duty to Promote Sustainable Development

On a broader level, we feel there is a need for the Mayor to play a leadership role in encouraging the development of commercial food growing in London by taking an integrated strategic approach.

We recommend that the Mayor should promote and develop food-growing activities as part of his duty to promote sustainable development, and reflect this in all relevant strategies, not just the London Plan.

Both London Plan policies on waste and energy, and any Mayoral strategy on either waste or energy, should recognise the significant opportunities and contributions urban agriculture can provide in terms of the recycling of compost and production of biogas as a form of renewable energy.

Reference to urban agriculture should also feature in any Mayoral strategy dealing with water in order to recognise its potential for grey water use and water recycling.

At a local level, we said the Mayor should encourage all boroughs to adopt a food strategy that includes advice on growing and buying food locally. A number of boroughs in London and elsewhere in the UK are already doing this with some success.

Regionally, the London Food Strategy supports food growing in London. Whilst London Food has a broad remit in relation to food in the capital, we believe cross-referencing the Food Strategy and the London Plan could further assist in achieving and implementing a common objective.

Integration of all relevant strategies – from food to energy – is key to ensuring that support for agriculture in the capital becomes embedded in the way the Mayor and other agencies set their priorities.

We urge the Mayor to ensure that the London Plan contains stronger links with the existing policies of the London Food Strategy that are relevant to planning matters. We also asked the Mayor to direct London Food to consider our report and integrate our recommendations in any future work.

Conclusion

There is so much to do before London truly achieves its potential for growing food, but we need to put the building blocks in place to enable this to happen for a more secure, sustainable future.

Those building blocks can be aided with revised planning policies. Food security is becoming a global problem. With more people to feed, adverse climate change impact on yields, increasing water demand and finite agricultural lands, it is obvious that cities such as London cannot continue to demand ever more resources, but should strive to produce as much as they possibly can.

To enable this, we need the Mayor to make changes to the London Plan to prioritise food growing as a land use, and for local authorities to amend their policies to give growers more flexibility and support.

There needs to be a more practical approach to planning applications from farmers who want to diversify and modernise their operations so they can flourish. Surely it is preferable to allow some sympathetic development in the Green Belt than to see farms fail.

On a smaller-scale, the Mayor should encourage local authorities to routinely include growing spaces in new housing schemes and to haggle with developers about including allotments when planning permission is negotiated.

We are encouraged by the Mayor's positive response to our recommendations and his indication that he will incorporate them into his policies. Our next step is to make formal submissions at the Examination in Public of the London Plan over the summer to try to maximise support for food growing in the policies set out in the final document.

Growing more food in London, and the rest of the UK, is going to become more and more critical over the next ten years. For the sake of our economy, our health, our security and our environment, the Mayor needs to put sustainable local food production at the heart of his policies now. [i]

Full report and case studies can be found at http://www.london.gov.uk/who-runs-london/the-london-assembly/publications/housing-planning/cultivating-capital-food-growing-and-planning-system-london

Case Study 1

Watts Farm – an example of how the planning system restricts development of commercial farming

Watts Farms is a 300 acre farm situated within the Green Belt on the outskirts of Orpington, Kent, which is in the London borough of Bromley. It specialises in the growing of herbs, spinach, baby leaf products, soft fruit and vegetables in the UK growing season, and importing a similar range from continental Europe out of season.

The farm won a planning appeal to build a new packhouse. However, this followed a six-year battle with the local authority. During this time Watts Farm has not been able to develop and become more efficient to keep up with the demands of the modern-day customer, according to their farm manager. The farmers were faced by what they felt was a complete lack of understanding by the local planning committee who repeatedly went against the advice to grant permission given by its agricultural consultants, the Mayor of London's office and its own planning officers.

At the final planning inquiry the inspector heard that Watts Farms' proposal for a pack-house on the edge of the Green Belt was not an expansion of the business but a rationalisation to bring all its activities under one roof. The proposed new facilities will allow Watts Farms to become more efficient and to improve working conditions for employees.

The planning inspector noted that 'the farm is sensitively managed, contributing positively to the visual qualities of this part of the Green Belt'. The inspector also agreed with the applicants that the proposed new building, although taller than existing ones, would improve the look of the site as it would result in the removal of unattractive structures.

Case Study 2

County Farms - how they could play a key role in retaining and expanding food production in London

Some of the consultation responses which the Assembly received, highlight the value of retaining and expanding the 'County Council[4] Smallholdings scheme'. We understand that the former Greater London Council (GLC) had an extensive estate of let smallholdings and farms in the London area, which passed to the respective Local Authorities where they were located when the GLC was abolished.

There are no complete records regarding the status of this land. Some boroughs provided the Assembly with information on council-owned farmland, others stated that they have no records or have not responded at all. Council-owned farmland tends to be leased out to individual tenants, often through commercial property managers. The remaining farmland could make a valuable contribution to retaining and perhaps expanding, commercial food production in London.

A Suffolk County Council Scrutiny Commission carried out a consultation on their County Farm Service in the year 2000 and found that most county councils have been disposing of their Agricultural Estates since the late 1990s. Of the counties bordering London, only Hertfordshire have developed a Rural Estate Masterplan setting out a number of policy objectives on managing principles for both environmental and commercial parts of the estate.

A 2003 report by the Tenancy Reform Industry Group (TRIG) recommended that the Department for Environment, Food and Rural Affairs "should use the powers under the Agriculture Act 1970 to scrutinise plans for re-organisation and disposal of smallholding estates

Case Study 3

Growing Communities – an Example of Social Enterprise Working to Create a More Sustainable Food System

to require Local Authorities to account for their future management strategies". Five years later a report by Sir Don Curry concluded that county council smallholding estates are an important, strategic, national asset that should be retained and receive more support and investment from local authorities.

Cambridgeshire County Council, whilst not bordering London, is a good example, having the largest county farms estate in England and Wales, and is said to have a strong record of achievement and support. The estate aims to promote and encourage commercial farm enterprises, making the best use of land and encouraging new entrants.

The National Farmers Union voiced their support for the retention of county council farms recognising them as valuable contributions towards providing an opportunity for pursuing a range of policy objectives linked to the environment. A number of individual consultation responses gave support to county farms in their function as a stepping stone for new farmers and indicated that they should be treated in the same way as education services if there was an established need for it that cannot be met otherwise.

As part of our investigation we visited a social enterprise with two small 'urban market gardens' in the London borough of Hackney, selling produce at a Farmers' Market and operating an organic box scheme in the area.

Growing Communities is a social enterprise run by local people in the Borough of Hackney, East London. It is working to create a more sustainable food system, supporting small organic farmers through a box scheme (the sale of boxes of salads and vegetables to customers in Hackney) and farmers' market, and growing salad crops on parkland in Hackney. Its two main growing sites are at Springfield Park, in Upper Clapton, which has a polytunnel and a greenhouse, and Allens Gardens on Bethune Road, Stoke Newington.

It currently employs 18 part-time members of staff and is supported by up to 80 volunteers working throughout the year. It also offers apprenticeships and offers a start-up programme to help community groups and businesses to replicate the scheme elsewhere. Since 2006, Growing Communities has been financially self-sufficient.

Growing Communities started life as a Community Supported Agriculture scheme that linked members up with a farm in Buckinghamshire. The box scheme started in 1993. In 1997 Growing Communities got its first London site and in 2003 set up the UK's first all-organic farmers' market currently operating from Stoke Newington Church Street.

These days Growing Communities provides a weekly selection of seasonal organic produce from £6 per week. The scheme allows members of the box scheme to collect their boxes from five pick-up points across Hackney, as well as one in Islington and one in Tower Hamlets. It supplies over 480 households every week.

Elsewhere in Hackney, the Stoke Newington Farmers' Market supports small environmentally sustainable farmers and producers based within a 100 miles of Hackney. It runs every Saturday and currently provides space for 14 farmers and producers to sell direct to the public. Over 1,500 people shop at the Stoke Newington Farmers' market every Saturday.

The Urban Market Gardens, where organic vegetables are grown on three small sites which are certified by the Soil Association, specialises in mixed salad bags and aim to supply all the salad needs of the box scheme from those sites.

Future projects include setting up "patchwork farms" made up of small plots in the local area and "Starter Farms" comprised of groups of urban growers on peri-urban land, which are located at the fringe of metropolitan centres and form the boundary between urban and rural areas.

Growing Communities' organic market garden in Hackney, London

Capital Growth

Rosie Boycott

"In the late autumn of 2008, the Mayor of London and the London Food Board launched Capital Growth, a publicly funded scheme to create 2012 Growing Spaces in the capital by the end of 2012. To date the scheme has attracted widespread publicity and in the early summer of 2010 we opened the 500th space, with the knowledge that we have around another 500 commitments from the 33 boroughs which make up the city.

It is important to stress from the outset that these spaces are both new and different from the existing allotment programmes which exist in all boroughs and indeed across the country as a whole. Allotments are spaces handed out to individuals who wish to grow vegetables. They are on land which is council owned but, under planning laws, deemed as agriculture space in perpetuity. They are hotly competed for in this new climate where many people want to become vegetable gardeners and in some boroughs the waiting lists are over 20 years! To try to create new allotment spaces is nigh on impossible as neither councils nor private landowners want to 'give away' land permanently. Capital Growth Spaces, on the other hand, are on short term (Meanwhile) leases, for temporary periods of time, say five years. That way, both boroughs and landowners are happy to allow gardeners to work on pieces of their land, confident in the knowledge that they can reclaim the space if and when needed.

Capital Growth has proved to be not only a popular city initiative but also a very vital one. In the eighteen months the scheme has been running many benefits have come to light, proving that inner city vegetable growing isn't just

City Hall's very own Capital Growth plot, in the shadow of Tower Bridge

about providing some good and free food to a few individuals: the range of benefits are far broader than that. All the schemes that the LFB has funded are community based. We do not fund individuals who want to work alone. We believe that vegetable growing on a community basis helps people to connect not only with the process of how food is produced, but also with each other; and we have seen some remarkable results which have been literally transformational to the immediate area.

Rosie Boycott launcing Capital Growth Schools Competition, 2010

Example One:
The Project is based on an estate in west London. Prior to the building of the garden, the estate was rough. In the afternoons - i.e. after school - the common areas would be full of teenagers, drinking, smoking, taking drugs. There was a lot of litter. The area was regularly policed, but despite that, single mothers and the elderly felt afraid to leave their homes. The estate is multi-cultural and there were tribal feuds. One estate tenant, Mike Howell, applied for a small grant (£500) and, in a small disused concrete triangle behind a tower block he installed 20 builders' bags (measuring one metre square), filled them with earth and offered them for rent for just £3 a year. Within a couple of months he had sixteen bags being gardened by (mainly) women on the estate. Within a year this had risen to thirty. The women found that the garden gave them confidence: they met and bonded with their neighbours and thus felt less alone. As the garden took shape they felt a pride of ownership and this spilt over into the common areas of the estate around the car park and the small, heavily fenced net ball ground. They picked up the litter and started to confront the gangs that hung around in the early evenings. Over time the gangs dispersed. Fruit trees have been planted round the sports ground. A second garden has been built by the neighbouring homeless women's hostel. Space is now being sought for another estate garden. The police say the levels of crime have fallen dramatically. The women feel empowered - they share meals with each other and share what they have grown.

Urban isolation is a very real modern problem and this example demonstrates that the simple act of food growing has provided a bonding structure which provides a workable solution.

Example Two:
Capital Growth funded a garden development in the back garden of a couple who had no time to look after it. The garden in question is large and when two women in the street took it over, it was covered with brambles. It is now a garden which is is used by five different families and the home-owner receives a supply of fresh vegetables in return. The scheme has provided bonding, plus a big change in attitude among the many children who help out. They now eat, cook and enjoy their fresh vegetables. The scheme has had many tangential benefits -not just neighbourhood bonding

and a sense of community but also inspiration. The group have planted a wildflower garden on a derelict piece of land by the nearby railway line, they are planting a communal street orchard (3 or 4 trees per household and all the fruit shared) and they are taking over another garden to grow veg in. Capital growth's investment was just £500.

I hope these two examples will illustrate just some of the benefits of the scheme. We are working with existing estates as well as with new ones to encourage the provison of community vegetable gardens within planning. We are also working with all the councils across the city to encourage them to help residents establish such schemes in their areas - in parks, on canal banks, river banks, beside railways, in either dis-used or little used places, in office grounds, car parks and on roof tops. London already boasts a considerable quantity of roof gardens, but we are still only utilising a fraction of this space. Roof gardens help mitigate climate change (through the actual garden) as well as via reduced costs of energy for both heat and air conditioning and flooding.

Community gardens on the ground also support the climate change agenda, but another benefit is reconnecting people with how their food is grown and what proper food is. This, we believe, is a first and crucial step in changing eating habits, especially among the young. Currently 25% of all children in London entering primary school are overweight or obese. The obesity epidemic is growing in our capital, leading both to childhood and adult illness as well as imposing a great strain on public health resources. Initiatives to combat obesity are largely unsuccessful but a recent survey from the Year of Food and Farming (conducted by the National Farmers' Union) showed that 93% of primary school children who grow their own begin to change their eating habits. Thus another part of the Capital Growth agenda is to encourage all primary schools to start vegetable gardens in their play grounds. Over the last two academic terms we have seen over 100 new ones open."

—

Endnotes

1. Jenny Jones is the author of the first part of this article. She was the Chair of the London Assembly's Planning and Housing Committee during the 'Cultivating the Capital, Food Growing and the Planning System in London' investigation which was published in 2010. The London Assembly is part of the Greater London Authority. She is currently the Deputy Chair. Rosie Boycott, Chair of the London Food Board is responsible for the final section, entitled Capital Growth.

2. An allotment, at its simplest, is a piece of land, usually around 250 square metres (299 square yards), which can be rented by an individual for growing fruit and vegetables. Most, but by no means all, are owned by local authorities. The rent paid by allotment gardeners across London varies enormously across the city, but the average is around £50-£60 annually. Source: The London Assembly's Environment Committee's report "A Lot to Lose – London's disappearing allotments" published in October 2006

3. City Limits - a resource flow and ecological footprint analysis of Greater London, 2002. This report estimates that 81% of food consumed in London was imported from outside the UK.

4. County Councils generally form the top tier of local government outside London and the larger cities in England. When the Greater London Council was formed in 1964 it took over parts of areas previously run by the county councils such as Middlesex, Essex, Kent, Surrey and Hertfordshire.

04 The ISOCARP Awards for Excellence

The 2009 ISOCARP Awards for Excellence

Dirk Engelke

ISOCARP Vice President Awards and Communication

The Historic Old Town Hall in Gdansk, Poland set an excellent environment for the ceremony of the 2009 ISOCARP Awards for Excellence on the World Town Planning Day at 8 November 2009. The award ceremony and an accompanying international seminar on "Planning for Urban Change" the next day were hosted by the City of Gdansk, the Society of Polish Town Planners (TUP) and the Gdansk University of Technology. The seminar was sponsored by INVI, Investment Environments.
An ISOCARP Award for Excellence is the highest honour the Society can award to a city, region or institution and is a bench mark for an excellent plan or project, where excellence is based on the "ISOCARP triple perspective": the knowledge of its members from practice, from academia and from policy. So, an ISOCARP project of excellence has to be excellent in all these three perspectives. The composition of the jury not only reflects this idea of the ISOCARP triple perspective, it also reflects the geographical spread of the Society. The jury's members were:
Ismael Fernández Mejía, (ISOCARP President / Mexico); Thomas Kiwitt, (Technical Director Greater Stuttgart Region / Germany); Pierre Laconte,

The winners of the 2009 ISOCARP Awards for Excellence

(former ISOCARP President / Belgium); Mairura Omwenga, (ISOCARP Liaison Office Nairobi / Kenya); David Prosperi (Florida Atlantic University / United States of America); Shi Nan, (Secretary General, Urban Planning Society of China / People's Republic of China; Pablo Vaggione, (ISOCARP Secretary General / Spain); Alfonso Vegara (Fundación Metropoli / Spain); Dirk Engelke (ISOCARP Vice President Communication and Awards / Germany / Chair).

The jury established three categories:
(a) District planning/urban design;
b) Urban and city planning; and (c) Strategic and regional planning, recognising the different levels at which spatial planners work. The awarded projects also had to answer to climate change aspects, linking to the theme of the 2009 ISOCARP congress "Low Carbon Cities".

Projects, submitted from Asia, Europe, the Middle East and North America were considered, but it became clear that the most exciting, excellent projects are those that are to be planned and realised in Asia and the Middle East. The jury decided to give the 2009 ISOCARP Awards for Excellence to the three projects below:

Beijing Changxindian Low Carbon Community Concept Plan

Joint Submission by Arup and Beijing Municipal Institute of City Planning and Design

> **Jury comment:**
> The Concept Plan is a well developed and presented project which utilizes several technical parameters and design criteria to plan and evaluate the overall project objectives. The notion of "low carbon zoning codes" highlights a traditional tool for planning as a means for obtaining current and future sustainability initiatives and goals. It is an excellent example in district planning/urban design in response to the global climate change concern and the urbanization pressure.

Planning Area
The Changxindian Low Carbon Community, located in Fengtai's Hexi District is one of the most important development areas along the south-western corridors of Beijing city. The project is 500 ha in area and includes a future residential and commercial area, an industrial research park and open space. It will be served by a Light Rail Transit line as part of the city-wide mass transit system. The future population will be approximately 70,000.

Background and Context
Climate change is already a critical global issue. Rising trends in China's carbon dioxide and other greenhouse gas (GHG) emissions will have a significant impact both on China and the world as a whole.

Rapid urbanization, together with rising living standards over the past two decades in China, have resulted in an increasing pressure on energy usage, resources and the environment. Without any energy and policy measures to manage GHG emissions, this unprecedented rate of urbanization will result in significant increase in GHG emissions. The country is urgently searching for sustainable ways to ease the negative implications of growth and urbanization. China has committed to reduce emission and energy intensity levels in her national 11th Five Year Plan. Innovative methods and tools are to be developed and incorporated in China's urban planning system to enable the creation of low carbon communities in the future.

Objectives
- To prepare a mixed-use community concept plan that is guided by a sustainability framework and performance indicators; and to establish a low carbon, economically viable, socially inclusive, environmentally friendly and resource efficient community.
- To pioneer the preparation of a set of innovative "Low Carbon Zoning Codes" that incorporate these sustainability indicators, and that are implementable as statutory zoning plans to manage climate change impact.

Steps of the Realization Process
The Fengtai – Hexi District Plan (2006-2020) was prepared by the Beijing Municipal Institute of City Planning & Design (BMICPD) on behalf of the City Government, in accordance with the Beijing Urban Master Plan.

Arup has subsequently been commissioned by a local developer (who acts on behalf of, and in partnership with, the Fengtai District Government) to review the existing statutory District Plan and to produce a "low carbon" concept master plan for the 500 hectares site.

Conventional planning processes in China focus mainly on spatial elements. In this project innovative planning tools driven by resource management objectives were introduced in a two-stage planning process as part of the decision making process.

In Stage One (Innovative Strategies & Tools) three elements were developed:
- A Sustainability Framework, including Vision, Objectives and 20 Key Performance Indicators

- An Integrated Resource Management (IRM) system and the use of an Eco-Footprint to assess the efficiency of the master plan options.
- Application of Participatory Planning & Village Upgrading, enhancing Social Improvement

Stage One resulted in a master land use plan that meets the 20 performance indicators.

In Stage Two the preparation of Low Carbon Zoning Codes as Statutory Zoning Plans (Regulatory Plans) was pioneered.

Innovation and Achievements

The current Chinese statutory planning system has focused on setting out site specific development parameters at the local detailed plan level – the statutory "Regulatory Plan". The list of mandatory planning parameters does not have an adequate breadth and depth fully relevant to low carbon planning objectives. This is a key challenge for planners in China.

Hence, the Beijing Changxindian Community Concept Plan is of prime importance as a pilot in addressing this implementation issue, as it involves an institutional solution. It is a pioneering case study aimed at building low carbon development models that can be implemented, enforced, and replicated in China through innovative low carbon zoning codes.

This new approach should greatly improve the feasibility and the enforceability of implementing the low carbon planning concept in China. This pilot project clearly demonstrates the need for institutional reform in China's planning system in response to the challenge of climate change.

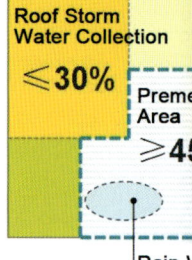

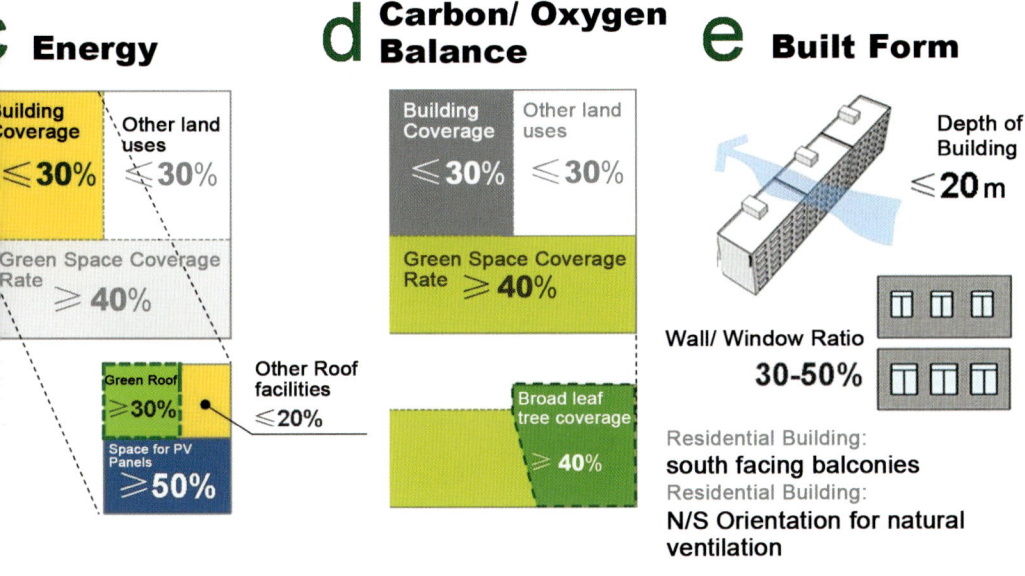

Sustainable Urban Design Guidelines

New Comprehensive Planning of Wuhan

Wuhan Planning and Design Institute, People's Republic of China

Jury comment:
The "New Comprehensive Planning of Wuhan" is setting the ecological framework for the sustainable metropolis region. The entry shows an advanced technology in problem identification, analysis and presentation. It also shows a sophisticated understanding of the relationship between microclimate considerations, open space provision, transportation and building strategies as key elements of sustainable comprehensive planning in Wuhan.

Planning Area
Wuhan, capital of the Hubei province, covers an area of 8,5 km² and has 8.97 million permanent inhabitants. It is a central metropolis in central China.

Background and Context
Wuhan, a nationally famous city of history and culture, major industrial, scientific research and education base, traffic and communication terminal, will have a population of 11.8 million by 2020.

It used to be one of the four famous "stoves" in China because of the problem of urban heat island effect, with temperatures ≥35 °C in summer.

Ecological problems in the rapid urbanization period are increasingly prominent. The City's water area, arable land, forests and other ecological resources are being encroached upon, while green space in the central city amounts to less than 9 m² per capita.

China's longest river, the Yangtze joins the Hanjiang River in the city center. The City's water area covers one quarter of its total area. Wuhan is the most typical riverside & lakeshore city.

Objectives
The overall objectives of the project are: Promoting Urban Ventilation (channelling fresher and cooler air into the city), Stack Control (technical design measures to enhance or, where appropriate, avoid this ventilation), an Ecological Framework & a Sustainable Metropolis Region
- Expand and introduce population distribution based on six development axes, applying a Transit Oriented Development (TOD) mode based on "expressways, main roads and rail" along multi-mode transportation corridors
- Encourage a green traffic network by preferential public traffic, developing a rapid, high volume public transport system .
- Establishment of a livable city focusing upon community construction, encouraging a balance between homes and jobs to reduce commuting and carbon emissions
- Strengthening measures for urban sustainable development
- The use of ecological methods based on natural circulation leading toeffective mitigation of the urban heat island effect

Steps of the Realization Process
In 2007, Wuhan Urban Circle was granted the "Experimental Area for Comprehensive Reform of Two-Oriented Society" status.

Thus, building a resource-efficient and environmentally- friendly eco-city has become a new aim for the spatial development strategy in Wuhan. This aim shall be met by adopting TOD Mode for sustainable metropolitan axial expansion as well as seeking urban ecological framework control for rapid urbanization period. This is supported by applying natural circulation of ventilation stack control to reduce the heat island effect.

Strategy Content:
- Create a spatial development pattern of "Mixed Axes & Wedges"
- Master Planning involving six new intensive urban groups and six ecological green wedges at the core of the main city zone", and a new approach to urban development, away from resource-oriented extensive development to an intensive ecological development pattern. The planned land area for ecology control is up to 83%.
- Construct an urban ecological framework based on the ventilation and stack control by setting up six large-scale ecological green wedges that run through the whole city mainly based on water areas, wetlands, mountains and woodlands along the Yangtze and Hanjiang rivers

- Provide extensive public green space in the urban area based on the climatology theory
- Emphasise the role of open space and the construction of main roads along river corridors in order to channel high quality air from the surrounding areas to the city center, accelerating mitigation of thermal island effect.

Innovation and Achievements

The new comprehensive planning of Wuhan helps the finding of solutions to the ecological dilemmas typical for metropolises in central China. It sets an ecological framework for the sustainable metropolis region and shows an advanced technological approach to problem identification, analysis and

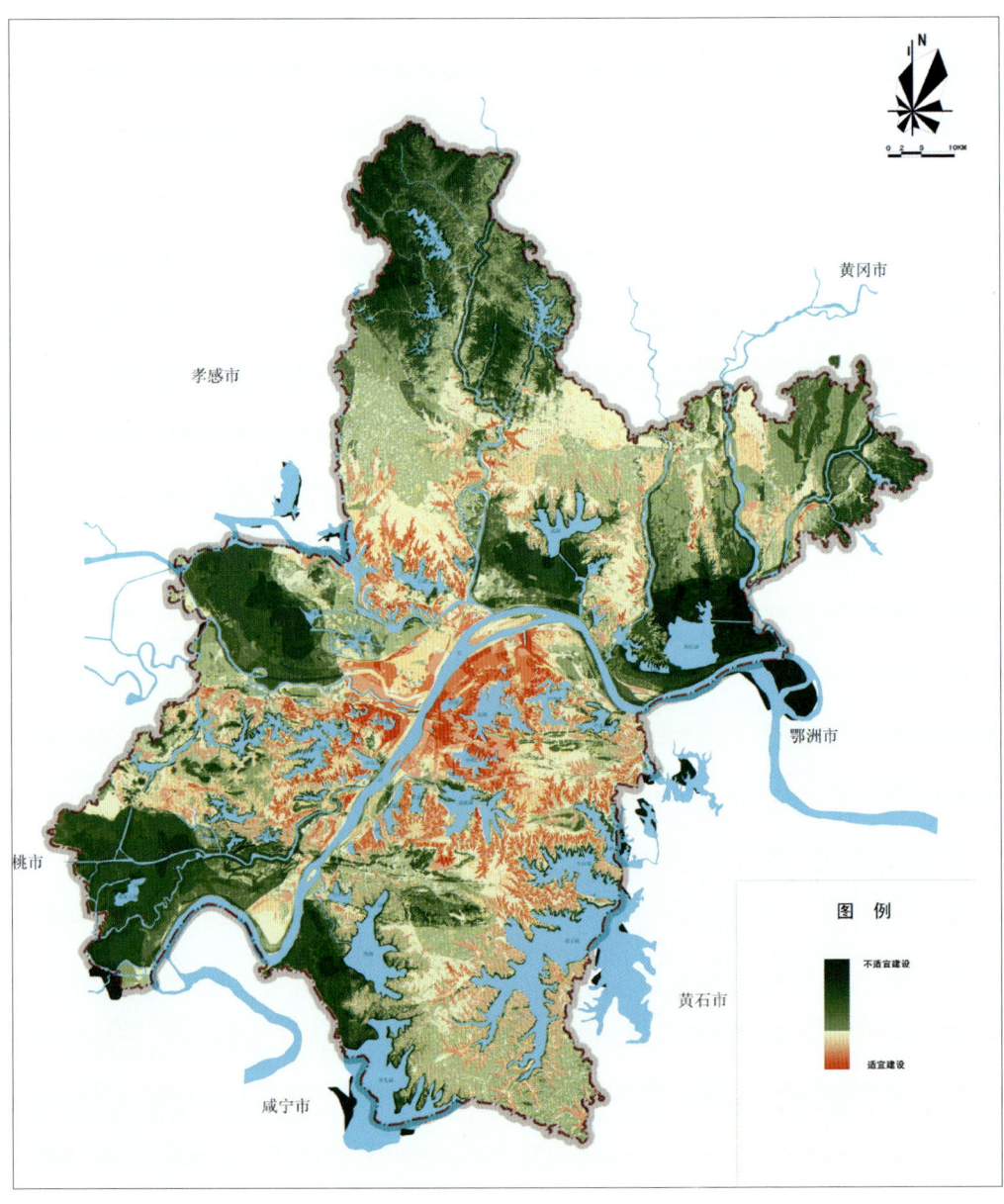

presentation. That framework effectively integrates microclimate considerations with green infrastructure provision, transportation and the location of built development as key elements of sustainable comprehensive planning in Wuhan.

Since 2003, high temperatures during summer days have apparently decreased by 1 °C on average in the urban areas of Wuhan. It means that the city has successfully shaken off its nickname "stove".

Evolution of land construction and urban development structure plan

Plan Al Ain 2030: Urban Structure Framework Plan

Abu Dhabi Urban Planning Council, United Arab Emirates

Jury comment:
The "Plan Al Ain 2030" is an ambitious plan for an ecologically extreme fragile region. It carefully balances between facing globalisation on the one hand and local/ethnical identities on the other by focussing on physical development and environmental concerns. Using a traditional approach the plan combines a strategic consideration based on local identity with a structural framework. The "Plan Al Ain 2030" is considered an excellent example of strategic/regional planning.

Location and Planning Area
Al Ain (meaning "The Spring" in Arabic) is located approximately 150 kilometres east of Abu Dhabi city and 150 kilometres south of Dubai in the United Arab Emirates (UAE). The fourth largest city in the UAE, it has an estimated metropolitan population of just over 400,000 residents.

Background and Context
The contemporary city lies at the site of an ancient nomadic crossroads that has offered reliable water supplies to human settlements for the past 5,000 years. It still has six oases originally fed by an ancient irrigation system known as falaj, some parts of which date to 1,000 BC. Al Ain Oasis, the largest of the six oases, is located adjacent to the city's central business district. Al Ain also possesses the UAE's richest architectural heritage, including 50 historic structures within the oases.

Contemporary Al Ain has reached a crucial turning point in its physical and economic development. A rapidly expanding population and a policy of very large plot allocations have filled out most of the available land. The city must now decide how to develop in order to preserve its character, heritage, and the relaxed lifestyle it offers.

Objectives
The "Plan Al Ain 2030" is an ambitious plan for an ecologically extreme fragile region, carried out by the Abu Dhabi Urban Planning Council (UPC). It carefully balances between facing globalization, on the one hand, and local/ethnical identities on the other. Using a traditional approach it combines a strategic consideration based on local identity with a structural framework, intended to foster the authentic Arabic identity of Al Ain while supporting continuous evolution and growth.

Plan Al Ain 2030 promises special treatment for the city's oases, ensuring that they remain at the heart of the community for generations to come. It supports traditional Bedouin living too.

Key environmental principles of Plan Al Ain 2030 include preserving the city as an oasis and protecting the natural environment. Key cultural principles include protecting the cultural heritage and cultural homeland. The key social principle of Plan Al Ain 2030 is a high quality of life, and a living Arabic community. The key economic principle is a diversified economic development. These key principals are laid down in four frameworks of the Plan Al Ain 2030:
- Environmental Framework
- Land Use Framework
- Transportation Framework
- Open Space Framework

Steps of the Realization Process
The UPC has already defined three phases for the delivery of the plan but the timing is subject to evolving circumstances and requirements. UPC is already working with private developers to incorporate Plan Al Ain 2030 principles into their development proposals.

During Phase 1, the major structural elements of the Land Use Framework will be planned, including a redevelopment plan for the City's Central District, key transportation and transit improvement initiatives, and the advancement of Emirati housing projects.

For Phase 2, the major structural components of the Gateway Transit Corridor will be planned, and development at key transit nodes will intensify. Planning work on the surface tram system will begin and the development of Emirati housing will continue. Through the implementation of Phase 3 by 2030 the majority of Al Ain residents and commerce will be housed.. A second north-south axis will also contain higher density accommodation, creating a crossroad where the two major axes meet.

Innovation and Achievements

Plan Al Ain 2030 is a conceptual document that articulates a clear vision for Al Ain, expressed through principles, policies, geographic plans, urban design details, and architectural guidelines, serving as an interim tool for evaluating development and growth propositions until detailed district-specific plans are completed,

Plan Al Ain 2030 strikes a delicate and much-needed balance between conservation and development. It explores the need to conserve ground water resources and protect natural habitats.. Creating a comprehensive network of protected areas and limiting urban sprawl, Plan Al Ain 2030 proposes projects that exploit existing economic wealth to develop renewable energy production and reduce the consumption of non-renewable resources.

—

Plan Al Ain 2030 Transportation Framework: Transit

ABOUT THE EDITOR

Chris Gossop
BSc MA PhD MRTPI is a chartered town planner with a broad range of experience that has embraced both local and central government, as well as a non governmental organisation, the Town and Country Planning Association (TCPA). He served in three local authorities, including Leicester City Council where he managed substantial environmental programs. Later, as Deputy Director with the TCPA, he became involved in numerous campaigning issues, at many levels, from the local to that of the European Union. In 1995, he joined the former Department of the Environment to coordinate United Kingdom preparations for Habitat II, the United Nations conference on human settlements. He currently serves as a planning inspector with responsibility for the scrutiny and determination of planning and environmental appeals, combining this with his work for ISOCARP where he is a Vice President. In 2009 he was the General Rapporteur for ISOCARP's 45th World Congress on Low Carbon Cities and, associated with that, he was joint editor of Review 05, which is the predecessor to this present book. Also in 2009, he became a trustee of the National Energy Foundation which is based in the new city of Milton Keynes, where Chris has his home.

ABOUT THE AUTHORS

Kenya: Urban Settlements and Development Profile
—

Mairura Omwenga
Mairura Omwenga is a trained civil engineer and urban and regional planner from the University of Nairobi. Presently he is completing his PhD research on school transportation in Nairobi. He is currently a lecturer in the Department of Urban and Regional Planning, University of Nairobi. He has wide working and research experience both in the public and private sector and runs a private consulting firm.

Mairura Omwenga holds a number of public and professional offices. He is the Chairman of the Architectural Association of Kenya (Town Planners Chapter) and Honorary Secretary of the Architectural Association of Kenya. He is also a member of the Physical Planners Registration Board. Mairura Omwenga is the coordinator of the ISOCARP Africa Region and ISOCARP Nairobi Liaison office.

Project Preparation and its Crucial Role in Enabling More Effective and Sustainable Development – The South African Experience
—

Mark Misselhorn
Mark Misselhorn is the CEO of Project Preparation Trust of KZN, an organization which specializes in the preparation of a wide range of developmental projects for poor communities in South Africa. Mark has been involved in development in South Africa for a period of 15 years with a particular emphasis on the conceptual, feasibility and planning stages of initiatives. His typical role is at the programme and project management level. He is also involved in a range of policy and strategy work. Mark's main areas of expertise include informal settlement upgrading, participative

local level spatial planning, pro-poor local economic development, sustainable livelihoods, low income housing and related infrastructure, and special needs housing for especially vulnerable groups such as orphans and vulnerable children.

Urban Africa – Challenges and Opportunities for Planning at a Time of Climate Change
—
Laura Petrella
Laura Petrella is an architect and urban planner trained at the Istituto Universitario di Architettura di Venezia IUAV, in Italy. After specialising in urban and regional planning for developing countries, she has worked in Colombia, Niger, and the Venice Lagoon, before joining UN-HABITAT Slum Upgrading Progamme. With UN-HABITAT she has been working on urban poverty and has been in charge of the Safer Cities Programme. More recently she has been in charge of urban planning and working within the urban environmental planning branch, with the task of developing the agency's urban planning content and activities, in partnership with various stakeholders at global and country level.

Climate Change, Cities and the IPCC
—
Jean-Pascal van Ypersele
Jean-Pascal van Ypersele (Brussels, 1957) has a PhD in Physics from the Belgian Université catholique de Louvain (UCL). He has specialized in climate change modelling and the study of the impact of human activities on climate.

As professor at UCL (www.climate.be), he directs the interdisciplinary Master programme in Science and Management of the Environment. He is the author of numerous scientific articles and popular works regarding climate change and sustainable development. He was a Lead Author for the WGII contribution to the Third Assessment Report of the IPCC and was elected in 2002 Vice-Chair of its Working Group II. In 2008, he was elected Vice-chair of IPCC.

Jean-Pascal van Ypersele has been a member of the Belgian Federal Council for Sustainable Development since 1993. He chairs its Working Group on "Energy and Climate". He was science advisor in the Belgian delegations to a dozen United Nations conferences from Rio (1992) to Copenhagen (2009). Among other prizes, he received in 2006 the Special Prize "Energy and Environment Award 2006" from the International Polar Foundation. Together with Al Gore and the thousands of scientists working for IPCC, he shared a (small) piece of the 2007 Nobel Peace Prize awarded to IPCC.

Sustainable Urbanism in Abu Dhabi
—
John P. Madden
John Madden is Senior Planning Manager of the Department of Sustainable Development and Urban Design for the Abu Dhabi Urban Planning Council (UPC). John's current role is managing and directing development growth within the Emirate of Abu Dhabi and helping to implement the principles and objectives of Plan Abu Dhabi 2030 with a strong emphasis on sustainability and urban design.

Before joining the UPC, John had worked in varying planning capacities within the Central Area Planning Division at the City of Vancouver, Canada. He had played a key role in the delivery of innovative programs and land use plans including the Trade and Convention Centre expansion program, an industrial lands strategy, mega waterfront and downtown historic preservation plans, as well as the award winning Downtown Transportation Plan. Before joining the UPC, John was one of the lead project planners for privately-held lands within Southeast False Creek, Vancouver's most recent mega development on the edge of Vancouver's central downtown. John was responsible for overseeing the implementation of an aggressive plan to transform a former heavy-industrial brown-field site into one of North America's leading sustainable communities.

Energy Saving and Emission Reduction: Chinese Low Carbon Strategy in 11th Five Year Plan Period
—
SHI Nan
Secretary General, Urban Planning Society of China (UPSC); Executive Chief Editor, City Planning Review (CPR); Associate Chief Editor, China City Planning Review (CCPR);

Senior Planner, China Academy of Urban Planning and Design (CAUPD).

Dr. Shi Nan has 28 years of planning experience and is specialized in policy analysis and master planning. He has been very active in major planning and research projects including the Revision of National Planning Act. He has more than 15 years of experience working with major international organizations including the World Bank, UNDP, IFHP, the Rockefeller Foundations etc. He is currently a Member of the National Board for Planning Education Accreditation and the National Board for Certified Planner Examination and Registration. His major publications include Some Observations concerning China's Urban Development, China Urban Development Report and Reader of Urban Planning etc.

YU Taofang
YU Taofang, PHD, Lecturer of Urban and Regional Planning, in School of Architecture, Tsinghua University Beijing. Yu Taofang has research interests in urban and regional planning, the mega-city region of East China, and urban competitiveness. He is the author of Urban Competition and Competitiveness (2004), Urbanization in China (2008) and of numerous research papers in scientific journals.

From 2005 onwards: Lecturer at the School of Architecture, Tsinghua University; 05-2008-05-2009: Visiting Scholar at the Department of Geography, London School of Economics and Political Science, London, UK; 06-2003-05-2005: Post Doctorial Research at the College of Architecture and Urban Planning, Tongji University, Shanghai, China; 01-2001-03-2001: Visiting Scholar at the Department of Geography and Resource Management, the Chinese University of Hong Kong (CUHK), Hong Kong.

Low Carbon Kunshan: Towards a Sustainable Future
—
Zhang Quan
Zhangquan, born in 1954, took a master degree in 1984 from the Architecture Department of Nanjing Institute of Technology. He is now the deputy director of the Housing and Urban-rural Construction Ministry of Jiangsu Province, the senior urban planner as professor-level, adjunct professor of Nanjing University, Vice President of the Urban Planning Society of China, and the chief director of the Ecology Planning Committee of the Urban Planning Society of China. He was in charge of several famous plans, such as "Urban System plan of Jiangsu Province", "Regional Plan of Nanjing Metropolis", "Master plan for Lhasa City",

"Master plan for Kunshan City", and "Regulatory Plan of ecology demonstration plot in Wuxi City".

The Carbon Footprint of UK Cities: 4M: Measurement, Modelling, Mapping and Management
—
Kevin Lomas

Kevin Lomas is Professor of Building Simulation in the Department of Civil and Building Engineering at Loughborough University, having previously been the Director of the Institute of Energy and Sustainable Development at De Montfort University. Loughborough is one of the twelve most highly funded UK research institutions in engineering and the physical sciences with a particular strength in energy demand, renewable energy and associated fields.

A member of the Building Energy Research Group, Lomas has particular interests in the application of computer models to the design and assessment of buildings and the actual energy and environmental performance of occupied domestic and non-domestic buildings. In recent years this has broadened into studies of energy use, carbon dioxide emissions and climate change at the city scale. He led the Carbon Reduction in Buildings Consortium (http://www.carb.org.uk/) and currently leads the 4M consortium that is examining routes to reducing the carbon footprint of UK cities (http://mmmm.lboro.ac.uk/).

Practice-based research into the architectural design and post-occupancy performance of advanced naturally ventilated buildings has been funded through energy and environment consulting. Notable projects include: the Queens Building, De Montfort University; Coventry University Library; the Olympic Stadium in Sydney; Lichfield Garrick Theatre; the School of Slavonic and East European Studies, University College London; and, latterly, a new Faculty Building for a college campus just west of Chicago, USA. These buildings have received numerous architecture and environmental design awards.

Lomas is the Loughborough Director of The UK Doctoral Training Centre for Energy Demand Reduction. A joint initiative with University College London, the Centre is the UK champion for multi-disciplinary postgraduate training in building energy demand and associated areas - policy and economics, design and construction, performance monitoring, etc. (http://dtc.lboro.ac.uk/).

He has supervised 27 PhD students and 31 research projects and published around 110 journal and conference papers. He currently holds a Leverhulme Research Fellowship.

Further authors:
Bell MC[2], Firth SK[1], Gaston KJ[3], Goodman P[4], Leake JR[3], Namdeo A[2], Rylatt M[5], Allinson D[1], Davies ZG[3], Edmondson JL[3], Galatioto F[2], Brake JA[2], Guo L[1], Hill G[2], Irvine KN[5], Taylor SC[5] and Tiwary A[2]

1. Loughborough University, Building Energy Research Group, Department of Civil and Building Engineering

2. Newcastle University, Transport Operations Research Group, School of Civil Engineering and Geosciences

3. University of Sheffield, Department of Animal & Plant Sciences

4. University of Leeds, Institute for Transport Studies

5. De Montfort University, Institute of Energy and Sustainable Development.

Rebuilding after a Natural Disaster: Using the Opportunity to be 'better than ever'

—

Dhiru A. Thadani

Dhiru A. Thadani, AIA, is a consultant, architect, urbanist, and educator who has been in practice since 1980, and has worked on projects in Asia, Europe and North and Central America. Since its formation in 1993, Dhiru has been a charter member of the Congress for the New Urbanism, and was appointed to the Board in 2005.

Dhiru was born in Bombay (Mumbai), India and moved to Washington, D.C. to study architecture. During his thirty-seven years in Washington, D.C. he has taught, practiced, and has worked to place architecture and urbanism in the public eye. Dhiru has been involved in new developments, urban retrofits, neighborhood revitalization, and infill densification. His goal has been to create neighborhoods that are walkable, and contain a diverse range and balance of workplace and housing. In addition, these new developments support regional planning for open space, and architecture that is responsive to the culture, climate and context.

For the past twenty years, Dhiru has been the lead designer for several major projects in developed and developing countries. The projects range in scale from government-sponsored autonomous new towns for 500,000 inhabitants to smaller resort communities for 900 residents, as well as small-scale residential infill interventions in revitalizing neighborhoods.

A 804 page reference book titled, The Language of Towns & Cities: A Visual Dictionary, which Dhiru authored will be published by Rizzoli in October 2010.

The Loss of Green Spaces in and around City Areas: Learning from Syria. (The Use of Medium Resolution Satellite Images in Examining the Impact of City Expansion on Urban and Peri-Urban Green Areas in Syria)

—

Peter Ross

Peter Ross is an urban planner of considerable senior experience; he has a strong work record in countries in transition, helping reform urban planning processes to meet the needs of a rapidly changing world. He has spent long periods leading major projects in Syria, China and Indonesia, as well as in Europe. He has directed high profile European Union funded projects, and has worked on World Bank and United Nations projects. In 2003, in China, he was honoured with the Shenyang Rose Award as an 'Elite Foreign Expert'. Most recently Peter Ross has been the Municipal Administration Modernisation Urban Development Team Leader in Syria, coordinating the project work on urban planning, traffic and transport planning, and urban development in six of the most important cities in the country, the extensive work with the old city of Damascus, and the work on the sustainable development of Palmyra, one of the most important heritage landscapes in the world, and a premier Syrian tourist destination. Peter Ross has had many articles published in both professional journals and in lay magazines and newspapers; he serves on the editorial board of Urbanistica pvs (University of Rome).

Cultivating the Capital: How the Planning System is Vital to London's Ability to Grow its Own Food

—

Jenny Jones

Jenny Jones is an ex-archaeologist and former chair of the Green Party. She has been a member of the London Assembly since 2000 and was elected as the first Green member on Southwark Council in 2006.

In May 2009, Jenny was appointed Chair of the Planning and Housing Committee in the Assembly and has overseen reports such as Cultivating the Capital, looking at urban agriculture in London. She also sits on the Transport Committee.

Since elected to the Assembly, Jenny has worked to secure safer roads, improved facilities for pedestrians and cyclists, reductions in road crimes and traffic, and excellent public transport for all users.

Jenny is also a member of the Metropolitan Police Authority, and has consistently called for greater police resources for the enforcement of road traffic laws, for stronger protection of civil liberties, and for a better police response to violence against women.

In the previous mayoral administration Jenny was the chair of London Food, the Mayor's road safety ambassador, and the Mayor's green transport adviser. Jenny is also the former Deputy Mayor of London.

In all her roles Jenny has raised awareness of the dangers of climate change and the urgent need to reduce greenhouse emissions. Jenny has been a member of the project board that has led the delivery of the East London Green Grid of open spaces.

In 2004, Jenny was named as one of 200 'women of achievement'.

Rosie Boycott

Rosie Boycott - Food Advisor to Boris Johnson, Mayor of London, and Chair, London Food Board

Rosie Boycott is a journalist and author. In 1971 she co-founded the feminist magazine Spare Rib with Marsha Rowe. Two years later she and Rowe co-founded Virago Press, a publishing concern committed to women's writing. She has worked on The Daily Mail, The Sunday Telegraph, Harpers and Queen and Esquire but is probably best known for her role as editor of The Independent on Sunday, The Independent, and The Express.

Rosie has written several books including an autobiography: A Nice Girl Like Me: A Story of the Seventies; a novel, All For Love; and a non-fiction book about running a small-holding, Spotted Pigs and Green Tomatoes: A Year in the Life of Our Farm.

In August 2008 she was appointed as Chair of London Food as part of Conservative Mayor Boris Johnson's attempt to help improve Londoners' access to healthy, locally produced and affordable food.

ISOCARP